MODERN CHICANO WRITERS

TWENTIETH CENTURY VIEWS

The aim of this series is to present the best in contemporary critical opinion on major authors, providing a twentieth century perspective on their changing status in an era of profound revaluation.

Maynard Mack, *Series Editor*
Yale University

MODERN CHICANO WRITERS

A COLLECTION OF CRITICAL ESSAYS

Edited by

Joseph Sommers and Tomás Ybarra-Frausto

Prentice-Hall, Inc. A SPECTRUM BOOK *Englewood Cliffs, N.J.*

Library of Congress Cataloging in Publication Data

MAIN ENTRY UNDER TITLE:

Modern Chicano writers.

(Twentieth-century views) (A Spectrum Book)

Bibliography: p.

1. American literature—Mexican American authors
—History and criticism—Addresses, essays,
lectures. 2. American literature—20th century—
History and criticism—Addresses, essays, lectures.
3. Mexican American literature (Spanish)—History
and criticism—Addresses, essays, lectures.
I. Sommers, Joseph, (date) II. Ybarra-
Frausto, Tomás, (date)

PS153.M4M6   810'.9'0052   78-25605

ISBN 0-13-589721-1

ISBN 0-13-589713-0 pbk.

Editorial/ production supervision by Betty Neville
Cover design by Stanley Wyatt
Manufacturing buyer: Cathie Lenard

10   9   8   7   6   5   4   3   2   1

PRENTICE-HALL INTERNATIONAL, INC. *(London)*

PRENTICE-HALL OF AUSTRALIA PTY. LIMITED *(Sydney)*

PRENTICE-HALL OF CANADA, LTD. *(Toronto)*

PRENTICE-HALL OF INDIA PRIVATE LIMITED *(New Delhi)*

PRENTICE-HALL OF JAPAN, INC. *(Tokyo)*

PRENTICE-HALL OF SOUTHEAST ASIA PTE. LTD. *(Singapore)*

WHITEHALL BOOKS LIMITED *(Wellington, New Zealand)*

For Antonia Castañeda

Acknowledgments

Fragments of "El corrido de Kiansis," "Los mexicanos que hablan inglés," and "Desde México he venido" from Américo Paredes, *A Texas-Mexican Cancionero* are reprinted by permission of the University of Illinois Press. © 1976 by the Board of Trustees of the University of Illinois.

Fragments of "Muerte del afamado Bilito" and "Personal, La Voz de mi conciencia" from Aurora Lucero—White Lea, *Literary Folklore of the Hispanic Southwest* are used by permission of John D. Lawson, West Southwest Book Publishing Company.

The first two stanzas of "The Corrido of Cesar Chavez" from *La Raza: The Mexican Americans* by Stan Steiner are used by permission of Harper & Row, Publishers, Inc. and Harold Matson Co., Inc. © 1969, 1970 by Stan Steiner.

The poem from *The Single Rose* by Fray Angelico Chavez is used by permission of the author.

The poems "My Certain Burn Toward Pale Ashes," "This the Place," and "The Space of Death" from Tino Villanueva, *Hay otra voz Poems* (New York: Editorial Mensaje, 1972) are used by permission of the author.

"Gata Poem" from *Restless Serpents* by Bernice Zamora is used by permission of the author.

Fragments of the poem "El Louie" by José Montoya and an excerpt from his interview with Tomás Ybarra-Frausto are used by permission of the author.

Scattered quotes from "Las dos caras del patroncito," "Los vendidos," "La conquista de Mexico," and the introductory pieces from *Actos: El Teatro Campesino* by Luis Valdez are used by permission of the author.

The quotation from Octavio Romano, "The Historical and Intellectual Presence of Mexican Americans," which appeared in *El Grito* (Winter 1969), is used by permission of Quinto Sol Publications.

Quotations from Tomás Rivera,... *y no se lo tragó la tierra* (1971) bilingual edition *and the earth did not part* are used by permission of Quinto Sol Publications. Those from the second edition are used by permission of Editorial Justa Publications, Inc.

Fragments of the poem from Rodolfo Gonzales *I Am Joaquin* are used by permission of the author.

The fragment of "Aztec Angel" from Luis Omar Salinas' *Crazy Gipsy* is used by permission of the author.

The fragment of "Hijos de la Chicangada" by Felipe Campos-Mende is used by permission of *Revista Nosotros.*

The fragment of "smile out the revolu" from *Canto y grito mi liberación* by Ricardo Sánchez is used by permission of the author. © 1971 by Ricardo Sánchez, Ph.D.

"Comfort," "I speak in an illusion," and "Jail—Life Walk" from "Memoriam: Poems of Judy A. Lucero," which appeared in *De Colores* (Winter 1973), are used by permission of the publisher.

Fragments of "to be fathers once again," "el maguey en su desierto," "las tripas y los condes," "must be the season of the witch," "wheat paper cucarachas," and "cuervo chicano" from *Floricanto en Aztlán* by Alurista are used by permission of the author and the publisher. Copyright 1971 by the Regents of the University of California, published by The Chicano Studies Center Publications, UCLA.

Fragments of "cuete chispas," "ameridian circle," "luna llena," and "corazon nos conocemos" from *Timespace Huracan* by Alurista are used by permission of the author and Pajarito Publications.

Fragments of "come down my cheek raza rosa," "turn on," and "tuning flower tones" from *Nationchild Plumaroja* by Alurista are used by permission of Alurista, as are two fragments of an interview with Tomás Ybarra-Frausto.

"Mis ojos hinchados" from *El Espejo—The Mirror* by Alurista is used by permission of the author and Quinto Sol Publications.

Contents

Introduction
by Joseph Sommers and Tomás Ybarra-Frausto   1

I.   A Conceptual Framework

The Folk Base of Chicano Literature
by Américo Paredes   4

Mexican American Literature: A Historical Perspective
by Luis Leal   18

Critical Approaches to Chicano Literature
by Joseph Sommers   31

Spanish Codes in the Southwest
by Rosaura Sánchez   41

Toward a Concept of Culture
by Juan Gómez-Quiñones   54

II.   The Narrative: Focus on Tomás Rivera

Notes on the Evolution of Chicano Prose Fiction
by Juan Rodríguez   67

Tomás Rivera's Appropriation of the Chicano Past
by Ralph Grajeda   74

Narrative Technique and Human Experience in Tomás Rivera
by Daniel P. Testa   86

Interpreting Tomás Rivera
by Joseph Sommers   94

III.   Poetry: Alurista, Villanueva, Lucero, Zamora, Montoya

An Introduction to Chicano Poetry
by Felipe de Ortego y Gasca   108

Alurista's Poetics: The Oral, The Bilingual,
The Pre-Columbian
  by Tomás Ybarra-Frausto   117

The Other Voice of Silence: Tino Villanueva
  by Bruce-Novoa   133

Judy Lucero and Bernice Zamora:
Two Dialectical Statements in Chicana Poetry
  by Marta Sánchez   141

Linguistic Structures in José Montoya's "El Louie"
  by Ignacio Orlando Trujillo   150

IV.   Theater: Focus on El Teatro Campesino

The Development of Chicano Drama and Luis Valdez' *Actos*
  by Carlota Cárdenas de Dwyer   160

Brecht and Chicano Theater
  by Barclay Goldsmith   167

From *acto* to *mito:* A Critical Appraisal of the
Teatro Campesino
  by Yvonne Yarbro-Bejarano   176

Notes on the Editors and the Authors   186

Selected Bibliography   189

MODERN CHICANO WRITERS

Introduction

by Joseph Sommers and Tomás Ybarra-Frausto

This volume treats the literature of a people whose presence and role on the cultural stage of the United States have often been denied and certainly never recognized adequately. Numerical estimates of the Mexican—descended population in our country vary: the figure of ten million is a moderate projection. What is certain is that for several decades, Mexican Americans have been the most rapidly growing minority in the nation, a fact which is explained not only by internal demographic growth, but also by the constant arrival (Texas Rangers and border immigration agents notwithstanding) of new immigrants. Thus Chicano culture is subject to constant modification thanks to the contribution of these successive bearers of innovative language and of dynamic folk cultural traditions. Not the least of their traditions is literary expression, usually transmitted orally in its several generic variants: poetic, dramatic, and narrative.

Chicano literature is not, however, merely a reflection of modern demographic patterns or recent socio-political movements. Its history begins in 1848, when the consequences of an expansionist war dictated that tens of thousands of Mexicans should become U.S. citizens. Through the remainder of the nineteenth century, as railroads, mines, and urban areas were developed in the Southwest, and continuing through the twentieth century, when the turmoil and violence of the Mexican Revolution (1910-1920) uprooted vast sectors of society in the mother country (one million Mexicans died!), this Mexican-descended population in the United States grew steadily and extended its cultural roots ever more deeply into North American soil.

Our fundamental assumption in making this collection is that Chicano literature is a form of cultural expression by a people who have survived and grown through responding to conditions of domination. The literary consequences of these conditions have been crucial. One is a lack of access to education and a resulting cultural emphasis on oral expression and transmission rather than print. A second is the conception of literature as a local or regional phenomenon. Yet another consequence lies in the series of issues associated with language. To write in Spanish, say, at the turn of the century in Texas was to retain contact and closeness to one's community, because publication would be limited to local newspapers or regionally distributed journals. To write in English, on the other hand, required erasing from one's literary discourse shadings of localism or colloquialism, and adjusting one's thematic lens to the narrow range of perception of the predominantly Anglo-middle-class audiences who constituted the readership of the few journals willing to publish the writings of Mexican-descended authors.

Accordingly, we have tried to serve two purposes in planning the colection. To begin with, we hope to introduce Chicano literature to a broad readership. We have addressed the book simultaneously to students and teachers of Chicano literature; to critics and teachers involved with the cultural expression of other minority groups, particularly Afro-American and Puerto Rican literatures; and to members of the academic community whose interests center on the mainstream of American literature, many of whom have explicitly voiced the desire for better access to Chicano literature in order better to define the nature and scope of American literature as a whole. Our second purpose is to provide a stimulus and challenge to literary critics both in academia and in the Chicano community itself. For while literary texts have been generated and circulated for more than a century, critical evaluation and response are only now becoming defined. By way of making that stimulus real, we have commissioned eleven articles expressly for this volume. Thus our contributors include not only recognized senior scholars such as Américo Paredes, Luis Leal, and Felipe Ortego, but also younger critics at the threshold of their careers, such as Yvonne Yarbro-Bejarano, Ralph Grajeda, and Marta Sánchez.

Our own critical outlook, as reflected in the choices, omissions, and emphases we have made, is, of course, partisan. We have consciously highlighted certain qualities, while attempting to avoid what we consider misapprehensions. It has been our aim, for example, to stress implicitly and explicitly that Chicano literature has a history. While many of the critical studies we present focus on modern works, we have tried to show that a perspective indispensable to full critical understanding is the historic process of cultural continuity and change. This dimension is present in the "framing" articles by Luis Leal and Joseph Sommers, and in the introductions to each of the three generically organized sections, by Juan Rodríguez, Felipe Ortego, and Carlota Cárdenas de Dwyer.

Similarly, we have wished to demonstrate the important links between popular oral expression and print culture, suggesting that even the most developed and polished literary text, whether a personal poem by Tino Villanueva, a Rulfo-like passage from Tomás Rivera, or an allegorical scene from the Teatro Campesino, is understood more clearly when seen against its sub-surface of popular experience, language, and culture. In one way or other, consciousness of these links underlies the framing articles by Américo Paredes and Juan Gómez-Quiñones, as well as the studies by Ralph Grajeda, Tomás Ybarra-Frausto, and Marta Sánchez.

Language problems have also received our attention. The nature of bilingualism and the relation between language and class are treated from different angles by Américo Paredes, Rosaura Sánchez, Tomas Ybarra-Frausto, and Orlando Trujillo. On a practical level, we have presented some Spanish quotations in translation, rendered some texts in English alongside the Spanish originals, and left still others with their bilingual qualities intact. Further, the work of able women has been sought out, and the volume is enriched by contributions from Rosaura Sánchez, Marta Sánchez, Carlota Cárdenas de Dwyer, and Yvonne Yarbro-Bejarano. In our opinion, the article by Marta Sánchez on two largely unstudied poets, Judy Lucero and Bernice Zamora, will stimulate a number of potential studies now in various stages of elaboration.

With these as our positive emphases, we have been at pains to clear up old misapprehensions and avoid disseminating new ones. For example, we have tried to make it obvious that Chicano literature is not "newly emerged." We have questioned the desirability of assimilating Chicano literature into traditional American literature. We have been careful not to adjust our texts and evaluations to the usual criteria of the Anglo-middle-class reader, and not to accept uncritically the many cultural and racial stereotypes which have sprung from the asymmetrical relationships between Anglo-America and Mexican America.

While recognizing that Chicano literature has roots in both Mexican and Anglo-American literatures, we have tried to imply that its own cultural sources and development patterns are identical with neither. A careful reader of this volume will, we think, be convinced of the need to amplify or reinterpret the categories conventionally applied in Anglo-American literary history. Terms such as "romanticism," "frontier epic," "alienation," or "national consciousness" demand special handling if they are to be applied at all to the interpretation of Chicano texts. So do concepts derived from Mexican literary and cultural criticism like "neo-realism," "hermeticism," "the dialectics of solitude," *peladismo, malinchismo.*

On the other hand, it has seemed to us neither possible nor desirable to attempt to prescribe a canon. The criticism of Chicano literature (in comparison with the quality of the literature itself) is still underdeveloped, and much critical trial and error will be needed to raise even the right questions. For this reason, we have devoted the first section to the conceptual terrain underlying literary criticism: popular culture, literary history, sociolinguistics, culture theory, critical theory. To the same end, we have included articles and formulations which contrast with or criticize each other. The introductions by Juan Rodríguez and Felipe Ortego, for example, are based on contrasting assumptions about literary history. The articles by Joseph Sommers and Juan Bruce-Novoa are at odds in their premises about the nature and function of literary criticism. And the studies by Carlota Cárdenas de Dwyer and Yvonne Yarbro-Bejarano represent differing evaluative approaches to the Teatro Campesino. It is our hope that this volume illustrates dialectical criticism at its best and that from contrasts, differences, and debates will come clarification and higher levels of analysis.

The Folk Base of Chicano Literature

by Américo Paredes

I

In the Forties, around the time of the Second World War, a folk-in-spired Mexican song was very popular. It went like this:

Como México no hay dos	There are no two like Mexico
No hay dos en el mundo entero	There aren't two in the whole world
Ni sol que brille mejor	Nor a sun that shines brighter...
Como México no hay dos.	There are no two like Mexico.

And some Mexicans would observe with a characteristic irony, "¡Gracias a Dios!" ("Thank God.")

Both the author of the song and those who commented on it were mistaken, since it is well known that there are in fact two Mexicos. Every Mexican knows that there are two Mexicos, just as he knows that there being two is not a purely metaphysical concept, although it has its transcendental implications. The concept of two Mexicos refers to facts to be understood in the world of things. One Mexico—the "real" one, in the Platonic as well as in the ordinary sense—is found within the boundaries of the Mexican Republic. The second Mexico—the "México de Afuera," (Mexico abroad) as Mexicans call it—is composed of all the persons of Mexican origin in the United States. My present theme is the folk culture of this "México de Afuera," as manifested in folklore.

Mexican folklore and that of "México de Afuera" are commonly thought of as two related but distinct entities. There is no general agreement, however, about the differences which exist between the two. Scholars have distinguished Mexican from Mexican-American folklore in at least three ways. I will call these 1) the Hispanophile, 2) the diffusionist, and 3) the regionalist views. To express the first view in its extreme form, we would have to stress the pronounced differences between Mexican-Americans and Mexicans from Mexico. Mexican-American folklore, we would say, is almost totally Spanish—Peninsular, in other words—in its origins, having come

"The Folk Base of Chicano Literature" (editor's title), by Américo Paredes. This essay appeared in more extensive form as "El folklore de los grupos de origen mexicano en Estados Unidos" in *Folklore Americano* (Lima, Peru), 14:14 (1964), 146-63. The translation is by Kathleen Lamb. Reprinted by permission of the author.

directly from Spain to the parts of the United States where it is found today. It has no more than a remote likeness to the folklore found south of
the border between the United States and Mexico, since the latter is mixed
with indigenous elements which have diluted its grace and elegance.

A less extreme Hispanophile view is based on chronology. While folklore
of Spanish origin in the United States, we are told, has its sources in colonial Mexico, this folklore reached the Southwestern United States long
ago, when Mexico was New Spain, centuries before modern Mexico was
formed. The Spanish folklore of the United States is thus superior to that
of Mexico, not only because it is *criollo* (Spanish-American) with impec-
cable colonial credentials, but also because it represents survivals of ancient
and valuable European forms. Adapting two terms well known in *Romancero* (ballad) Studies, the Spanish folklore of the United States is considered
antiguo while the folklore of Mexico is simply *vulgar*.

The Hispanophile view does not appear in its extreme form in the work of
any serious folklorist, though it is found in that of many amateur collectors,
commentators and novelists of the Far West. Interested persons can find
all the necessary examples in the work of Cecil Robinson, *With the Ears
of Strangers*.[1] This attitude is based on a racial snobbery of which no nation
on earth is completely free, but which reached one of its high points in the
United States in the late 19th and early 20th centuries. The less extreme
form of Hispanicism, which relies on chronology, has in fact influenced
serious studies of Mexican-American folklore. It is the tacit assumption
on which the first studies of Mexican folklore were made in the United
States, especially those in New Mexico. The renowned scholar Aurelio M.
Espinosa, for instance, made admirable discoveries of remnants of Spanish
folklore in the Southwestern United States, but in general he was rarely concerned with the purely Mexican elements, which were decidedly in the majority—or if he did collect them, very seldom did he recognize them as
Mexican. Among his materials were Mexican *corridos* of very recent creation, and of undoubted Mexican origin, like "De Ignacio Parra," yet he
did not recognize them as Mexican because he was convinced of the purely
Hispanic character of New Mexican folklore.[2] His prestige, in fact, made
a sort of dogma of the supposed Peninsular origins of New Mexican folklore. For this reason, when in 1933 Arthur L. Campa affirmed its basically
Mexican character, his observations seemed almost revolutionary, though
they merely indicated what was evident to those who wished to see.[3]

The second way of interpreting Mexican-American folklore—which we

---

[1]Cecil Robinson, *With the Ears of Strangers: The Mexican in American Literature* (Tucson,
Arizona, 1963).

[2]See for example Espinosa's "Romancero nuevomejicano" in *Revue Hispanique* XXXIII:
84 (1915) 446-560; XL: 97 (1917) 215-217; XLI: 100 (1917) 687-680.

[3]Arthur L. Campa, "The Spanish Folksong in the Southwest," *University of New Mexico
Bulletin* IV: 1 (1933) 7-8, 13, 32-33, 54-56, 66.

call diffusionist—sees it as a slight isolated ripple, moving far from its origin in the great waves of Mexican folk culture centered in Jalisco, land of the *machos*. There is no need to insist on the attractions of this view for any Mexican folklorist. The converse of the Hispanophile opinion, it regards Mexican-American folklore as in no way different, original, or important, since it is merely a collection of decayed chips scattered far from the trunk. We might perhaps find a few variants of texts well-known in Mexico, variants which would serve as footnotes to Mexican folklore. That would be about all. Most native Mexican folklorists have viewed Mexican-American folklore in this way, as the detritus of Mexican folklore, when they have taken it into account at all.

Mexican-American and Mexican folklore can also be differentiated by considering the former a "regional folklore" and the latter a "national folklore." A regional folklore tradition in the United States is defined as the offshoot of some distant trunk of national folklore, which has put down deep roots in North American soil and developed characteristics of its own. The members of a regional folk culture, according to Richard M. Dorson in *American Folklore:*

> are wedded to the land and the land holds memories. The people themselves possess identity and ancestry through continuous occupation of the same soil.[4]

In his survey of United States regional folklore in *Buying the Wind*, Dorson includes Mexican-American folklore among regional folklores like those of the Pennsylvania Dutch and the Cajuns of Louisiana, thus giving Mexican-American folklore an identity of its own.[5] This is the point of view, naturally enough, of the modern North American folklorist who is interested in identifying the various threads making up the complex fabric of North American culture.

None of these three ways of seeing Mexican-American folklore is completely wrong. If we are looking for survivals, we must admit that the Mexican folk culture of the United States is often more conservative than that of Mexico, and retains folkloristic data originally from Spain which seem to have disappeared in Mexico. The ballad "La bella dama y el pastor" is an example. Apparently Mexican folklorists have been unable to collect it in their country, although it is well known both in New Mexico and southern Texas.[6] No serious folklorist nowadays would doubt, however, that "La bella dama y el pastor" reached the Southwestern United States from Mexico, in line with the most classic diffusionist principles, or that the groups of Spanish-speaking people in those areas are strictly Mexican in

[4]Richard M. Dorson, *American Folklore* (Chicago, 1959) p. 75.
[5]Richard M. Dorson, *Buying the Wind: Regional Folklore in the United States* (Chicago, 1964) 415-95.
[6]I should mention that I have collected versions of this ballad within the boundaries of Mexico, in the city of Matamoros, Tamaulipas. But Tamaulipas is the old province of Nuevo Santander, together with southern Texas.

origin and culture.[7] Neither is it wrong to refer to the cultures of these groups as "regional cultures." They are Mexican-Americans who have been established for centuries in the regions where they live, and far from being "immigrants" themselves, can view the North American as the immigrant.

II

But this is not the whole story. The attention of folklorists has been limited almost exclusively so far to regional groups, that is, to groups established for generations in certain parts of the Southwest. Only a minority of the Mexicans in the United States, however, live within these groups. If we consider Mexican-Americans folklore as a totality, we find other kinds of groups besides regional ones. We also find evidence of a series of exchanges between endemic Mexican folklore and that of the "México de Afuera," a continuous mutual influence moving in both directions which is not typical of other regional cultures in the United States. This is the result of a simple geographical fact: the Atlantic Ocean divides Pennsylvania from Germany, and Louisiana from France, but only an imaginary line divides "México de Adentro" (Mexico as a territorial unit) from "México de Afuera." This line is easy to cross, legally or illegally.

At least three kinds of folklore groups of Mexican origin can be found in the United States. First, there are the truly regional groups; second, the groups composed of rural or semirural immigrants; and third, the urban groups. The first, as we have said, are composed of descendants of the early settlers on the northern frontiers of New Spain. At present, they are found in only two areas. One, more or less equivalent to the former province of Nuevo México, includes the present state of New Mexico, West Texas, parts of Arizona and Colorado, and the Mexican state of Chihuahua. The second area, corresponding to the former province of Nuevo Santander, is comprised of southern Texas, from the Nueces River to the Río Grande, the Mexican state of Tamaulipas, and nearby areas of Coahuila and Nuevo León. Two similar regions existed in California and the former province of Texas, but it has been some time since they sustained Mexican-American folk cultures of the regional type. After 1849, Mexican settlements in California were engulfed in the wave of North American immigration caused by the discovery of gold, so that only traces remain of *californio* traditions. The Mexicans who lived in the province of Texas— the region east and north of the Río Nueces—were almost all driven from their homes after Texas gained independence in 1836. Only in the areas which earlier formed part of the provinces of Nuevo México and Nuevo Santander have Mexican-American folk groups of the regional type sur-

[7]Of course I am not referring to recently immigrated groups like the Basques and the Sephardic Jews.

vived. In those areas, folklore materials from Spain and Mexico have been kept alive for many generations, and local adaptations have been made as well. These two regions are well known to folklorists. What is often not known is that their limits are not defined by the Customs and Immigration offices at the border. Parts of northern Mexico are included within the boundaries of each. These regional folk cultures thus include regions of two nations.

The folk groups composed of rural or semi-rural immigrants are formed to a large extent by *braceros* (migrant workers) from the interior of Mexico, who began to enter the United States in growing numbers at the turn of the century. In Border areas they frequently displaced the day laborers born and brought up in those areas, who were forced to emigrate to the northern United States. In successive waves, *braceros* from southern Mexico established themselves among the regional groups, reoccupied formerly Mexican areas of California and Texas, and penetrated into parts of the United States to which Mexican culture had not extended before. Since they are almost all agricultural workers they have congregated in farming communities, where they constitute a pool of badly paid labor. Their folklore has much in common with that of the regional groups, but it is enriched by material recently brought from the interior of Mexico. For example, the water spirit which haunted the shores of the Papaloapan in Veracruz now appears by the banks of the Río Grande in Texas, or the Colorado in Arizona.

The third type of Mexican-American folk group (the urban) is found in the *Mexiquitos* of North American cities like Los Angeles, Chicago and San Antonio. Some members of these urban groups come from the regional groups, displaced by *braceros* migrating from Mexico. Others are enterprising ex-*braceros* who came to work in the fields and stayed on as employees in the factories of the big cities. Children and grandchildren of political refugees who left Mexico during the Revolution are also almost always found in cities. The folklore of these urban groups comes, for the most part, from the regional groups and from the immigrant farm workers, although it has been adapted to the needs of life in the city. A marked emphasis is given to such forms as the *caló* (dialect), the *albur* (word play), the *blazon populaire*, and to the *chascarrillo* (joke) known to all the ethnic groups of the city.

Of the three groups, those least affected by the process of transculturation are the immigrant field workers; it would be difficult to decide which of the other two—the urban or the regional—has experienced a greater degree of transculturation, since both types are bilingual in varying degrees. The member of the urban groups is more subject to external influences, and is thus also the object of greater hostility, caused by the pressures and complexities of urban life. As a result, he feels less at ease in his environment than the member of the regional group. The latter, in turn, while his regional consciousness may permit a more favorable synthesis, finds himself more isolated from North American cultural traditions. These three folk groups which make up "México de Afuera" are constantly influencing one another at the same time that they are the object of all sorts of influences from Mexico as well as from the United States. They also exercise a certain influence in both Mexico and the United States. Mexican folklore, that is, like the concept of a "México de Afuera," knows no borders.

III

The first Mexicans to become permanent residents of the United States —with the exceptions of a few political refugees—were the inhabitants of the Mexican territories ceded to the United States in 1848. This was the origin of the regional folk-groups, and these were the first Mexican-Americans—the majority of them very much against their will. They were at once involved in a long-drawn-out struggle with the North Americans and their culture. Cultural differences were aggravated by the opportunism of many North American adventurers, who in their desire for riches treated the new citizens from the start as a conquered people. Names like Juan Nepomuceno Cortina, Aniceto Pizaña, Gregorio Cortez and Elfego Baca—all men who, as a *corrido* (narrative folk song) puts it "defendieron su derecho" ("defended their right")—were immortalized in songs and legends. This was the birth— ten years after the war between Mexico and the United States—of the first examples of Mexican-American folklore. Some of these rebels against the government of the United States were killed or taken prisoner by the North American authorities, who naturally treated them as bandits and law-breakers. Others escaped to Mexico, where they lived out their lives as symbols of Anglo-American injustice.

If we look at the history of Mexico from a general point of view, Mexican nationalist feeling does not define itself until the last third of the Nineteenth Century and owes a great deal to the French occupation during the reign of Maximilian of Austria. In the northern frontiers, however, and in the parts of the United States recently taken from Mexico, nationalism begins to be felt toward the end of the 1830s, if we may take the folklore of those regions as an indication. It is a blaze stirred up by the daily conflict between the quietism of the Mexican and the power, the aggressiveness, and the foreign culture of the Anglo-American. On the one hand, this conflict was expressed almost immediately in folkloric data, in *corridos* and other songs, semi-historical legends, insulting labels for North Americans. On the other hand, these folk artifacts reinforced psychological attitudes toward the United States and helped to isolate the regional groups, making them more typically "folk" than ever.

The Mexican saw himself and all that he stood for as continually challenging a foreign people who treated him, for the most part, with disdain. Being Mexican meant remaining inviolable in the face of overwhelming attack on one's personality. Under those circumstances, for a Mexican to accept North American values was to desert under fire. Such a situation—creative of folk groups defined as minorities—is not historically unique. It has been repeated many times with other peoples whose identity has been menaced. Among people within their own borders—the Poles, let us say, the Finns, the Irish or the Greeks—such a situation has created an intensified nationalism. In contrast, other peoples who have existed as minorities within a dominant group—the Jews in Europe, for example—have maintained their identity through very close cultural bonds. The Border Mexican-American, because of his special relationship to the United States, made use of both these solutions.

It is not until 1890 that the immigration of new Mexican elements to the United States really begins, as part of a reciprocal movement: at the same time that North American capital invades Mexico, the Mexican *bracero* invades the United States. The cause is the same: the expansion in industry and finance which occurred in the United States in the decades after the Civil War (1861-1865). By 1890 North American capital was strong enough to look for foreign investments, and the government of Porfirio Díaz welcomed it to Mexico. It was around this time that the Díaz government became oppressive. The exploitation of the nation's natural resources by foreign capital worsened the already miserable situation of the Mexican peasant.

Migrant work was nothing new to the field worker from the interior of Mexico, but now he began to extend his trips from the states neighboring his own to the northern part of the country, and finally across the border. In the United States everything was ready to welcome him. The Civil War had initiated a shift in population from rural areas to the city, at the same time that the nation's total population increased, causing a greater demand for agricultural products. European immigrants were arriving in great numbers, but they remained in the big cities as factory workers, or if they turned to agriculture it was in the northern part of the country. There were harvests to reap and railroad tracks to lay in the South and the Southeast. This demand was met by the *bracero*. *Braceros* immigrated to Texas at first, and to other Border regions, but with time they moved farther and farther north—to the railroads of West Virginia and Pennsylvania, to the sugar beet fields in Michigan, and finally, to the factories of the Great Lakes. According to the Twelfth Edition of the Encyclopedia Britannica, in 1908 there were 71,000 Mexican immigrants in Texas alone; in 1920 there were a quarter million. In 1910, 2% of all the immigration to the United States was from Mexico; in 1920 it was 12%.

IV

The Mexican *bracero* in the United States became a more or less permanent source of labor—and a minority made up of immigrants in a situation little superior to that of the former slaves, with whom they competed for work. The great antagonism between Blacks and Mexicans which resulted was often the cause of violence between the two groups. Also the Mexican *bracero* was identified with the Black in the mind of the Anglo-American. In this way racial prejudices were added to prejudices based on linguistic differences and other cultural factors, resulting in exclusion from restaurants, beaches, and theatres, and segregation in special schools. As the number of Mexican immigrants in the United States grew, these discriminatory practices increased as well, including lynchings of Mexicans accused of raping North American women.

Treatment of the *bracero* has varied with the use which could be made of him, and the Immigration Laws have been applied at the convenience of the American farmers who hired him. In times when labor has been in short supply he has been well received. When the need for him was not so great, efforts were made to prevent his passage from Mexico to the United States, not only by legal means but also by intimidation and insults from Customs and Immigration agents. In times of economic depression, he has been suddenly deported and forced to abandon family ties formed during a stay of twenty or more years in the United States. In fairness, we must note that the Mexican immigrant's sense of continuing to "pass through" after twenty years or more of residence in the United States contributed to his problems, since he remained a perennial visitor in a foreign country, without exercising the rights and the duties of citizenship. And he brought up his children born in the United States in his own way of thinking. Here we see an extension of the concept of a "México de Afuera" already described in discussing the regional groups.

A brief mention of the urban groups remains to be made. Of course Mexicans have always lived in North American cities like San Antonio, where the Mexican element has been present since Texas was part of Mexico. But we do not find really large groups or "colonies" of Mexicans in the cities of the United States until the Mexican Revolution, that is from 1911 on. With the Revolution comes another type of Mexican immigrant: the refugee from fratricidal wars and the political exile, among whom were many of Mexico's intellectuals. These people naturally went to the cities—to suffer all the anxieties of exile in an environment hardly noted for its sympathy with the Mexican and his culture. These exiled intellectuals lost no time in becoming the leaders and models in the "Mexican colonies" of the big cities, so effectively that some cities like San Antonio and Los Angeles became Mexican cultural centers in exile for a time. But these "colonies" were not composed only of exiles; they also included many other Mexicans who had come to the United States not in flight from the Revolution, but in search of work. During the First World War large numbers of *braceros* — and Mexican-Americans from the regional groups as well — abandoned rural areas and small farms for the cities, where they found work in the industries promoted by the war.

While others formed the majority in the "colonias mexicanas," the refugees imposed the intellectual and emotional tone. To them, all the Mexicans in the United States were living in unhappy exile, outlawed from the homeland they longed for and eager to return at the first opportunity. Here once more the concept of "México de Afuera" appears, but with intellectual embellishments which were lacking in the viewpoints of the regional groups and the immigrants — all of this developing in *barrios* very similar to the *ghettos* of European Jews. As in the case of the Jews, segregation in the *ghetto* was in part imposed by external circumstances and in part was the result of cultural preference. This "exile" — that is, "exile" as a state of mind — lasted until the administration of Lázaro Cárdenas issued a general amnesty. Some few Mexicans abandoned "el México de Afuera" and returned to their homeland; the majority stayed in the "Mexiquitos" of North America's cities, without completely giving up the idea that they were living in exile. This is the older generation, of course. An entire generation of Mexicans has since been born and grown up in the big cities of the United States which does not understand the "exile" attitude adopted by its parents, yet through their behavior feels the differences which distinguish it from Anglo-Americans. These young people have in self-defense adopted many ways of behaving different from those of their parents, exaggerating these traits as much as those they have inherited in the desire to create a new personality of their own. This is the origin of the "pocho," the "pachuco" — the child born in the *ghetto* — although his "mores" have been extended in many cases to the regional groups and the rural immigrants.

V

At this point, the reader may well ask the reason for so much attention to the relations between the United States and Mexico, and to the social and economic conditions of Mexicans within the United States, in a work whose theme is Mexican-American folklore. The reason is that the shock of cultures and peoples in a continuing situation of cultural conflict has given Mexican-American folklore the traits which distinguish it from other folklores, including that of Mexico. The rest is Mexican folklore, and by extension, Spanish-American, Spanish, or universal folklore. *Märchen* registered in the Aarne-Thompson index of types can be collected from Mexican-Americans as from other folk groups, as Aurelio and José Manuel Espinosa demonstrated many years ago. The same may be said of the tales and *romances* (ballads) found especially in New Mexico. The links between Mexican-American folklore and all of Spanish America were pointed out by Arthur Campa as far back as 1933, while already in 1891 Captain John G. Bourke was collecting in southern Texas folk material as typically Mexican as the "Pastorelas" (Christmas plays).[8] This is all material of importance, worthy of the study it has received and continues to receive. But it does not mark Mexican-American folk groups as the possessors of a distinctive folklore. A purely Mexican-American folklore must be sought in the conflict of cultures. Its initial genre is the Mexican-American or Border *corrido* (narrative folk song), which appears as an anticipatory phase of the Mexican *corrido*. Vicente T. Mendoza tells us that the "*corrido mexicano* begins in the last quarter of the nineteenth century, with the singing of the deeds of various rebels against the government of Porfirio Díaz...[this was] the real beginning of the period in which the courage of the protagonists and their disregard for their lives was underlined and given emphasis."[9] But in southern Texas and nearby areas of northern Mexico, *corridos* of this type which sing the feats of the first Mexican-American rebels against the North American government already exist at the end of the 1850s. The uprising led by Juan Nepomuceno Cortina in southern Texas in 1859 was celebrated in *corridos* of which we still have fragments. From the *corridos* of Cortina on, this Mexican-American genre develops in a form similar to its Mexican counterpart, but with characteristics peculiarly its own. The hero is always a Mexican whose rights or self-respect are trampled upon by North American authority. Very often the conflict begins with the cruel and unjust death of the hero's brother at the hands of Anglo-Americans. The hero takes vengeance and is attacked by large numbers of *rinches* or "Texas Rangers." He kills large numbers of the enemy but it is impossible for him to win a final victory because the odds are so unfair. One of these protagonists, Gregorio Cortez, describes such a situation: "¡Ah, cuánto rinche montado, para un solo mexicano!" (Ah, how many mounted Rangers, against one lone Mexican). This is clearly an expression of the Mexican's general state of mind on seeing himself attacked on every level of his existence by a people more powerful and more numerous than his own.

Another type of Mexican-American *corrido*, also older than the *corrido mexicano*, is that dealing with the adventures of a group of Mexicans whose work forces them to travel deep into the United States. Always narrated in the first person plural, these *corridos* recount the perils of the trip, the foreign cities and the strange things seen by the adventurers. An example is "El corrido de Kiansis," from the 1860s, which relates the journey of a group of *vaqueros* (cowboys) driving a herd of cattle from South Texas to the ends of the railroad lines in the south of Kansas:

[8]Aurelio M. Espinosa, "Comparative Notes on New Mexican and Mexican Spanish Folktales," *Journal of American Folklore* XXVII (1914) 211-31. José Manuel Espinosa, *Spanish Folktales from New Mexico* (New York, 1937). Campa, op. cit., pp. 16, 23-33. M. R. Cote, *Los Pastores: A Mexican Play of the Nativity* (Boston and New York, 1907).

[9]Vicente T. Mendoza, *El corrido mexicano* (Mexico City, 1954) XV. *Lírica narrativa de México* (Mexico City, 1964) 14.

14

Américo Paredes

Cuando salimos pa' Kiansis	When we left for Kansas
con una grande partida,	With a great herd of cattle
!Ha, qué camino tan largo!	Ah, what a long trail it was!
No contaba con mi vida.	I was not sure I would survive.

Sixty years later the type persists in "El Corrido de la Pensilvania," which narrates the adventures of other Mexicans who go from Texas to Pennsylvania, not driving steers this time but to work on the railroad. The same narrative pattern is preserved, and the same tone and style of narration:

De la suidá de For West (Fort Worth)	From the city of Fort Worth,
a las seis de la mañana	at six o'clock in the morning
salimos en un enganche	we left on a labor contract
para el estado de Pensilvania.	for the state of Pennsylvania.

Other *corridos* about migrant workers are concerned not with adventures on the road but with the injustices and sufferings endured by the *bracero,* whether from his North American bosses, from racial discrimination, or from Immigration agents. We find *corridos* with titles like "Los Deportados," ("The Deported Ones"), "La Discriminación," "Los Enganchados," ("The Work Gang") or "Tristes Quejas de un Bracero" ("A Bracero's Plaint"). The expression of grievances—or more properly social protest—is evident in them:

Los gringos son muy maloras,	The gringos are very tricky;
se valen de la ocasión;	they take advantage of the opportunity,
y a todos los mexicanos	and treat us all
nos tratan sin compasión.	without compassion.

In the *canción* we find happier themes—comic compositions in bilingual form, and other satirical texts which ridicule North American customs. In some the Mexican-American satirizes his situation, making use of his own propensity to mix Spanish with English:

En Texas es terrible	In Texas it is terrible
por la revoltura que hay;	how things are all mixed up:
no hay quien diga "Hasta mañana";	no one says "hasta mañana,"
nomás puro "Goodbye".	it is nothing but "Goodbye."

In another a newly arrived *bracero* criticizes the freedom of the North American woman:

Desde México he venido,	From Mexico have I come,
nomás por venir a ver	just to come and see
esa ley americana	this American law that says
que aquí manda la mujer.	the woman is the boss.

In prose narratives, the legend and the belief tale, as well as the comic anecdote are used to develop themes of cultural conflict. "La Muerte de

Antonio Rodríguez" (The Death of Antonio Rodríguez), for example, is a story based on an historical event: the lynching of a young Mexican who was apparently burned alive in a small town in Texas in 1910. In a variant collected in 1962, the story retains its tone of outrage and indignation after half a century, but the additions of universal motifs like K 2111, Potiphar's Wife, have converted the story into legend. Another example is the legend of José Mosqueda, which dates from the 1890s. Although Mosqueda was an ordinary train robber, his legend has been given traces of cultural conflict. In addition, some versions approach the *Märchen* in the variety of motifs which have been woven into the narrative: for example, G 303.10.5, Where the Devil Can't Reach He Sends An Old Woman, and S 241, Child Unwittingly Promised: "First Thing You Meet..." At the end of the tale, the malevolent old woman sells José Mosqueda for a large sum in dollars but the North American she is working with betrays her and doesn't give her a single cent. If old women are worse than the devil, then according to this legend North Americans are worse than old women.

VI

My intention has been not only to present a rapid overview of the genesis and development of Mexican-American folklore but to demonstrate the importance of cultural conflict in its formation. I have also wished to point out the necessity of studying these factors, to which folklorists have given scant attention. Let us go back for a moment to the three points of view which most scholars have adopted toward Mexican-American folklore. Naturally, nothing of what has interested us here can be hoped for from the Hispanophiles. A fragment of a ballad about El Cid inevitably has more interest for them than three dozen examples of folkloric data such as those I have given. True, Aurelio Espinosa was interested not only in Spanish survivals in New Mexico but in folkloric data which seemed to be genuine products of New Mexican folk groups. True, also, that his mistakenly identifying these with Mexican materials was less his fault than the result of the state of folklore studies at that time, which took little interest in its social context. Nevertheless, the contribution of the Hispanophiles to a modern understanding of these materials has been small.

The same may be said of "diffusionists" like Vicente T. Mendoza. As late as 1954, when *El corrido mexicano* appears, he is ignorant of an entire tradition of Mexican-American border *corridos*. It is true that he includes a variant of "El corrido de Kiansis" in *El corrido mexicano*, but he identifies it as proceeding from the mountains of Chihuahua. Not until 1964, in *Lírica narrativa de México* does he recognize the existence of a type of *corrido* which deserves to be called *fronterizo* in a summary reference to "El corrido de Gregorio Cortez"—but he later identifies this same "Corrido de Gregorio

Cortez" as from Coahuila!¹⁰ This is strange indeed, since I do not have the least doubt that by 1960 Mendoza was aware that "El corrido de Gregorio Cortez" comes from South Texas.

The "regionalists" are a separate case for two reasons: first, because they have been relatively numerous and active in the collection of Mexican-American folklore; second, because the perspective they have taken toward that folklore sets it apart as something individual. They are interested in the Mexican-American as such [in his role as Mexican-American] and much might be hoped for from them in analysis of the folklore of "El México de Afuera." But they disappoint us. The "diffusionist" may not be aware of the origin of Mexican-American folklore or may ignore it; the "Hispanicist" may show a great preference for cultural survivals; yet authentic folklore texts can be expected from each. In contrast, many of the texts published by the "regionalists" have been vitiated by a limited knowledge of the language and by either a too romantic vision of the folk or an attitude of arrogant condescension. Their supposed "informants" talk like Castilian grandees or else stereotyped Mexicans in a third rate film.

Most "regionalists," moreover, have been romantics through and through. The romantic point of view deals not with living things but with idealizations of them, in a world where there are no contemporary problems. This romantic attitude very often follows the conquest of new territory. In the history of Spanish folklore, the vogue for everything *morisco* (Moorish) after the fall of Granada is well known. It is this tendency to sentimentalize a conquered people, with its elements of condescension, which directs the efforts of the majority of "regionalists." They have focussed their energies on the regional groups, that is to say on the "Romantic Southwest." They look for local color, for the rare, the archaic, the bizarre, and as a result the sort of folklore with which we are concerned has small place in their collections.

Combine this with lack of personal communication between collector and informant, and you have the regionalists' most serious flaw. This is why J. Frank Dobie, for example, could spend his life among Mexican informants in Mexico as well as in the United States without ever really getting to know them; why John A. Lomax and others collected Mexican songs in South Texas without being aware of the existence of a whole tradition of Border *corridos* dealing with cultural conflict. They collected variants of the "Corrido de los Sediciosos" ("Corrido of the Seditionists") which relates the uprising in 1915 of a group of Texas Mexicans commanded by Aniceto Pizaña, but they were variants which ridicule the "sediciosos" and give the role of hero to the Texas Rangers, hated so strongly by the regional folk groups!

A certain mistaken delicacy, or the desire not to offend, not to bring up painful matters which we all know have existed and which we all want to remedy, has convinced some folklorists that it would be in poor taste to ex-

---

¹⁰Mendoza, *Lírica narrativa*, 35 and 204.

pose the conflict between the Mexican and North American cultures. But this is to deny folklore study its place as a scholarly discipline. It belongs with the opinion that anyone who studies obscene folklore is an obscene person and that anyone who studies popular beliefs must be superstitious as well.

For one or several of the reasons given, the folklorists of the past paid little attention to the most characteristic aspects of Mexican-American folklore. The task of making these known remained for investigators whose primary interest was not folklore—sociologists, economists, linguists, and anthropologists. The first published variant of the "Corrido de Gregorio Cortez"—the synthesis of the *corrido* of cultural conflict—appeared in 1930 and owes its appearance to don Manuel Gamio.[11] The economist Paul S. Taylor published a variant of the "Corrido de la Pensilvania" in 1931, and both Gamio and Taylor have made various *corridos* of the *braceros* known through their writings.[12] Linguists have studied gestures, insulting names, and *caló* (dialect) in general, and there have also been studies of the social context by sociologists and anthropologists.[13]

Meanwhile, in the United States we have a new generation of folklorists with a different orientation and a better training in languages. They are responsible for a new and greater interest in Mexican-American folk culture. In this way we are beginning to recognize throughout the United States that "como Mexico sí hay dos."

[11]Manuel Gamio, *Mexican Immigration to the United States* (Chicago, 1930) 96.

[12]Paul S. Taylor, *Mexican Labor in the United States* (Berkeley, California, 1931) cii-ix.

[13]Charles E. Kany, *American-Spanish Semantics* (Berkeley, California, 1960) and *American-Spanish Euphemisms* (Berkeley, California, 1960). Munroe Edmonson, *Los Manitos* (New Orleans, 1957).

Mexican American Literature:
A Historical Perspective

by Luis Leal

Mexican American literature of all genres is being written, published, and appraised at a striking rate. In addition to established journals such as *El Grito, Aztlán,* and *Con Safos,* new periodicals dedicated to the dissemination of Chicano culture continue to appear.[1] In 1970, at its meeting in New York City, the Modern Language Association included a workshop on Chicano studies; at its meeting in Detroit in 1971, the Midwest Modern Language Association accepted a paper on Chicano literature; and in December of that same year the American Association of Teachers of Spanish and Portuguese, meeting in Chicago, dedicated an entire section of its program to the examination of Mexican American literature. This condition of affairs has been aptly called by Philip D. Ortego a "Chicano Renaissance."[2]

It is our belief that an effort should be made to trace the historical development of Mexican American literature now that it has been recognized as a subject worthy of serious study. It has not yet been determined, however, whether Mexican American literature should be considered as an entity in itself, as a part of American literature, or even, perhaps, as a part of Mexican literature. It has been pointed out that since Chicanos are Americans, their literature should not be separated from American literature. On the other hand, since a large part of Mexican American literature is written in Spanish, or is bilingual, its study has often been assigned to critics and professors of Spanish American literature, primarily those acquainted with Mexican literature, for Chicano literature is a living organism: its roots are to be found in the long literary tradition of Mexico, while its flowers grow

---

"Mexican American Literature: A Historical Perspective" by Luis Leal. This essay is an updated version of the article which appeared in *Revista Chicano-Riqueña,* I, no. 1 (1973), 32-44. Reprinted by permission of the author and the publisher.

[1] This paper was prepared with the collaboration of my wife, Gladys Leal. I take this opportunity to thank her for her generous contribution. It first appeared in the *Revista Chicano-Riqueña,* 1:1 (1973), 32-44. Since its publication the interest in Chicano literature, as well as the number of new periodicals that have appeared, has been tremendous. Some of the other literary periodicals that have contributed to this renaissance are: *De Colores, Grito del Sol, Mester, Revista Chicano-Riqueña,* and *La Luz.* These notes have been updated.

[2] Philip D. Ortego, "The Chicano Renaissance," *Social Casework,* 52-5 (May, 1971), 294-307.

for the English or bilingual reader, and especially for the Chicanos who form part of that reading public. Though the use of a dual language poses a problem for critics, excellent contributions of criticism and analysis have already been made by specialists in both English and Spanish American studies, such as Philip D. Ortego, Gerald Haslam, Robert Blauner, Edward Simmen, Octavio Ignacio Romano-V., Herminio Ríos C., Tomás Rivera, and José R. Reyana.[3] The training of Chicano specialists conversant not only with American literature but with Mexican letters and Chicano culture will accelerate the formation of a tradition in Chicano literary criticism. Better still would be the training of Chicanos themselves to evaluate their own artistic productions. In regard to this, Teresa McKenna has said, "The Chicano must not only address himself to the creation of a distinct literature emergent from his own reality, he must also contribute to the further richness of his art through the development of a body of criticism that approaches Chicano literature from a Chicano perspective."[4]

To consider Chicano literature as a part of American literature is an object too idealistic, at least for the time being, for socially Chicanos are considered a group apart. The rejection of the Mexican American in the United States is well documented. One of the best studies is that of Carey McWilliams who, in 1949, published *North from Mexico*, one of the first books to explore the plight of the Chicano in the United States with a sympathetic attitude.[5] The rejection of the Chicano is also reflected in literature, as demonstrated by Cecil Robinson in *With the Ears of Strangers: The Mexican in American Literature*[6] and in the short stories collected by Simmen in his anthology, *The Chicano: from Caricature to Self-Portrait.*[7]

Neither can we say that Chicano literature is a branch of Mexican literature even though it has, as we have said, its roots there, and still derives inspiration and a model from it. That the Chicano is rejected in the United States does not mean that he has always been accepted in Mexico, or even by Mexicans visiting the United States. Amado. Nervo, passing through the United States in 1900 on his way to Europe, wrote: "Walking the streets of San Antonio, Texas, I come across one or another type of Mexican, but all so distasteful that I dare not approach them, because I know that from their

[3]Also Rolando Hinojosa S., Francisco Jiménez, Charles M. Tatum, Juan Bruce-Novoa, Guillermo Rojas, Roberto Cantú, Frank Pino, Juan Rodríguez, Joseph Sommers, Francisco A. Lomelí, Tomás Ybarra-Frausto, Arturo Madrid, and others.

[4]Teresa McKenna, "Three Novels: An Analysis," *Aztlán*, 1:2 (Fall, 1970), 47.

[5]Carey McWilliams, *North from Mexico* (Philadelphia and New York: J. B. Lippincott Co., 1949). This book has been recently translated into Spanish, *Al Norte de México* (México: Siglo XXI, Editores, 1968). A recent article is that of John Womack, "Los Chicanos (1)," *Plural,* 12 (Sept., 1972), 3-8.

[6]Cecil Robinson, *With the Ears of Strangers: The Mexican in American Literature* (Tucson: The University of Arizona Press, 1963).

[7]Edward Simmen (ed.), *The Chicano: from Caricature to Self-Portrait* (New York and Toronto: Mentor, 1971).

lips I can expect only gutter sentences, and I do not wish to witness the profanation of the harmonious treasure of my old Latin language."[8] In more recent years, walking down the streets of Los Angeles, another American city with a large Chicano population, the poet Octavio Paz had this to say: "Something similar occurs with the Mexicans whom one meets in the street; although they have lived there for many years, they still wear the same clothing, speak the same language, and are ashamed of their origins. No one would confuse them with authentic North Americans."[9] The same point is made from a different direction by José Vasconcelos in defining *pocho*: "A word that is used in California to designate the outcast who rejects Mexican culture although he has it in his blood, and who attempts to adjust all his actions imitatively to those of the present rulers of the region."[10]

This attitude is not confined to writers alone. The new immigrant too, often considered himself superior to the conforming Mexican American. The sociologist, Manuel Gamio, in 1931 collected this testimony from Anastacio Torres, of León, Guanajuato: "I don't have anything against the *pochos*, but the truth is that although they are Mexicans, for they are of our own blood because their parents were Mexicans, they pretend that they are Americans. They also want to talk in English and they speak Spanish very badly. That is why I don't like them."[11] In recent years, of course, this attitude has changed in Mexico mainly as a result of the Chicanos' struggle for civil rights. The Chicanos and their problems are now viewed with sympathy, and an effort is being made to understand them, as is evidenced by recent articles in the weekly review *Siempre!*, in the important *Cuadernos Americanos*, and in books such as those written by Gilberto López y Rivas and Hernán Solís Garza.[12]

If the Chicano was rejected by both the Anglo-American and the Mexican national, he himself rejected both groups. "The 'Pachuco'," says Paz, "does not wish to return to his Mexican origin; nor it would seem does he wish to blend into North American life." (p. 13). This desire to establish an identity has resulted in the creation of a unique literature which reflects Chicano culture and possesses characteristics that differentiate it from Anglo-American as well as Mexican literature.

[8]Amado Nervo, *El éxodo y las flores del camino* (Madrid: Biblioteca Nueva, 1920), p. 15. The 1st edition of this book appeared in 1902.

[9]Octavio Paz, *El laberinto de la soledad* (México: *Fondo de Cultura Económica*, 1959), p. 12. The 1st edition of this book appeared in 1950.

[10]José Vasconcelos, "Asoma el pochismo," *La tormenta*, in *Obras*, I (México: Libreros Mexicanos Unidos, 1957), p. 781.

[11]Manuel Gamio, *The Mexican Immigrant: His Life Story* (Chicago: The University of Chicago Press, 1931), p. 58.

[12]See *La Cultura en México*, Supplement of *Siempre!* No. 463 (Diciembre 23, 1970), Adolfo G. Domínguez, "El chicanismo: sus orígenes y actualidad política," *Cuadernos Americanos*, 175:2 (marzo-abril, 1971), 64-76; Gilberto López y Rivas, *Los Chicanos: una minoría nacional explotada* (México: Ediciones Nuestro Tiempo, 1971); Hernán Solís Garza, *Los mexicanos del Norte* (México: Editorial Nuestro Tiempo, 1971), ch. 4.

Before the word Chicano became naturalized, no one spoke of a Mexican American literature or a Mexican American art. On this account, some critics have tended to identify Chicano literature with that written during the last decade by militants. Simmen, in the Introduction to his collection of short stories, claims that Chicano literature did not exist before our own days. To explain its absence, he argues that Chicano society did not permit the appearance of the Chicano writer. The rich, educated minority were not interested in writing, and the poor were not trained to do so. The emerging middle class, the so-called *vendidos*, were not concerned, Simmen holds, to preserve their way of life, and therefore had no will to give it expression in literary works. To prove his theory, Simmen cites his own bibliography of Chicano literature, in which the earliest Chicano work dates from 1947. But this is argument by fiat. For Simmen, a Chicano can only be an American of Mexican descent who has liberal or radical ideas about the social and economic order. Necessarily, then, Chicano literature is of recent origin, appearing at the same time as the social and economic movement called "El movimiento."

A less restrictive definition is that of Luis Dávila. He holds that Chicano literature is literature written by Americans of Mexican descent "regardless of what they might prefer to call themselves." If it is of recent origin this is because "the bicultural Mexican-American writer of yesteryear often found himself in awkward relation to the supposedly monolithic cultures of the United States and Mexico. For this reason he virtually did not exist."[13] For a definition still less restrictive, one may point to Herminio Ríos C., who identifies Mexican American (or Chicano) literature as that written by the Spanish speaking inhabitants of the Southwest since 1848.[14]

During the 1930s and before, Americans of Mexican descent and "Americanized" Mexicans were called *pochos* by the recent immigrants. In return, the "pochos" called the immigrants *chicanos* (short for *mexicanos*[15]). The terms *chicano* and Mexican American thus came to be used interchangeably.[16] The review *El Grito*, founded by Chicanos and a stout defender of *chicanismo*, calls itself in its subtitle "A Journal of Contemporary Mexican American Thought."

On these grounds, we shall consider Chicano literature here to be that literature written by Mexicans and their descendants living or having lived in what is now the United States. We shall consider works, especially those

---

[13]Luis Dávila, "On the Nature of Chicano Literature: En los extremos del Laberinto," MMLA Convention, Detroit, Michigan, 1971, Spanish Section III, p. 1.

[14]Herminio Ríos C., "Introduction to Tomás Rivera, *...y no se lo tragó la tierra* (Berkeley, California: Quinto Sol Publications, 1971), p. viii.

[15]A possible explanation could be that the word *mexicano* was shortened to *xicano* (pronounced *chicano*, due to Aztec influence).

[16]Luis Valdez in his "Teatro Campesino," however, makes a clear distinction between *chicano* and Mexican American. For him the Mexican Americans are the so-called *vendidos*, or Americanized persons of Mexican descent. See especially his play "Los vendidos" in *Actos: El teatro campesino* (San Juan Bautista, California: Cucaracha Publications, 1971), pp. 35-49.

dating before 1821, written by the inhabitants of this region with a Spanish background, to belong to an early stage of Chicano literature. We are not overlooking the fact that before 1848 Mexican Americans legally did not exist as a group; they have, however, a long uninterrupted literary tradition. Though in 1848 English became the official language of the Mexican territory annexed to the United States and for this reason affected the development of the literature of the region, it did not interrupt the tradition.

Accepting this definition of Chicano, we can say that Chicano literature had its origin when the Southwest was settled by the inhabitants of Mexico during Colonial times and continues uninterrupted to the present. We shall divide its course into five literary periods and cite a few representative authors of each. A great deal of research must yet be done to give Mexican American literature the attention it deserves. Here we can only hint at the possiblities.

1. The Hispanic Period (to 1821)

This first period is characterized by prose writings of a historical or semi-historical nature including many descriptions left behind by explorers of the region where the majority of Chicanos now live. Among them we find the *Relaciones* of Alvar Núñez Cabeza de Vaca, Fr. Marcos de Niza (*Relación del descubrimiento de las Siete Ciudades*), and Fr. Francisco Palou; the *diarios* of Juan Bautista de Anza, Miguel Costanso, Fr. Juan Crespi, Fr. Tomás de la Peña, Gaspar de Portalá, and Fr. Junípero Serra; also, a number of *historias, memorias, recuerdos, anales,* and *apuntes*. More significant, perhaps, is the *Historia de la Nueva México*, a rhymed history of the conquest of New Mexico in 34 cantos by Gaspar Pérez de Villagrá.

Essentially, these works do *not* belong to the history of Spanish literature. In the words of Federico de Onís, "The originality of Spanish American literature exists from the very beginning, from the very moment at which America itself commences to exist. ...'Originality' derives from 'origin,' and American originality lies in the fact of being America and not Europe."[17] Somewhat earlier, another critic, Menéndez Pelayo, recognized that Spanish American writers, even those born in Spain, confronted a new environment that modified their attitudes. Spanish American literature had its origins, he said, "in the contemplation of a new world, in the very elements of its landscape, in the modification of human beings by the environment, and in the energetic style of life which they created, first in the effort of colonization and conquest, later in the wars of separation, and finally in their periods of civil strife."[18]

[17]Federico de Onís, "La originalidad de la literatura hispanoamericana," *España en América* (San Juan, Puerto Rico, 1955), p. 120.

[18]Marcelino Menéndez Pelayo, "Prólogo," *Antología de poetas hispanoamericanos* (Madrid, 1927(, I, ix.

Philip D. Ortego, in his article "Chicano Poetry: Roots and Writers," mentions Ercilla's *La Araucana* and calls it "the first modern epic in the New World dealing with an American theme."[19] Pérez de Villagrá's poem, if in comparably less artistic than Ercilla's, also deals with a distinctly American theme. If *La Araucana* belongs to Chilean literature, why cannot the *Historia de la Nueva México* be a part of the literature of Aztlán? As Ray Padilla has said, "all works prior to 1848 can be treated as pre-Chicano Aztlanense materials."[20]

Popular literature brought to the Southwest by early settlers from Mexico resembles the popular literature of Mexico in all its aspects. The many *romances, corridos*, folktales, and religious plays are often difficult to assign to a place of origin with any assurance. In 1600, for example, Juan de la Peña wrote a religious play, *Las cuatro apariciones de la Virgen de Guadalupe*.[21] Since nothing is known about the author, we cannot determine if it belongs to Mexico or New Mexico. We do know, however, that it was very popular in New Mexico and that it is not mentioned by the historians of the Mexican theatre. With another play, a *pastorela*, we are more fortunate. We know that it was written in California in 1820 by Fray Francisco Ibáñez of Soledad Mission.[22]

The *corrido*, a typical poetic form of the Mexican populace, is very common in the Southwest and wherever Chicanos live. Apparently derived from the Spanish *romance*,[23] it expresses brilliantly the oral impulse that runs deep in Chicano literary culture, and, as a "form of the people" has served that culture as a primary vehicle toward self-understanding and self-definition.

No less important than the *corrido* is the folktale, where we often find modified forms reflecting the psychology, not only of the Mexican Indian, but also of the American Indian. The folktale, it is well known, is one of the popular forms that can most easily adopt cultural motives to give ex-

---

[19]Philip D. Ortego, "Chicano Poetry: Roots and Writers," *New Voices in Literature: The Mexican American*. A Symposium, Pan American University, Edinburg, Texas, October 7-8, 1971, pp. 1-17; quotations on p. 3.

[20]Ray Padilla, "Apuntes para la documentación de cultura chicana," *El Grito*, 5: 2 (Winter, 1971-72), 3-36; quotation on p. 19. Other *cronistas* are Pedro de Nágera Castañeda and Alonso de Benavides. This article gives a good documentation of this early period.

[21]See Aurora Lucero-White Lea, *Literary Folklore of the Hispanic Southwest* (San Antonio, Texas: The Naylor Company, 1953), pp. 16-21. The play is reproduced on pp. 86-106. Another popular play in New Mexico and Colorado was *Los Comanches*, commemorating the defeat of the Indians by the Spanish in Colorado. The play was edited by Aurelio M. Espinosa in 1907. See also A. L. Campa, "Los Comanches, a New Mexico Folk Drama," *University of New Mexico Bulletin*, 7:1 (April, 1942).

[22]See Antonio Blanco S., *La lengua española en la historia de California* (Madrid: Ediciones Cultura Hispánica, 1971), pp. 653-729.

[23]See Vicente T. Mendoza, *El romance español y el corrido mexicano* (México: Universidad Nacional Autónoma, 1939). For a contrary view see Celedonio Serrano Martínez, *El corrido mexicano no deriva del romance español* (México: Centro Cultural Guerrerense, 1963).

pression to the desires and aspirations of the people.[24] Aurora Lucero, who has collected popular literature in her native state of New Mexico, has said of those who brought this literature to the region, "They recited her prayers, they retold her stories, they sang her songs, they reenacted her plays. The fervor that went into the doing, the reciting, the telling and the acting was of such nature as to result in a tradition that was to take roots in the soil — roots that flowered into a pattern that has constituted the basis for living in the Hispanic New World, and a tradition that still endures."[25]

2. The Mexican Period (1821-1848)

When Mexico's Independence was finally achieved from Spain in 1821, the northern provinces, the land now called Aztlan by the Chicanos, became part of the Republic of Mexico. This second period, although short-lived and unstable — it ended in 1848 with the Treaty of Guadalupe Hidalgo — represents an important link in the development of Mexican American literature, since it was during this period that the Hispanic-Mexican inhabitants of the region had to decide if they were to remain loyal to Mexico or fight for their own independence. This spiritual struggle gives uniqueness to the literature produced during these years. The clashes with the Mexican authorities began almost immediately. In 1830, while celebrating the Independence on the 16th of September in the house of the Governor of California, a violent fight occurred between some young Californios and "los de la otra banda." In another incident, a certain José Castro was imprisoned for posting derogatory remarks about the Mexicans. According to the memoirs of Governor Alvarado, Castro later beat up the Mexican Rodrigo del Pliego because he had insulted Californios by calling them ill-bred.[26]

The case of the writer Lorenzo de Zavala is instructive. Having defended the independence of Texas, he lost his Mexican citizenship and was ostracised in his own country. His *Viage a los Estados-Unidos de Norte América* (Paris, 1834) definitely belongs to this period of Mexican American literature. Typical of the poetry of the time are the verses of Joaquín Buelna, who in California between 1836 and 1840 wrote compositions dedicated to the native *rancheros*. History, memoirs, and diaries are represented by José Arnaz, Juan Bandini, and Juan Bautista Alvarado. An interest in the cultures of the native Indians also appears. Gerónimo Boscana (1776-1831) wrote a historical account of the origin, customs, and traditions of the Indians of the Mission

---

[24] See Lucero-White Lea's book, Part III; Jóse M. Espinosa, *Spanish Folk Tales from New Mexico* (New York: American Folklore Society, 1937); Juan B. Rael, *Cuentos españoles de Colorado y de Nuevo México*. 2 vols. (Stanford, California: Stanford University Press, 1957).

[25] Lucero, p. 4.

[26] See Blanco S., p. 148.

of San Juan Capistrano under the title *Chinigchinich*.[27] Popular literature
continues to offer the familiar genres. There are several religious plays,
among them a *Pastorela en dos actos* dated from 1828 and signed with the
initials M.A. de la C. In New Mexico this popular play was performed reg-
ularly. An *Auto pastoral*, of Mexican origin, was performed in Taos as early
as 1840[28]

3. Transition Period (1848-1910)

The third period begins in 1848 and ends in 1910, the year of the Mexican
Revolution. It is a period during which Mexican American literature lays
the basis from which Chicano literature is to develop; a period in which
Mexicans living on the land taken over by the United States had to make
up their minds if they wished to return to Mexico or stay and become American citizens with all the accompanying requirements of learning a new
language and going to new schools. Most decided to stay but to remain at
the same time faithful to their Mexican traditions and language. In this
way they became trapped, forming, politically, a part of a society that socially rejected them. Poised between two cultural worlds, they developed
ambivalent attitudes that were to mold their way of thinking for some time,
and expressed themselves in the literature of the period, often by use of
both languages, Spanish and English. But there were times when the new
citizens were able to break through the rigid social barriers and pass on to
become part of Anglo-American society. Such was the case of Miguel A.
Otero, who was appointed Governor of the Territory of New Mexico in 1897.
He is the author of an interesting book, in English, about life in the Old
West, *My Life on the Frontier*, as well as a book on Billy the Kid.[29] How this
transition from the use of Spanish to English takes place in Mexican American
literature is an area not yet sufficiently investigated. Naturally, writers
using Spanish still predominate at this time. As an example we shall mention
the works of Francisco Palou, the biographer of Fr. Junípero Serra.[30]

Popular literature was perhaps the least affected by the political change.

[27]Boscana's manuscript was made known by Alfred Robinson in his book *Life in California*
(New York: Wiley and Putnam, 1846), in which he included an English translation (pp. 227-341).
Another edition: Oakland, California: Biobooks, 1947.

[28]See Juan B. Rael, *The Source and Diffusion of the Mexican Shepherd's Plays* (Guadalajara,
México: Librería La Joyita, 1965); Arthur L. Campa, *Spanish Religious Folktheatre in the Spanish Southwest. University of New Mexico Bulletin*, Language Series, 5:1 and 2 (1934).

[29]Miguel Antonio Otero, *The Real Billy the Kid* (New York: R. R. Wilson, 1936). See also
My Nine Years as Governor of the Territory of New Mexico, 1897-1906 (Albuquerque: The
University of New Mexico Press, 1940).

[30]Fr. Francisco Palou, *Noticias históricas de la Antigua y Nueva California* (1875), trans. by
Bolton as *Historical Memoirs of New California* (Berkeley, 1926); *Relación histórica de la vida
y apostólicas tareas del venerable padre Fray Junípero Serra* (Madrid: Aguilar, 1958).

The people continued to produce *corridos, romances, pastorelas,* and *cuentos.* Nevertheless, even here, subject matter was expanded to include events related to non-Mexicans, such as the *corrido* "Muerte del afamado Bilito," in which the death of Billy the Kid is related:

El Bilito mentado	This well-known Billy the Kid
por penas bien merecidas	for punishment he well deserved
fue en Santa Fe encarcelado	was jailed in Santa Fe
deudor de veinte en la vida	for he owed twenty people their lives
de Santa Fe a la Mesilla.	from Santa Fe to la Mesilla.

Another *corrido,* ("La voz de mi conciencia"), is significant because it introduces the theme of social protest. This *corrido* corroborates Romano's theory that the Mexican American was not a passive, resigned person expecting all salvation from without.[31] The *corridista* says:

Treintitrés días de cárcel	Thirty-three days in jail
injustamente he sufrido	unjustly have I suffered
por un falso testimonio	because of a false witness
de un crimen no cometido.	of a crime I did not commit.
Cuando el juez nos sentenció	When the judge handed down his sentence
fue cosa de reír —	it almost made me laugh —
al culpable casi libre	the guilty one would go free
y al inocente a sufrir.[32]	while the innocent was left to suffer.

Still another writer of this period, mentioned by H. Herminio Ríos C., is León Calvillo-Ponce.[33]

4. Interaction Period (1910-1942)

Immigration from Mexico to the United States between 1848 and 1910 was negligible. After 1910, a large influx of immigrants crossed the border in search of security and work in the green fields of Texas, New Mexico, and California, as well as in the factories of more remote states. Most of these immigrants never returned to their native land (except during the depression years of the thirties), and their sons and daughters became American citizens by birth, although still attached to the way of life of their parents. The new immigrants brought new blood into the Mexican-American community and reinforced the Mexican traditions. The same thing occurred in intellectual circles with the interchange of ideas among writers such as José Vasconcelos, Martín Luis Guzmán, Mariano Azuela, Ricardo Flores Magón, and others who lived in the United States.

[31]Octavio Ignacio Romano-V., "The Anthropology and Sociology of the Mexican-American: The Distortion of Mexican-American History. A Review Essay," *El Grito,* 2: 1 (Fall, 1968), 13-26.
[32]Lucero, pp. 136-137.
[33]Ríos C., p. viii.

This period, which comes to an end with the Second World War, is characterized by the appearance among Mexican Americans of a group consciousness that manifests itself in the formation of societies whose purpose is mutual help and protection of the needy. Some of these associations became politically oriented and spearheaded the struggle for equal rights. Their periodicals, as well as the many newspapers which sprang up during the period, included poetry, short stories, and scholarly articles as well as news.[34] The pages of *LULAC News, Alianza,* and others are a good source for the literary production of this period. Ortego, in his study of Chicano poetry, has brought to light the names of some of the poets who published in these periodicals. He also discusses the poetry of Vicente Bernal and Fray Angélico Chávez, the former the author of an early book of poems, *Las primicias* (1916), and the latter a representative of the mystic tradition in three works, *New Mexico Triptych* (1940), *Eleven Lady-Lyrics and other Poems* (1945), and *The Single Rose* (1948).[35]

As a consequence of the Revolution, Mariano Azuela published his famous novel, *Los de abajo,* in the pages of the newspaper *El Paso del Norte,* of El Paso, Texas, in November, 1915. Later, in 1935, Teodoro Torres, who lived nine years in the United States and was editor of *La Prensa of San Antonio, Texas,* published *La patria perdida,* a novel whose first part takes place in the United States and deals with life among Mexican Americans. Another Mexican, Alberto Rembao, who lived in New York and edited the review *La Nueva Democracia,* published novels with Mexican themes and settings. A novel entitled *The Journey of 'The Flame'* (1933), dealing with early life in California, was written by Antonio de Fierro Blanco, about whom little is known. In general, the novel and short story of this period need study. Research will undoubtedly uncover many novels written by Mexican Americans, both in English and Spanish.[36]

The *corrido* continues at this time to be a popular form of expression, with social protest and politics entering more prominently into its content. In 1936 a *corrido* was written about some Gallup coal miners who had been subdued with gunfire by the sheriff and his men during a strike. Senator

[34]For a listing of these newspapers see Herminio Ríos and Lupe Castillo, "Toward a True Chicano Bibliography: Mexican-American Newspapers: 1848-1942," *El Grito,* 3: 4 (Summer, 1970), 17-24. Also Guillermo Rojas, "Chicano/Raza Newspaper and Periodical Serials Listing," *Hispania,* LVIII, 4 (December, 1975), 851-863.

[35]Other works by Fray Angélico Chávez are: *Clothed with the Sun* (Santa Fe: Writers' Editions, 1939); *La Conquistadora. The Autobiography of an Ancient Statue* (Paterson, N.J.: St. Anthony Guild Press, 1954; *The Virgin and the Port Lligat* (Fresno: Academy Literary Guild, 1956); *The Lady from Toledo* (Fresno: Academy Literary Guild, 1960); *Selected Poems* (Santa Fe: Press of the Territorian, 1970).

[36]An example of this are the two short novels *El hijo de la tempestad; Tras la tormenta la calma* (Santa Fe, New Mexico, 1892) by Eusebio Chacón, a native of New Mexico. See Francisco A. Lomelí and Donaldo W. Urioste, *Chicano Perspectives in Literature* (Albuquerque, New Mexico: Pajarito Publications, 1976), pp. 42-43.

Bronson Cutting's defense of the lawmen elicited a protest poem which ended with the following lines:

Ud. se come sus coles	You eat your cabbages
Con su pan y mantequilla	With your bread and butter
Y yo me como mis frijoles	And I eat mine with beans
Con un pedazo de tortilla.[37]	And with a bit of tortilla.

During this period, serious scholarship and literary criticism begin to appear with the works of Carlos Castañeda, Juan B. Rael, George Sánchez, Arthur L. Campa, and Aurelio M. Espinosa.

5. Chicano Period (1943—to the present)

June of 1943 marks the beginning of a new period in the history of the Mexican American. The so-called Zoot Suit Riots which took place in Los Angeles that month began an open confrontation that was to be intensified during the post-war years by the presence of thousands of returning Mexican American veterans. A new type of literature emerges animated by a rebellious spirit often inspired by the revolutionary leaders of Mexico, such as Villa and Zapata. Characteristic of this writing is the Chicano's search for identity, often probing for the roots of his being in the Indian past. This quest is found in the poetry of Luis Omar Salinas, Miguel Ponce, Alurista, Sergio Elizondo, and Rodolfo "Corky" Gonzales, the last of whom expresses this sentiment in *I am Joaquin* (1967):

> I am Cuauhtemoc,
> Proud and noble
> leader of men
>
> I am the Maya Prince.
> I am Nezahualcoyotl,
> Great leader of the Chichimecas
>
> I am the Eagle and Serpent of
> the Aztec civilization.

In his metaphoric prose, "Tata Casehua," Miguel Méndez M. goes back to more recent, but timeless Indian ancestry. He dedicates his story "To My Indian Ancestors, nailed to the sign of Omega, and to their tragic fate."[38]

Other writers find inspiration for their poetry and prose from their barrio experiences. Sometimes the language is that of the barrio, and almost always there is the use of Spanish and English in a juxtaposition that is often

[37]From Mabel Major and T. M. Pearce, *Southwest Heritage: A Literary History with Bibliography.* (Albuquerque: University of New Mexico Press, 1972), p. 38. Reprinted by permission of the publisher.

[38]See *El Espejo/The Mirror: Selected Mexican-American Literature.* (Berkeley, California: Quinto Sol Publications, 1969; 3rd Printing, 1970), pp. 30-43; English translation by Octavio I. Romano-V., pp. 44-58.

startling in effect. We find this in the tender poem of José Montoya, "La jefita," about a barrio mother.[39]
Several anthologies of Mexican American literature have already been published. In addition to *El Espejo*,[40] which contains prose and poetry, we have Ed Ludwig and James Santibáñez (eds.), *The Chicanos: Mexican-American Voices* (1971); Antonia Castañeda Shular, Tomás Ybarra-Frausto, and Joseph Sommers (eds.), *Literatura Chicana: texto y contexto* (1972); Luis Valdez and Stan Steiner (eds.), *Aztlán. An Anthology of Mexican American Literature* (1972); Philip D. Ortego (ed.), *We are Chicanos* (1973); and Luis Omar Salinas and Lillian Faderman (comps.), *From the Barrio: A Chicano Anthology* (1973) and many others.[41]

Three novels, *Tattoo the Wicked Cross* (1967) by Floyd Salas, *The Plum Plum Pickers* (1969) by Raymond Barrio, and *Chicano* (1970) by Richard Vásquez, are reviewed by Teresa McKenna in her article, "Three Novels: An Analysis."[42] An earlier novel, *Pocho*, by José Antonio Villarreal, was first published in 1959. *Barrio Boy* by Ernesto Galarza appeared in 1971, and *Bless Me Ultima*, by Rudolfo A. Anaya in 1972. The book ...*y no se lo tragó la tierra* (1971) by Tomás Rivera is an artistically written collection of stories. Other short fiction has appeared in...periodicals...anthologies.[43]

The possibilities of the drama have not yet been explored, though El Teatro Campesino has carried on its traditions under the directorship of

[39]*El Espejo*, pp. 188-189.
[40]For reviews of *El Espejo* and other Chicano literature see Gerald Haslam, "¡Por la Causa! Mexican-American Literature," *College English*, 31 (April, 1970), 695-709; Robert Blauner, "The Chicano Sensibility," *Trans-Action* (February, 1971), pp. 51-58; Philip D. Ortego, "Mexican-American Literature," *The Nation* (September 15, 1969), pp. 258-259.
[41]Short summaries of these anthologies and other literature can be found in Charles M. Tatum, *A Selected and Annotated Bibliography of Chicano Studies* (Society of Spanish and Spanish-American Studies, 1976). (Department of Modern Languages, Kansas State University, Manhattan, Kansas.)
[42]See above, n. 4.
[43]More recent novels are: Oscar "Zeta" Acosta, *The Revolt of the Cockroach People* (New York, Bantam Books, 1973); Miguel M. Méndez, *Peregrinos de Aztlán* (Tucson, Arizona: Editorial Peregrinos, 1974); Ron Arias, *The Road to Tamazunchale* (Reno, Nevada: West Coast Poetry Review, 1975); Alejandro Morales, *Caras viejas y vino nuevo* (Mexico City: Joaquín Mortiz, 1975); Aristeo Brito, *El Diablo en Texas* (Tucson, Arizona: Editorial Peregrinos, 1976); Rolando Hinojosa, *Klail City y sus alrededores* (La Habana, Cuba: Casa de las Americas, 1976), and others. Some collections of short stories are: Rolando R. Hinojosa-S., *Estampas del valle y otras obras* (Berkeley, California: Quinto Sol Publications, 1972); J. L. Navarro, *Blue Day on Main Street* (Berkeley, California: Quinto Sol Publications, 1973); Estela Portillo Trambley, *Rain of Scorpions* (Berkeley, California: Tonatiuh International, 1975); and Sabine R. Ulibarrí, *Cuentos de tierra amarilla* (Albuquerque: The University of New Mexico Press, 1971). Some studies of Chicano fiction are those of Donald F. Castro, "The Chicano Novel: An Ethno-Generic Study," *La Luz*, 2: 1 (April, 1973), 50-52; Juan Rodríguez, "El desarrollo del cuento chicano: del folklore al tenebroso mundo del yo," *Fomento Literario*, 1: 3 (Winter, 1973), 19-31; Guillermo Rojas, "La prosa chicana: Tres epígones de la novela mexicana de la Revolución," *Cuadernos Americanos* (1975), pp. 198-209; and Gustavo Segade, "Un panorama conceptual de la novela chicana," *Fomento Literario*, 1: 3 (Winter, 1973), 5-18.

Luis Valdez.[44] The *corrido*, the most enduring of the popular genres, is still being composed and sung by Chicanos, especially the *huelguistas*; unfortunately, very few have been written down. One is "The Corrido of Cesar Chávez," which in part says:

> The seventeenth of March,
> First Thursday morning of Lent,
> César walked from Delano,
> Taking with him his faith.
>
> When we arrive in Fresno,
> All the people shout:
> Long live César Chávez,
> And all who follow him.[45]

In conclusion, it may be reemphasized that Mexican American literature is not just a by-product of the struggle for civil rights. By this I do not mean to minimize the efforts of the Chicano movement or to underestimate the new energy that it has sparked. The very term Chicano, whatever connotation it may eventually receive,[46] has spurred the production of literature. Even so, it is only when we look at Mexican American literature from a historical perspective that we understand its true nature. From Mexican literature it has derived its forms, both erudite and popular, as well as its spirit of rebellion. And although the more recent phase of it may emphasize social protest or a search for Chicano identity, its roots reach far back to poets like Bernal who write simply about mystic experience, or other universal themes.

[44] For information on this theatrical group see Luis Valdez, "El Teatro Campesino, its Beginnings," *The Chicanos: Mexican American Voices* (Baltimore: Penguin Books, 1971), pp. 115-119. The development of Chicano theatre has been studied by Pedro Bravo Elizondo, "El teatro chicano," *Revista Chicano-Riqueña*, 1: 2 (Otoño, 1973), 36-42; Roberto J. Garza (ed.), *Contemporary Chicano Theatre* (Notre Dame, Indiana: University of Notre Dame Press, 1976); Jorge A. Huerta, "Chicano Teatro: A Background," *Aztlán*, 2: 2 (Fall, 1971), 63-71; Francisco Jiménez, "Dramatic Principles of the Teatro Campesino," *The Bilingual Review*, 2: 1/2 (January-August, 1975), 99-111.

[45] Stan Steiner, *La Raza: The Mexican Americans* (New York: Harper & Row, 1970), p. 315.

[46] For discussions on the concept of the Chicano, see Jesús Chavarría, "A Precis and a Tentative Bibliography on Chicano History," *Aztlán*, 1: 1 (Spring, 1970), 33-141, and Fernando Peñalosa, "Toward an Operational Definition of the Mexican American," *Aztlán*, 1: 1 (Spring, 1970), 1-12.

Critical Approaches to Chicano Literature

by Joseph Sommers

I

The ideas which follow are part of a longer study entitled, "From the Critical Premise to the Product: Critical Modes and their Applications to a Chicano Text." It is a study in three parts. The first attempts to gauge the social and cultural context of Chicano literature and literary study at the present moment. The second part, from which the ideas below are abstracted, tries to single out three critical approaches to Chicano literature, examining them in terms of assumptions, methods and consequences. The approaches are termed formalist, culturalist and historical-dialectical. Part three is in many ways an acid test, since it represents an effort to demonstrate how each approach functions when applied to a specific literary work. I have chosen the narrative text by Tomás Rivera,....y no se lo tragó la tierra,[1] which is rich and complex in both form and meaning, thereby pro-' viding a formidable challenge to any critic.

The aim here is to avoid twin dangers which might undermine the arguments presented. One danger might be termed pluralism, a tendency to assume a neutral posture and to infer that all approaches are equally valid, perhaps leading to the same objective. The other danger is to be prescriptive, assuming that one approach is totally correct and that other views must be totally rejected. My intention is to demonstrate the possibilities and the shortcomings of the first two critical approaches and to make clear why I advocate the third. I assume that to disagree is not to censure, that disagreement can be based upon respect, and that the process of testing and contrasting ideas can be productive.

A brief summary of the first section of the longer study will help to frame the ideas below, which are taken from the following part. The need to define critical strategies when analyzing and interpreting Chicano literature is greater than ever, because the social and cultural atmosphere in which this

"Critical Approaches to Chicano Literature" by Joseph Sommers. An enlarged version of this study entitled "From the Critical Premise to the Product: Critical Modes and Their Applications to a Chicano Literary Text" appeared in *The New Scholar*, 5, no. 2 (1977). Reprinted by permission of *The New Scholar*.

[1](Berkeley: Quinto Sol, 1971).

literature exists at present is more difficult and hostile than was the case a decade ago. In the first place there has been a withdrawal from academic commitments of the 1960s: to recruit minority students and faculty on all levels; to promote actively the study of minority literatures; to question and reform hardbound educational norms and traditional academic standards; to amplify accepted views of what constitutes our national ("American") literary tradition.

In the second place what legitimation has been accorded to Chicano literature and to related teaching and research in this field has been limited and ambiguous. The tendency has been to favor either the assimilation of the literature into an engulfing Anglo-American literary mainstream, or the dilution of critical perspective by means of newly validated formulae such as "cultural pluralism" or "ethnopoetics."

II

Of the three main lines of critical approach to Chicano literature, the most prominent in academic publications is that which attempts to apply the norms and categories of formalist criticism. It seeks to validate Chicano texts, for both Chicano and Anglo readers, as authentic modern literature.

The methodology varies, but the two most common features are reliance on comparative criteria and stress on textual analysis. Some comparatists focus on identifying literary influences (for example, Juan Rulfo on Tomás Rivera), tending to base their claims for the validity of the Chicano text on its derivation from sources of recognized excellence. Others refer to established definitions such as "modernism" to call attention to what for them is a "newly emerged" literature. Texual critics try to show that the criteria of stylistics and more recently of structuralist criticism can reveal in a Chicano poem or narrative the types of complexity and levels of formal coherence which are found in exemplary texts of modern literature. Other critics such as Juan Bruce-Novoa retain the formalist insistence on separating the text from historical reality or social context, but nonetheless seek to account for "meaning." This approach to "meaning" limits it to the realm of the imaginary, postulating the text as occupying "imaginary space,"[2] as being mental experience which provides an alternative to lived experience, to the chaos, injustice and temporality of the real world. Meaning, rather than reference to reality, becomes yet another index of the literariness of the work.

What underlying assumptions characterize this approach to a given text? For one, emphasis on accepted major works as models carries the assumption that literature is a phenomenon of print, with the most respected exemplars being those valued by the educated middle class. A corollary as-

---

[2]This is a central notion in his "The Space of Chicano Literature," *De colores* (Albuquerque), I, 4 (Winter, 1975), pp. 22-42.

sumption attaches relatively low value to oral literature, the product of a popular culture which introduces collective themes based on concrete experience, which relies upon oral transmission, which is frequently anonymous, and which historically has provided a source of resistance to the dominant ideology.[3] A second corollary is stress on the text as individualized creation. In this view, the act of literary production is the artist's private struggle to find a personal voice and to express an individualized response. The poet is seen as arbitrarily gifted with the quality of genius, as being endowed with special intuitive insights and access to the truth.

A further assumption is that the prime feature of a literary text is its aesthetic quality, which cannot be measured by the yardstick of meaning or cognition, for these are categories which normally rest upon criteria of reason and of reference to experienced reality. Aesthetic quality on the other hand can be uncovered by analysis of features contained within the text, features which when taken together yield "unity" and "complexity."

Finally there is a widespread tendency to value the quality of "universality." This quality is rarely defined, except by implication or by negation. Some critics seem to state that to be universal is somehow to transcend "social protest" (presumably they would strike Galdós, Neruda and the entire picaresque novel from the "universal" list). Others seem to suggest that literature achieves universality by avoiding the regional or the immediately historical in favor of the abstract, the metaphysical, the imaginary, or the timeless themes and myths of world culture (this would underestimate the importance of regional themes and historical issues in Balzac, Tolstoy, Malraux and the corpus of Spanish epic poetry). What seems involved beneath the surface of these notions is a fragmentation of categories which might otherwise be seen as interconnected, such as the artistic and the social, or the imaginary and the historical. Certainly one can infer from this view of universality a conception of literature as distraction, or as aesthetic object, or as distinct mode of mental activity from other disciplines, or as embodied in a succession of masterpieces insulated against the ravages of time by protective jackets of brilliant thematic colors.

What are the consequences when these assumptions constitute the critic's point of departure? On the positive side is a healthy stress on intensive analysis of the formal qualities of given texts. On the negative side, the bulk of this type of criticism tends to be ahistorical, concentrating on contemporary texts and their modernism. By extension this has meant a thrust toward the assimilation of Chicano literature, or more precisely of a select number of Chicano texts, into the standard reading list of the educated reader, primarily in academe. The critic's role, when these assumptions are

[3]Arturo Islas seems to imply this assumption of low value in "Writing from a Dual Perspective, *Miquiztli*" (Stanford University), II, 1 (Winter, 1974), p. 2: "More often than not, much of the fiction we do have is document, and sometimes not very well written document. Much of what is passed off as literature is a compendium of folklore, religious superstition, and recipes for tortillas. All well and good, but it is not literature."

primary, is, as Bruce-Novoa phrased it, "to lead the reader back to the literary work itself,"[4] for literature in this view constitutes a separate, non-referential transcendental reality.

III

The second line of critical approach, prominent during the 1960s, is based on the notion of *cultural uniqueness*. It values Chicano literature precisely because in it one finds expression of the distinctive features of Chicano culture. An earlier philologically oriented but nonetheless culturalist variant, practiced by Aurelio Espinosa half a century ago, stressed the survival of authentic Spanish forms in the Southwest.

The critical methodology tends to stress descriptive cultural features: family structures, linguistic and thematic survivals, anti-gringo attitudes, pre-Hispanic symbology, notions of a mythic past, and folk beliefs ranging from *la llorona* to the Virgin of Guadalupe. Some culturalist critics, waging a necessary struggle against the elitism which characterizes purist notions of literary Spanish, stress the distinguishing presence in Chicano literature of what sociolinguists term code-switching and what critics have called the binary phenomenon—a process by which linguistic symbols and syntactic structures of two languages interact in the same text. Others stress the presence of Aztec symbols or myths. Thus Herminio Ríos and Octavio Romano find special value in *Bless Me Ultima*, the novel by Rudolfo Anaya, because, "It is from our collective memory that he draws myths such as that of Cihuacoatl....And it is from our collective subconscious that the myth of the Golden Carp arises...Anaya takes us from the subconscious to the conscious, from the past to the present...in so doing, he has helped us to know ourselves."[5]

What assumptions underlie culturalist criticism? One is evident in attributing positive value to Anaya because his novel reveals traces of the Aztec world view. Stated in bare terms, it claims that present-day Chicano mental structures, by dint of a sort of Jungian operation of the collective unconscious, retain continuity with the thought patterns and cosmology of the Aztec past. Also implied is the notion that rediscovery of cultural origins imparts a healthy consciousness of uniqueness to the generations of the present. This notion that the distant past—and here I refer to a mythic, magical past rather than to the past in a historical process of change—shapes and controls the present, regardless of social and historical developments, is by no means original. A Mexican example embodying the same anti-historical view is the essay by Octavio Paz, *Posdata*,[6] in which the well known Mexican poet and critic attempts to explain the Tlate-

---

[4]"The Space of Chicano Literature," p. 39.

[5]"Introduction", *Bless Me Ultima* (Berkeley: Quinto Sol, 1972), p. ix.

[6](México: Siglo XXI, 1970).

lolco massacre of 1968 in terms of the persistence of pre-Hispanic values and attitudes. Comparable manifestations of this cultural pessimism can be found in the creative works of Carlos Fuentes, *La región más transparente* and *Todos los gatos son pardos*, as well as his essays, *Tiempo mexicano*.[7] It was this ingredient in Chicano thought which led Philip Ortego to state in 1971: "Perhaps the principal significance of the Chicano Renaissance lies in the identification of Chicanos with their Indian past."[8]

There are other related assumptions which form part of the matrix of culturalist thought. One is the positive value attached to tradition regardless of its content. For example, the traditional role of the church, whether in its mystical or its adaptive manifestations, is seen as integral to Chicano culture. A further tendency is to criticize the materialism, racism, and dehumanisation of contemporary capitalist society by counterposing idealistically the values of traditional culture, presenting these values as flawless and recoverable in unchanged form. Needless to say this thesis construes culture to be static and separable from the historic process, rather than dynamic, creative and responsive to experience.

Another notion of culturalist thought, embedded in the Plan de Aztlán, places primacy on the distinctive ethnic origins of Chicano culture, setting it apart from other cultures and indeed from other nations. Here the stress is on racial fusion, on Indian and Mexican constituent elements, with occasional references to a Hispano component. There is frequent harking back to José Vasconcelos' slogan, "la raza cósmica," and to *mestizaje* as being the distinctive feature characterizing the Chicano experience. The key assumptions here not only view culture as static, but also view race (and ultimately nature and the biological process) as the controlling element in culture, while positing culture as the central determinant of a people's experience. This line of thought tends to subordinate the idea that culture might be related to the social category of class, as well as the idea that cultural forms evolve in response to the specifics of the historical process. The upshot for critical practice is usually the adoption of one of the several variants of "myth criticism" which have been in vogue in academe recently, centered on archetypal qualities in human nature and archetypal patterns in human relations.

A further implicit assumption in some culturalist criticism, not in consonance with myth criticism, is that Chicano literature can be understood only by Chicanos and interpreted only by Chicanos. In this view Chicano critics writing from a Chicano perspective and publishing in Chicano periodicals are the only reliable sources of understanding of Chicano literature.[9] Accompanying this assumption is the idea that all literary expres-

---

[7](México: Joaquín Mortiz, 1971).

[8]"Chicano Poetry: Roots and Writers," in *New Voices in Literature: The Mexican American. A Symposium.* (Edinburg, Texas: Dept. of English, 1971), p. 11.

[9]I do *not* intend in my own departure from culturalist thought to imply that non-Chicano critics will have just as much light to shed as Chicano critics. I would suggest that while Chi-

sion by Chicanos constitutes a contribution to the body of Chicano culture. This assumes that *lo chicano* is good by definition, thus eliminating the critical function of literary criticism.

The consequences of such an approach are reductive. It conceives of Chicano literature as ethnic literature, designed for and limited to an ethnic readership, to be isolated academically within ethnic studies programs. It supposes that Chicano literature is distinct from other literatures which may in fact have comparable structural features (such as an oral tradition or the bilingual mode or historical trajectories involving confrontation with class exploitation and institutional racism). It abandons the struggle to redefine exclusivist views of American literature. And finally, whereas formalism tends to ignore the past, focusing on modernism and its virtues, a culturalist approach tends to ignore the present, stressing in nostalgic and idealized terms the predominance of the past.

IV

The third line of critical approach, espoused by this critic, rejects the classic distinction sanctified by René Wellek and Austin Warren between "intrinsic" and "extrinsic"[10] in favor of a criticism that is historically based and dialectically formulated. For the label-minded it can include the work of Marxists but is not practiced exclusively by Marxist critics. The working definition of "literary criticism," in this view, is ample and complex. It begins by explaining the singular formal qualities of a text which distinguish it from alternate modes of verbal expression. It must also account for the manner in which a given text rejects, modifies and incorporates features of other texts which have preceded it. Analysis, then, includes the notion of intertextuality, the response to literary tradition. Since the critic sees literature as a cultural product, the text is also studied in relation to its cultural ambience, which means in the light of an understanding of societal structures.

Finally the critic assumes that to experience literary texts, even in their most fantastic and abstract variants, is a form of cognition, for the text comments upon, refers to and interprets human experience.

Treating critical approaches dialectically, the critic does not reject formalism or culturalist analysis out of hand, but tries to incorporate their positive features into a system which transcends their self-imposed limitations. Hence this third approach incorporates into its methodology the con-

---

cano critics' insights are indispensable in the interpretation of key texts, particularly in regard to cultural meanings, symbols, and nuances, the contributions of other critics may be useful, particularly in establishing the extra-cultural merits and significance of such texts.

[10]This distinction underlies the entire structure of their important volume, *Theory of Literature* (New York: Harcourt Brace, 2nd ed., 1956).

cerns of the sociology of literature, which range from analyzing the material conditions and the intellectual climate of literary production to interpreting the reception and the impact of a given text. Another dialectical aspect of this approach is its attempt to identify an internal Chicano literary dynamic and simultaneously to account for interactions with both Mexican and North American middle class and popular literary traditions.

While no one critic has worked exclusively along these lines, three examples come to mind of different but important degrees and kinds of compatibility. One is the monograph of Américo Paredes, *With His Pistol in His Hand,*[11] which undertakes formal study of a *corrido,* situates it in the light of literary tradition on the Texas-Mexican border, presents variants of the basically established text, studies the relationship between historical fact and popular myth, and shows the *corrido* as part of the historical dynamic of cultural response to social repression. A second compatible critic is Luis Leal, in his rigorously researched article, "Mexican American Literature: A Historical Perspective,"[12] which explores the problems of historical periods and of literary development within different genres, providing valuable pointers toward future research in literary history. The third example is the study by the Mexican critic, Carlos Monsiváis, "Literatura Comparada: Literatura Chicana,"[13] published in 1974, examining parallels and divergences between Chicano and Mexican literatures in the modern period. He first studies the comparable ways in which both Mexican and Chicano literatures have in effect suffered the consequences of cultural imperialism. He then goes on to treat the contradictory lines along which, within Mexican literature, there have developed literary responses embodying internalization of the dominant ideology on the one hand, and resistance and critical perspective on the other.

Returning to our analysis of the historical-dialectical approach, perhaps three assumptions can be identified. One stems from the understanding that Chicano literary expression is bound up with the historic pattern of economic and social oppression prevailing since 1848. In economic terms this oppression has eliminated upward class mobility, consigning Mexican-descended Americans almost uniformly to working class status, whether urban or rural. This fact, compounded enormously by the racism of linguistic discrimination, has historically limited access to education, to literacy, to the print media including journals, libraries and publishing houses, and to the related distribution systems which shape the growth of a literary market. Logically, then, the trajectory of Chicano literature differs crucially from the mainstream models of both Mexico and the United States. The mapping of this literary tradition will have to account for an important popular stratum, only rarely available in print, which includes *corridos,*

[11](Austin: University of Texas Press, 1958).

[12]*Revista Chicano-Riqueña* (Gary, Indiana), I, 1 (Spring, 1973), pp. 32-44.

[13]"Literatura Comparada: Literatura Chicana", *Fomento Literario* (Congreso Nacional de Asuntos Colegiales), I, 3 (Winter, 1973), pp. 42-49.

folk tales, historical narrations, and *teatro de carpa y de revista*.[14] It must search out the work of artists whose impact was local or regional, and expect thematic emphases more centered on the social, cultural and historical than the personal, individualized, and psychologically introspective.

A second assumption incorporates ideology into critical evaluation. For example, where a culturalist critic would insist that all writing by Mexican-Americans deserves equal footing in the study and articulation of Chicano literary history, a critic of this approach would see the defining of literary history as part of the struggle for cultural expression in the face of oppression. Thus a text by a Mexican-American author celebrating the patriotism of New Mexicans fighting alongside Theodore Roosevelt in 1898 to suppress Cuban independence would certainly merit serious study stressing ideological contradictions, but would hardly be seen as progressive or as central by comparison, say, with the *corrido* tradition. Similarly, the critic would analyze the view of culture which is embedded in the literary makeup of a given text, with the question in mind: is the view of culture dynamic or static? Is the substance of Chicano culture, as interpreted in the text, its capacity to provide the forms and encourage the spirit of resistance, as is the case, for example, with Raúl Salinas' poetic reconstitution of the language and life-style of the *barrio* in his poem, "A Trip Through the Mind Jail"? Or is it rather the harking back in sadness and nostalgia to a forgotten, idealized and unobtainable past, as is true of *Bless Me Ultima* by Rudolfo Anaya?

Finally, the third premise is that literature, rather than merely reflecting historical experience, carries in its form and its structures an interpretation of this experience, an interpretation which is capable of impact upon the consciousness of its reader. By this logic, the writer is neither an omniscient *vates*, a seer, nor a self-anointed revolutionary, but rather a creative interpreter, whose identification with a social group connotes responsibility to it, one who must assume the contradictions of his or her social condition and struggle to resolve them.

As might be expected, different consequences derive from this approach to Chicano literature. For one, emphasis falls upon a *critical* criticism. The role of the critic is to challenge both writer and reader to question the text for meaning and values (which needless to say are inseparable from its formal configuration), and to situate this meaning and these values in a broad cultural framework of social and historical analysis.

Further there is a concern for comparative study. For example there might well, in the logic of this approach, be an examination of the ideas of Amiri Amamu Baraka (LeRoi Jones). In his essay, "The Myth of Negro

---

[14]Tomás Rivera stresses the importance of the *corrido* and other popular literary forms, and calls for study of Mexican American newspapers of the nineteenth century in "Into the Labyrinth: The Chicano in Literature," in *New Voices in American Literature: The Mexican American. A Symposium.* A point of departure for periodical research is the article by Her-

Literature,"[15] Baraka sustains the view that the authentic roots of black literature are in popular culture, in indigenous forms such as the "blues," while newly arrived genres like the novel are artificial creations of a bourgeois society. Questions of literary history such as this require comparative cultural study, with emphasis on the relationships across time between class structures, social institutions, and literary forms.[16]

A comparativist focus might address the question of how Tomás Rivera examines, in a particular linguistic, social and historical setting, the themes of boyhood, coming of age, and adolescent analysis of adult society, by contrast and comparison with other modern writers—such as Robert Musil, J. D. Salinger, Richard Wright and Mario Vargas Llosa.

Another consequence is insistence on multiple responses to the hostile cultural environment which now prevails, responses transcending the double trap of ghettoization or assimilation. On the one hand there is the need to define, study and teach Chicano literature in all academic settings, to devote scholarly meetings to it, to encourage historians and critics of Chicano literature by means of grants and other positive recognition. On the other, there is the simultaneous need to see Chicano literature incorporated into the purview of both Spanish and English departments. Chicano literature can be seen as nourished by Latin American literature, especially that of Mexico, and as contributor to these traditions. But this Latin Americanizing of perspective need not contradict an analogous North Americanizing process in teaching, rendering Chicano literature integral to the "American" literary tradition. Specialists in American literature should be expected to know Spanish in order to command a full understanding of their field.[17]

---

minio Ríos and Lupe Castillo, "Toward a True Chicano Bibliography: Mexican American Newspapers, 1848-1942," *El Grito*, III, 4 (Summer, 1970), pp. 17-24. Examples of recent research which has uncovered valuable material are two articles by Doris L. Meyer, "Anonymous Poetry in Spanish-language New Mexico Newspapers, 1880-1900," *The Bilingual Review/La Revista Bilingüe*, I, 2 (Sept.-Dec., 1975), pp. 259-275; and "Banditry and Poetry: Verses by Two Outlaws of Old Las Vegas," *New Mexico Historical Review* (Oct., 1975), pp. 277-290. A further example is the book by Anselmo Arellano, *Los pobladores nuevo mexicanos y su poesía, 1889-1950* (Albuquerque: Pajarito Publications, 1976).

[15]LeRoi Jones, "The Myth of Negro Literature," in *Home: Social Essays*. (New York: William Morrow, 1966).

[16]Another type of research involves the unearthing of texts which may not have circulated widely. A clue may be present in a footnote by John Rutherford, in his *Mexican Society During the Revolution: A Literary Approach* (London: Oxford University Press, 1971), pp. 48-49. He provides the titles of ten novels of the Mexican Revolution published in El Paso and San Antonio between 1915 and 1928. This indicates the presence in Texas of publishers and a reading audience. Is it not likely that Chicano novelists, poets and *cuentistas* may have also been published during these years? I agree with Luis Leal (See "Mexican American Literature: A Historical Perspective") that a *published* narrative tradition undoubtedly existed long before the appearance of *Pocho* in 1959.

[17]A good argument can be made for the incorporation of Yiddish texts into the study of American literature. Although fascinating comparisons and contrasts can be identified between

In sum, this approach, if practiced with creativity and openness, can be central to the challenging task facing scholars working in the field of Chicano literature—the gathering, ordering and evaluating of the countless literary texts, many of them presently unknown, which taken together constitute the record of a people's cultural responses to the history they have lived.

Jewish and Mexican minority experiences, an undeniable fact of American literary history is the existence and circulation, over a period of perhaps half a century, of a significant body of texts in Yiddish—poetry, narrative, and theater—linguistic discrimination notwithstanding. Unlike the Chicano model, this tradition no longer thrives. However its history is fundamental to the understanding of modern American literary expression.

Spanish Codes in the Southwest

by Rosaura Sánchez

To analyze literature adequately in terms of both form and content, one must take into account the historical context within which the work is written. In much the same way it is important to analyze the sign systems, both in society and in literature, in relation to the social conditions within which they evolve. In order to understand Chicano Spanish and its import in Chicano literature, thus attaining a deeper grasp of the literary message, we must analyze the linguistic continuum ranging from English to Spanish which permeates the community. As an introduction to Chicano language codes, this article will offer a brief analysis of the dynamic bilingualism current among Chicanos and a description of their Spanish codes in relation to the linguistic and social factors determining the contexts within which they function.

The Spanish codes to be analyzed here do not form part of the repertoire of each individual speaker in the community but instead can be said to form part of the collective repertoire of the Chicano community. Since historical, social, and economic reality can also be codified, it is possible to incorporate these social and cultural elements into the code as selectional features. The sign-vehicle /mecha/, "a wick," for example, with particular denotations and connotations in Latin America, would have an additional denotation, "match" in the Spanish repertoire of the Southwest. This additional denotation would necessarily be described in terms of circumstantial features restricting the denotation to Chicano community usage, just as contextual features in the general repertoire account for extension of meanings to include "lock of hair." Only a linguistic model which includes both social and linguistic contexts can serve to explain the generation and use of particular codes in the community. Thus a study of the communication system in a community must consider not only the different levels of meaning of the messages being transmitted by a particular code, the sender encoding the message, and the receiver decoding the message but also the conditions under which the communication act takes place. In this study we will be concerned only with Chicano transmitters and receivers of messages. This choice already offers enough complexity because the population is not homogeneous in terms of significant factors: nativity, generation,

"Spanish Codes in the Southwest" by Rosaura Sánchez. This article appears for the first time in this volume. It is used by permission of the author.

residency, occupation, and education. To facilitate this analysis in terms of determining social factors, we will begin with a review of the demographic and economic particulars of this population.

Recent statistics indicate that over eight million persons in the United States use Spanish as their first or second language.[1] This Spanish-speaking minority includes Chicanos, who make up 60.7 percent of the Spanish-origin population in this country and continue to reside primarily in the Southwest.[2] It is possible then to characterize the Mexican-origin population in general terms as bilingual. The term "bilingual," however, is apt to describe a variety of competencies ranging from bilinguals who function equally well in both languages to diglossic bilinguals who use each language for particular functions in particular domains, as well as to bilinguals for whom one of the languages plays an increasingly diminishing role. All of these varieties of bilingualism exist in the Southwest, from border bilinguals who shift diglossically each time they cross the border to third-generation Chicanos who have an aural competency in Spanish but never speak the language. Yet despite this trend to shift to English among third and fourth generations, the Spanish language is still very much alive in the Chicano community and not only among incoming Mexican immigrants.

Two major factors have contributed to the continued presence of the Spanish language in the Southwest; immigration and labor segmentation. Immigration of Mexicans has been steady throughout this century although critical economic periods in the United States have reduced the flow, producing forced deportation of thousands of Mexican immigrants, such as those occurring during the Depression and the period of the 1950s. This continuous influx of Mexicans has undoubtedly reinforced the maintenance of Spanish in the Southwest by increasing the opportunity for contact with the language. In a society where assimilation is the explicit aim of all immigrant groups and where English appears to function as a vehicle for social mobility, labor segmentation has further served to isolate the Mexican immigrant, limiting him to low-wage lower-level positions in secondary industry and services, restricting him to low-cost housing in barrios or housing projects, and concentrating his children in inadequate, poorly staffed schools. These economic consequences of labor segmentation have reduced the social and language contact between minority groups and the dominant English-speaking groups. The situation, however, is not that simple, for there are, at the same time, other factors, like urbanization and occupational shifts, which have taken the Chicano population from a primarily farm work category to one where only 8 percent of its labor force are

---

[1]Bureau of the Census, *Current Population Reports. Special Studies,* "Language Usage in the United States: July 1975 (Advance report)," Series P-23, No. 60 (Revised), July 1976.

[2]Bureau of the Census, *Current Population Reports. Population Characteristics,* "Persons of Spanish Origin in the United States: March 1976 (Advance Report)," Series P-20, No. 302, November 1976.

in agriculture.[3] Today Census data indicate that 67 percent of Mexican-origin workers are in blue-collar and service work and 76.8 percent of Mexican-origin families reside in metropolitan areas.[4] Urbanization and industrialization are thus counterforces dissolving social and language bonds in the community, increasing contact between Spanish and English speakers, and accelerating the process of acculturation. What results then is a dynamic bilingualism[5] whereby the Spanish language continues to survive even as it loses more and more of its functions among the younger generations.

Given the social and economic conditions in the Southwest, complete assimilation is not possible. On the other hand, neither is stable bilingualism with definite social functions for both languages. This would hardly be possible in an area where the minority language is constantly losing ground, where significant social roles are played in English, and where no value is placed on the maintenance of Spanish for particular roles. The presence of these contradictions creates the particular Spanish language situation that is prevalent throughout the Mexican-origin communities of the Southwest.

Several Spanish codes, or varieties, reflecting the different segments of the Mexican-origin population are spoken throughout the Southwest. Given the constant influx of immigrants, there is always a newly arrived group of Mexicans who speak a variety of standard and nonstandard urban and rural forms of Mexican Spanish. The Chicano population also includes several generations of descendants of Mexican immigrants who have continued to use their ancestors' varieties of Mexican Spanish while at the same time incorporating new elements into a vocabulary constantly in the process of elaboration to meet the needs of a complex, rapidly changing industrialized society. Today, although the majority of Chicanos are urbanized, there is still a significant 23 percent residing in nonmetropolitan areas and reflecting rural backgrounds. This rural segment includes the migrant labor family that travels north from the Texas valley to the Midwest, on through the Northwest and south to the valleys of California. Another important segment of the population includes the younger generations, some of whom reside in urban centers with large concentrations of Mexican-origin families where unemployment rates soar, the dropout rate in schools is high (24 percent of Mexican-origin persons complete less than five years of school),[6] and there is little or no chance for social mobility. Only a third of the Mexican-origin population completes four years of high school or more. Together all of these segments, young and old, reflect several language variety choices.

In all languages there exist different varieties of language to deal with

[3]*Ibid.*

[4]*Ibid.*

[5]Glyn Lewis, *Multilingualism in the Soviet Union* (The Hague: Mouton, 1972), p. 275.

[6]Bureau of the Census, "Persons of Spanish Origin," November 1976.

different situations and circumstances. All speakers then have a linguistic repertoire from which they select the appropriate code according to role, context, and domain. All varieties of languages are not, however, equally accessible to all speakers, since experience is different for members of different groups and different socioeconomic classes. Some reflect training or instruction or particular social settings. Educators and linguists often distinguish between standard and nonstandard varieties of language. Standard varieties are those which have undergone the process of standardization. This involves the selection of a particular variety; its codification in terms of norms, rules, and forms; its elaboration if it lacks important elements necessary for particular functions; and its dissemination through the media, education, government, printing, etc. Obviously only an influential group of people exercising control of social institutions can standardize a variety of language. Different norms may exist in different communities but the term "standard" generally refers to the official language variety in an area. What is important is that the process of standardization is a historical one, man-made and man-controlled.

All varieties of language have the potential, then, to be standardized and elaborated to meet specific needs; linguistically they are all equally valid, for they are all sign systems useful for communication. As a historical phenomenon, language is also constantly changing, evolving, and developing so that forms current at some particular period are superseded by developing forms. Often those forms making up the standard variety during a particular period are later replaced by other forms. The original forms may continue to exist in the repertoire of the masses even though the elite have discarded them from the standard varieties.

Socially, however, all language varieties do not share the same status. Language varieties in fact reflect the status of the speakers. Given a stratified society, the varieties of those speakers at the lower end of the scale will be stigmatized. In effect we find that social changes are reflected in language and language choice. Often a desire for social mobility will lead to language change and language shifts, for survival may call for appropriating the language of the majority in the area.

In the Southwest, all prestigious social roles and functions are the domain of the English language. Few formal domains call for the use of Spanish. Among these are the churches in Chicano barrios, radio and television stations in metropolitan centers, and local barrio newspapers. Often these enterprises are run by personnel educated in Spanish; consequently, standard varieties are the medium, although commercials and broadcasts featuring local speakers sometimes reflect local varieties of Spanish, as do sermons by locally ordained preachers. Bilingual programs in the public schools also attempt to use standard varieties of Spanish but given the lack of trained personnel to teach in Spanish, whatever the variety, what often occurs is constant code-switching and little or no instruction in Spanish.

Given the lack of Spanish instruction in the schools for so many years and in fact the prohibition of the Spanish language itself on school premises, plus the lack of institutional support for the Spanish language in Southwest society, it is not surprising that formal varieties have not flourished. Consequently, the Mexican-origin population in the Southwest is generally not literate in Spanish. The situation is one of oral proficiency in nonstandard or popular varieties, a situation common to many parts of the Spanish-speaking world where illiteracy runs high.

Although all Spanish language varieties share a common base, each country in fact has its own standard which differs from others and from Castilian in pronunciation, vocabulary, and/or morphology. Differences also exist between nonstandard varieties of Spanish, but here again several features appear in most of these varieties, particularly in the rural varieties. In fact rural dialects in Argentina, Chile, Peru, and Mexico share many features with rural dialects in Texas, New Mexico, Arizona, Colorado, and California. These shared characteristics include laxing or loss of voiced fricatives, conversion of *hiatos* into diphthongs, aspiration of sibilants and labio-dental fricatives, addition of epenthetic sounds, displacement of sounds in cases of metathesis and reduction of forms through loss of initial or final syllables.

One common phenomenon in language change is the simplification of grammar rules with an extension of rule application. One grammar may place particular constraints on the operation of a rule while another grammar removes some of those constraints, allowing the rule to apply in more cases. This type of rule extension and rule regularization occurs in the morphological component as well as in the phonological. In the following examples we can see cases of morphological regularization in popular varieties spoken in the Southwest. It will be important to describe these popular codes in comparison to standard codes which also function in the Southwest:

		Standard Codes	*Popular Codes*
A.	Present Tense	salimos	salemos
B.	Present Subjunctive	volvamos	vuélvamos
		sintamos	siéntamos
		comamos	cómamos
C.	II Person Singular Preterit Verbs	comiste	comistes

Examples under A reflect a logical restructuring of the -ir conjugations to reform to -er patterns. Verbs ending in -er indicate shift in tense through a shift in the thematic vowel from -e to -i in the preterit tense:

Standard Codes	Present tense:	comemos	salimos
	Preterit tense:	comimos	salimos

Standard conjugations for -ir verbs maintain the thematic -i vowel for both present and preterit tenses. Popular varieties have thus extended rules for

-er verbs to include -ir verbs as well to produce the following results and maintain the pattern:

> Popular Codes   Present tense: comemos salemos
>   Preterit tense: comimos salimos

The verb forms shown under example B reflect an irregular stem pattern with an underlying O vowel that diphthongizes whenever it falls in a stressed syllable. Otherwise it remains as o:

> vÓLv + a + s   — — vuelvas
> vOLv + á + mos — — volvamos
> Rule: Stressed O becomes diphthong [we].

In the popular varieties the rule affecting stressed O remains the same but the stress rule is changed to retain stress in the antepenultimate syllable as follows:

> vÓLv + a + s   — — vuelvas
> vÓLv + a + mos — — vuélvamos

These first person plural forms thus appear to have a stressed underlying O vowel. Once we examine other verb forms we find that the stress shift occurs in all these subjunctive forms, not merely in those with underlying O vowels:

Standard Codes	Popular Codes
comamos	cómamos
salgamos	sálgamos
pensemos	piénsemos
vivamos	vívamos

Thus the stem vowels in the popular variants have been regularized so that all forms have the stress on the same syllable:

piense	piénsemos
pienses	
piense	piensen

Another interesting phenomenon occurs to first person plural verbs in some Texas and New Mexico dialects. Here the person affix -mos becomes -nos whenever the verb form has the stress falling on the antepenultimate syllable as follows:

	Texas Variants	Other popular Variants	Standard Variants
Present Subjunctive	tráiganos	tráigamos	traigamos
Imperfect	vivíanos	vivíamos	vivíamos
Conditional	tomaríanos	tomaríamos	tomaríamos
Imperfect Subjunctive	comiéranos	comiéramos	comiéramos

Examples under C also show an instance of rule extension. Standard Spanish contains a rule which indicates that -s is the second person singular morpheme. Thus all *tú* verbs add -s at the end as the person-number affix: *comes, hablas, vives.* The standard variety, however, has an exception to the rule. The preterit ending for *tú* verbs is -ste with no -s at the end. In the popular varieties, the exception is eliminated and the preterit personnumber form becomes -stes. In some Texas varieties the second person singular ending is -tes instead:

Standard	Popular	Texas
comiste	comistes	comites
hablaste	hablastes	hablates
fuiste	fuistes	fuites

In these few examples we can see that popular varieties just as standard varieties can be explained in terms of logical grammar rules. In fact there is often little logic to irregular standard forms. Popular varieties, then, are not incorrect but rather correct according to their grammars. Needless to say, one can communicate just as well with *vuélvamos, dijites,* or *salemos* as with *volvamos, dijiste,* and *salimos.* Here it again becomes important to recall that the selection of some forms over others is simply a historical process revealing the preferences of some influential group rather than the forms' inherent suitability. Social reality rather than linguistic superiority makes it imperative that these standard forms be made accessible to all.

Language varieties can also differ in terms of vocabulary. Thus in some areas the term for "avocado" is *palta* (Argentina) rather than *aguacate.* In some areas a *carro* is a bus (Ecuador), while here in the Southwest it is a car. Puerto Ricans, on the other hand, ride *guaguas* and Mexicans *camiones,* while Chicanos ride *buses* or *boses.* Puerto Ricans eat *habichuelas,* while we eat *frijoles.* Regional lexical differences also are common in the Southwest. What is a *niño chiflado* (spoiled child) in Texas is a *niño chiqueado* in California. A farmworker works in a *labor* in Texas and in a *fil* in California. Much of the vocabulary in the Southwest is of course derived from terms brought in from various parts of Mexico. Thus, within a small community we can find speakers referring to a "kite" as *cometa, papalote,* or *huila* and to "bucket" as *balde, cubeta, tina,* or *cedrón.*

Rural varieties in the Southwest, as elsewhere in the Spanish-speaking world, also include old forms often referred to as *archaic* terms, which were acceptable variants and part of the norm in the 16th century. Later, in the process of standardization, other forms were preferred but codification did not mean the extermination of early forms from popular speech, particularly for those groups isolated from urban centers, where language change can be effected more rapidly through constant contact with newer forms and different variants. Among these archaic terms are forms like *vide, truje, haiga, semos, escrevir,* and *mesmo.* Some forms, like *haiga,* are part of the repertoire of the majority of Chicano Spanish speakers.

All previously discussed variants found in the Southwest are also common in Mexico and Latin America. There are, however, elements in Chicano Spanish that are unique not in terms of the phenomenon but simply in terms of the range of the phenomenon. These are the loanwords in Southwest Spanish taken from the English language and adapted phonologically and morphologically to the Spanish language. These loanwords reflect the process of acculturation initiated by immigrants upon crossing the border. Some loans reflect urbanization and consumerism. The loans are borrowed for various reasons. Often there is no Spanish equivalent with the same connotation as the English term. *Yard* and *patio*, for example, cannot be said to be equivalent, since the referents are different in the two cultures and have a different function. Wherever certain consumer goods were incorporated into a household which had never previously used such items or appliances, the English term was adapted: Words like *mapiador* (from *mop*), *mapear (to mop)*, and *suiche (switch)* or *plogue (plug)* were adapted phonologically and morphologically. Words of high frequency in the language, like *bill*, given the credit system functioning in this country, were adopted, as in *bil* and *biles*, and preferred over traditional terms, like *cuenta*. As new consumer products appeared on the market they were also incorporated: *la baica* (bike), *la juila* (wheeler), *el mofle* (muffler), *el cloche*, (clutch), *el estare* (starter), etc. A number of high-frequency loanwords have now become part of local Spanish varieties: *espelear, taipiar, puchar, wachar, troca, faite, daime, nicle, dipa, rula, waifa, norsa, broda,* and many others.

Other types of loans include loan-shifts, which involve direct translation of phrases, as for example, *correr pa presidente* for "to run for president" or *venir pa tras* for "to come back." In cases where cognates exist in the two languages, often the endings in Spanish are altered to resemble more closely the English equivalent. Thus we have words like *farmacista* for *farmacéutico* through the influence of *pharmacist,* and *telefón* rather than *teléfono* for *telephone.* Often the loans are false cognates, for in fact the Spanish standard equivalent has a different meaning. Thus we often say *librería* (bookstore) for *library* rather than *biblioteca,* or *realizar* (to achieve) for *realize* rather than *darse cuenta.* Borrowing is of course a common phenomenon wherever two language groups are in contact. The specific type of borrowing reflects the type of contact between the two language groups. Extensive borrowing in one language often reflects a hierarchical situation where one language occupies a dominant position and the other is subordinated.

The English language, for example, borrowed many terms dealing with ranching and mining because of the contact between Mexicans and Americans in the Southwest during the 19th and 20th centuries. Words like *placer, cowboy, lariat, rodeo, lasso, corral, barbeque, calaboose* all reflect this early contact. But Spanish loanwords in English are fewer in proportion, despite the fact that English also incorporated a number of Spanish place names as well as social and food terms.

The particular concentration of the Mexican-origin population in low-income housing, isolated from other language groups or in contact with other poverty-stricken minorities, has generated youth groups or gangs who invariably suffer from unemployment, high dropout rates, and boredom, since recreational facilities are difficult to find in the barrio or ghetto. Although these youths may sometimes fall prey to drug pushers and other types quick to take advantage of their desperate situation, most are in fact not delinquents but rather manual laborers, dishwashers, waiters and busboys, gardeners, hall sweepers, and the unemployed in large urban centers. Young males in the barrio develop their own slang, as do all youth groups in the United States. Chicano slang incorporates argot from Mexico and loan-words from English to produce an authentic variety characterized by its ironic humor which can be both light and derisive, and by its coining of original terminology to replace worn-out expressions. This variety, called *caló* or *pachuco*, became notorious during the 1940s when the California press waged a racist campaign against youth of Mexican origin who followed a particular dress fad and sported duck-tail haircuts. In their relative isolation amidst prosperity, the Mexican youth developed a "hip" fashion and a particular code. The caló of that decade is still around with further innovations and increased sophistication as it penetrates academia. It is still primarily the language of young males, now called *vatos locos* rather than *pachucos*, in large urban barrios and ghettos.

Caló, which can be subdivided into several subsets, is distinguished from other Spanish varieties by its lexical component. Morphologically, syntactically, and phonologically it resembles all other varieties and is especially marked by its extensive use of homophones, tropes, alliteration, synecdoche, and metonymy. Its sources are the standard variety, the popular varieties, the English language, English slang—particularly that taken from Black English—and Mexican slang. Some of the terms are common in the argot of all Spanish-speaking countries, particularly the jargon dealing with crime, violence, and prisons. Slang terms dealing with food, sex, and work are more apt to vary from region to region and often cease to be exclusively the language of youth, becoming part of the general population's repertoire. In these examples, followed by a standard Spanish version, we can see some of the described sources:

1. De su chante le talonió pal jale.
   De su casa se fue a pie para el trabajo.

2. Me periquió del escuelín.
   Me habló de la escuela.

3. Le apañó la vaisa a la güisa.
   Le tomó la mano a la muchacha.

4. Hazme esquina.
   Apóyame.
5. Se alivianó unos calcos, una lisa y unos tramados.
   Se robó unos zapatos, una camisa y unos pantalones.
6. Simón, ése. Se descontó con otro barco.
   Sí, se fue con otro vato (hombre).

In the first example we find a case of synecdoche and metonymy, where an element constituting the part is substituted for the whole at the same time that it is used figuratively. Thus *talón* (heel) is substituted for *pie* (foot) and for the entire phrase *ir a pie* (to walk). From the word *talón* is derived the verb *talonear*, pronounced *taloniar*, in the sense of "to walk" or simply "to go." The term *jale* comes from the verb *jalar*, a popular pronunciation for the standard *halar*, "to pull." An extension of meaning converts *jalar* into a word synonymous with "to work," for both connote "strenuous effort." The noun *chante*, on the other hand, is a loanword adapted phonologically and morphologically from "shanty."

In the second example the verb *periquió* from *periquiar* is a humorous figure of speech based on association, since *pericos* (parrots) are birds famous for their oral imitations. In English, of course, the word "parrot" is also a verb, but in Spanish it does not denote imitation or repetition but simply "to speak." The word *escuelín* is an example of extensive use made in caló of derivation through the addition of diminutives or augmentatives. The affix *-ín*, common in exotic words like *chile piquín*, is used simply to defamiliarize the word.

In the third example are three words which are marked as [+ caló] : *apañó*, *vaisa*, and *güisa*. The term *apañó* is a standard term meaning "to take" but it is not frequent in the Southwest or Mexico. Standard terminology may qualify as caló if it is not a familiar part of the general population's repertoire. The word *vaisa* is a loanword from *vise*, an English term for a griplike device, where meaning is then extended from "grip" to "hand." *Güisa*, on the other hand, is an argot term for "girl."

In the fourth example, the caló phrase is simply a figure of speech taken from carpentry, where a corner is a square structure of support for walls and roof. *Hacer esquina*, "to form a square or corner," is then used as an equivalent of "to support" in more ways than one.

In the fifth example, the dress items, *calcos*, *lisa*, and *tramados*, are all argot terms found also in the caló of Mexico. The verb *alivianar*, on the other hand, is a standard term meaning "to lighten a load," where meaning has been extended to connote "to steal."

The last example reflects a linguistic technique with a high frequency among Chicano youth. Here worn-out phrases are replaced with terms having homophonous initial sounds. A worn-out expression like *Ahi nos vemos* (I'll see you) is replaced by *Ahi nos vidrios*, where *vidrios* (glass) can substitute as a humorous synonym for the expected *vemos*. The selection of substitutes with homophonous beginnings is quite common, as in *Simón* for *Sí*, *estufas* for *estuvo*, *barco* for *bato* or *vato*. This last example also shows use of the singular demonstrative pronoun *ése* as a common calo equivalent for *tú* or *Vd*. Use of the verb *descontar* is again an extension of meaning, where the denotation "to subtract" is extended to indicate "to remove oneself from the premises."

Calo, then, is a highly creative code which utilizes a number of literary techniques. It increases the denotations and connotations of existing terminology, thereby creating a huge store of figurative expressions. Clichés and worn-out expressions are defamiliarized through the addition of suffixes and prefixes, and argot terminology is substituted for common items. As long as the Mexican-origin population continues to be concentrated in particular residential areas, the youth will continue to develop their unique variety for use among themselves. Caló is not a secret language but it does convey group solidarity and affiliation. Youth using this variety of course shift to other varieties when involved with older speakers, family members, women, and strangers.

The most common variety of language in the Chicano community among bilingual speakers is code-switching. This variety, characterized by the inclusion of both English and Spanish components within a single discourse, clearly reflects the contact between two language groups. The fact that English is the dominant language with most of the important functions in this society explains why it has encroached on intimate and informal situations formerly the domain of Spanish.

Code-switching occurs among bilingual Chicano students for intra-group communication, which requires that interlocutors not only share information but establish rapport as fellow Chicanos. What generally occurs is that the speech event calls for the English language for two reasons: 1) in all probability the situation was experienced in English and 2) the terminology associated with that topic was learned in English. Frequency plays an important part in language choice, since unfamiliarity with a particular topic or event in one language can trigger a shift to the language functioning in that domain.

Language shift, however, can occur for other reasons. As we know, the inclusion of items from another language within a discourse can serve to produce particular effects, whether humorous, cultural, or elitist. In Chicano code-switching the shift can also signal a change in mood or a shift to a different speech act within a speech event. Thus an informal conversation can shift to English when the discourse becomes serious. A formal presentation in English may call for a shift to Spanish to introduce a joke or an aside. A conversation in Spanish may be sprinkled with English shifts when the tone is light. Thus shifts from Spanish to English may occur not because of lexical gaps but because the shift changes the affective content of the message. Consider the following sentence:

Ponlo en el refrigerator so it won't spoil.

This sentence said entirely in Spanish (*Ponlo en el refrigerador para que no se eche a perder*) is perceived as a more formal command than the code-switched sentence, which can be taken as lightly as a suggestion. Thus any utterance said entirely in Spanish carries a tone of formality and may in fact sound pedantic, as in a) *Tenemos que enumerar los puntos principales* vs. b) "Tenemos que list todos los important points." We cannot assume that the speaker of (b) does not have the Spanish vocabulary to produce (a), for there are extralinguistic factors determining choice of (b) over (a). The context and circumstances where code-switching will occur can be summarized as follows:

1) Code-switching may occur if the discourse is marked [+ technical] where the interlocutors are both [+ Chicano]. In this case introductory words and connectives may be in Spanish but the discourse is primarily in English.

2) Code-switching may occur if the discourse shifts from [+ serious] to [+ informal] where the interlocutors are both [+ Chicano]. In this case a serious discussion in English may shift to Spanish for a joke or an aside. This applies also to serious discourse in Spanish where the shift to English signals lighter topics and informality.

3) Code-switching may occur where straight use of Spanish would not only signal [+ serious] but also [+ pedantic].

4) Code-switching may occur where terminology with high frequency is employed. A student who uses terms like "xerox copy" several times a day will not say *Fui a sacar una fotocopia* to his friends. *Fotocopia* has a very low frequency in the discourse of most Chicano students and consequently can produce a pedantic effect.

5) Phrases of high frequency, like crutch words or connectors, are often code-switched, especially in Spanish discourse when the speaker has used English throughout most of the day at work, school, and business. It is then common to hear complete sentences in Spanish sprinkled with "I mean," "like," "so," "so like que," or "I know" and "you know."

All of these varieties make up the collective repertoire of the Chicano community. We can summarize the Chicano Spanish code system through the presentation of these five sentences, which range from a standard code to a code-switching code:

1. ¡Qué barbaridad! Se han llevado mis cerillos.
2. ¡Chingáo! Se han lleváo mis ceríos.
3. ¿Las mechas? Las puse pa tras en la mesa.
4. ¡Esos guys! They took off con mis cigarettes y mis mechas.
5. ¡Ya estufas! Esos vatos se descontaron con mis trolas.

These five subcodes encompass numerous phonological, morphological, and lexical as well as semantic variations and could be further subdivided in terms of urban/rural varieties. Shifts from one variety to another could be predicted in terms of generational, residential, and language contact features as well as in terms of affective domain features. The multiplicity of speakers, backgrounds, and settings is not only part of daily life in the Southwest but is reflected in the literature of Chicanos, for literature, like language, reflects the historical and social context of the class involved.

Toward a Concept of Culture

by Juan Gómez-Quiñones

This article is dedicated to Américo Paredes

Why

This essay deals with culture among the people of Mexican descent in the United States. The problem of culture consists of understanding its makeup and its process historically and in contemporary times, and understanding the relation of culture to conflict both conceptually and specifically. Questions and answers on culture are basic to historical analysis and political discourse. Polemics, definitions and analysis rather than specific data form the core of the essay. The need to understand culture arose from studies on labor in the 19th and 20th centuries. Attempts to examine the problem of worker consciousness and the relation between class, conflict and culture raised the problem of culture. Unfortunately, there is great frustration in seeking answers to questions on culture from the existing literature...The essay is divided into the following parts: discussion on culture and its relation to domination; history; the border; class struggle; and the role of intellectuals. Essentially the essay is a call to debate on culture academically and politically.

The essay argues and asserts basic points. Culture is historically derived, fluid, composed of both positive and negative aspects and is malleable to conscious action. In domination and resistance to domination, culture is of salient importance. It is inseparably interrelated to the life of people and their struggle. Culture is the context in which struggle takes place; however, conflict or resistance is primarily economic and political and constitutes class resistance. The relation between culture and class is a historical phenomenon; it is observable over time. In contemporary times class and cultural expression take place in a matrix involving the world situation, socializing influences along the border and class and cultural divisions among the population....

Academic writers have not contributed much to clarifying the problem of culture, though attempts are presently underway. Traditionally the study of culture is the province of sociology and anthropology, rather than eco-

"Toward a Concept of Culture" by Juan Gómez-Quiñones. An extended version of this essay was published in *Revista Chicano-Riqueña*, 5, no. 2 (*primavera* ["Spring"] 1977), 29-47. Reprinted by permission of the author and the publisher.

nomics, history or literature. Academic writings often have the following not mutually exclusive conceptual frameworks or biases: folk culture model, value orientation model, and acculturation model. These writings stress assumptions based on the perception of Mexican culture as static and homogeneous, and measure the culture on the basis of its presumed backwardness or measure progress of the culture bearer in terms of acculturation, which is seen as the adoption of Anglo middle-class "values." These views were contested by the first stage of Chicano revisionist writings, when in the sixties writers discovered culture does exist, and Mexicans are not passive. After this great breakthrough, more critical writings began to analyze the historical relations between the economy, race and class and the internal dynamics within the Mexican community and its relation to consciousness. Examples of the latter are the writings of Tomás Almaguer, Carlos Muñoz, and Guillermo Flores. The best studies on culture of the Mexican people in the United States are those of Américo Paredes and José Limón. I draw from them. . . .

Culture

Culture encompasses the customs, values, attitudes, ideas, patterns of social behavior and arts common to members of a group and provides a design for living embracing specific historically derived material traits. Culture, ethnicity, identity, language, history, nationhood, nationality are all related; each may be seen as a part or as encompassing the others. Culture is both subjective and objective; it is both ideal and material. It stems from the base; however, culture can act upon the base. The base is an interaction between the economy, the ecology and social relations; it is an interaction between productive forces and mode of production. Culture is an expression of class relations. Culture is a process which undergoes change. The dynamic aspect of culture is in seeming conflict with the perception of it as stable and permanent, a perception which, though fallacious, follows from the fact that it is learned; thus from this fact, it is assumed to be stable. Culture is learned rather than "instinctive" or biological. Genetic inheritance may be separate from culture. Ethnic characteristics are meaningful culturally only when expressed in relation to other individuals of a person's own group and/or in relation to other groups. Identity involves a cultural framework. An individual consciously identifies with the culture and practices the sum of it. The absence of any one feature or several does not rule out the general sum of culture or the possible identification; nonetheless, an accelerating erosion of features passes from the absence of degree to a qualitative difference in culture. Individuals teach and learn culture from others. Culture is taught by people to other people, parents to children, peers to peers, elders to youth, generation to generation. Through repetition of teaching comes persistency which results in a relative consistency among individual bearers. However, culture is not "above" or "independent" of people.

Culture is social in that it is shared by people living and interacting in organized aggregates. One does not practice or "create" culture in isolation. The culture and the society are interdependent; culture does not survive the society. The historical outcome is mutual. This interdependence is expressed in the values of group cohesion which are in turn advanced by the cultural forms of social control, group protection and group perpetuation and expansion. Thus, in part, culture is a set of ideational norms. The ideational is not always the actual behavior. An individual's behavior may or may not conform to the norm depending on circumstances or will. There is neither an "ideal culture" above classes, nor a homogeneous culture for all peoples of a group independent of class aspects.

Continuity in elements of culture depends on functional validity and satisfaction. Culture provides pleasure which contributes to its reinforcement. If no longer satisfactory or pleasurable, change occurs. Culture changes through adaptation, borrowing and invention, in that order, as material and subjective conditions change. The contemporary and the historical functional elements of culture are not inconsistent. Rather, their interrelation renews culture. Culture rigidity is a sign of cultural death. In the course of change or renewal a "lag" occurs, which means an element is temporarily out of scheme with other elements, until integration occurs, which requires time. At no one moment is integration absolute. Nonetheless culture is on the whole integrative and this requires time which assumes the form of "tradition." To stress "tradition" is to view how culture is acquired rather than to see of what culture consists. Humans are actors within culture; they can and do act upon culture consciously. Art is an example of the conscious expression in aesthetic form of elements generative and degenerative of a culture and an expression of acting upon culture by people.

Domination and Its Rejection

Domination of a people by a foreign system principally involves human labor, material resources, and political hegemony. Domination interrupts the creation and continuity of culture, the process of development. Domination stifles the interaction between creation and continuity. It suppresses the people through force and control as it negates the historical process of the people. The historical culture is displaced by an ersatz culure, a counterfeit culture, a superimposed culture of domination.

Since through domination, labor is sought as a resource, ways and mystiques, however beset with contradictions, come into play to facilitate economic exploitation and political hegemony. Dominating cultural institutions do the following: 1) legitimize domination and those who hold power; 2) reinforce social hegemony and its allied interests; 3) attempt integration and alienate. In domination, cultural assimilation is both an ideological mystique and a social control policy, which is conditional and selective acting upon the oppressed people. In extreme form the existence of the people and their concurrent claims are in fact denied. However, assimilation deforms but never does it bring about integration or acceptance of the discriminated population by the dominant group, and those who accept the mystique are doomed to be marginal.

Domination is contested by people because they reject exploitation, which means subjugation and which in turn threatens national survival. Against domination various kinds of resistance take place: sporadic or consistent, individual or small group, armed or weaponless, juridical or civic— all the varied resistances which challenge social hegemony. But the most encompassing and persistent are those of class and culture. These subsume the others. Cultural resistance, the rejection of cultural domination, is the negation of assimilation. This may take two routes: "tradition" for its own sake, or a synthesis of tradition and creation. Heightened cultural expression, however, is not of itself political or an act of struggle. Within the boundaries of the acceptance of domination, cultural expression is permitted. The principal, most potentially subverting resistance is that against economic exploitation and political hegemony. When resistance occurs, crisis ensues. Political crisis intensifies cultural expression as a result of tightened group cohesion and sharper group values. Political dissent, class conflict and cultural resistance reinforce each other. To be an act of struggle, culture requires critical consciousness and collective participation in politics. Culture must be joined to politics of liberation for it to be an act of resistance. At this juncture cultural creation supersedes "tradition." In moments of crisis, class and cultural resistance assume political form which is all encompassing.

History and Culture

The cultural historical formation of the Mexican in what is now the United States spans two major periods: (a) Indian times to the Mexican-North American War, during which a provincial, agrarian, mestizo society was established, a process parallel and integral to the general formation of the Mexican nation; and (b) the war to the present during which the people in the previous provinces were partially separated from the historical formation of Mexico and the society enlarged by migration was subject to direct economic and cultural domination within the confines of a foreign cultural, urban and industrial framework. In the late 19th and early 20th centuries cultural change was the result of changes in land tenure relations, the introduction of early large-scale capital enterprises and the appearance of mass labor. Historical development involved both diversity and unity.

In the United States north of the Río Bravo, the space is vast and varied and the Mexican population diverse. Historically, regional variety is related to the regional economy, to the rate, length and type of settlement, the culture of local Indian groups, the relation with local Indian groups, rate and manner of displacement by Anglo North Americans. The local regional differences are, in addition, a result of differing regional Anglo economic-political, cultural, social, demographic complexes, and of culture brought over by succeeding generations of Mexicans to the communities at different times as general patterns of migratory preference shifted. Within each of the regional diversities, differences are determined by occupation of the person and his family, racial features, individual and family sense of history, identity and culture, length of residence, education, use of Spanish, type of English, acculturation, degree of participation in Anglo society, urban or rural residence and individual experience of exploitation and discrimination.

Across this diversity are factors of commonality, ethnicity, class, history, and domination. Important in this unity are race and ethnicity, that is Mexican descent and access to general Mexican culture. The genetic inheritance is Indio-Mestizo-Mulatto but the Indian is overwhelmingly predominant. Since the Mexican shares race and geography with the Indian, this relation is particularly important. This relationship has been varied: hostile, friendly, and neutral but there is a historical comradeship shared with the Indian felt by the Mexican at least that is not extended to whites. Most important, Mexicans are united by a common dependent relation to the economy: they are workers. In any region the vast majority of Mexican people are workers living in workers' conditions. Thus in regard to identity as well as objectively, class membership coincides generally with community membership and identity. Thus a particular relation to the means of production along national and class lines exists. There are other factors of unity. The circumstances and the social-cultural legacy of the Mexican community is a product of war. This affects all regions. Thus, Mexican people consciously or unconsciously perceive the Southwest as part of the homeland; the existing domination is perceived as a usurpation and unjust fact. Further, the historical legacy means that the Anglo is not only an imperialist, but also a historical enemy; to acculturate is not merely to exercise a culture preference but to go to the other side. The legacy of war, as well as other factors, means the Mexicans are viewed and treated as a subject people by Anglo individuals and institutions. Across class lines racism in a particular form, a pervasive rationalized anti-Mexicanism, has been experienced by and directed at Mexican people. In all areas of life social hegemony is a fact for Mexicans. Coexistence, the economy and subjugation have caused a continual cultural syncretic process, a culture of adaptation, of survival, of change which welds the people together. Historically, continuous resistance and conflict is the result of continuous oppression which can unite. ...

The Border and Culture

Since 1848 the question of culture and identity has involved a critical choice of consciousness for the people of Mexican descent living within the United States. Culture and identity are not critical to the majority of Mexicans in Mexico at this time. However, heightened cultural awareness is an aspect of consciousness shared by the Mexican population in the United States and the people residing in the northern Mexican border states. A special historical relationship is shared by the "Greater Mexican North," the provinces occupied in 1848, and the present Mexican border states. This relationship, besides being spatial and geographic, is a result of patterns of settlement, Mestizaje, and the economy of cattle raising, agriculture, mining, transportation and the society and values surrounding these. The greater Mexican north border area was relatively egalitarian, Mestizo and characterized by wage labor or commerce, independent rancheros and a local, often liberal, middle class which was on occasion radical. Politically, liberalism and rebelliousness, as well as nationalism, were features of this area. Along the border national feelings are historically strong.

Today the historical relation between the Mexicans in the Southwest and the people, the industries, the towns and countryside of the present Mexican border states and border towns is now mediated by the large border urban conglomerations from Tijuana to the Gulf of Mexico. Too often the cities in these areas have been seen only as depots of transient labor and as tourist-free zones. On one hand in fact, they are the base for a certain entrepreneurial element and on the other hand a base for a proletarizing process involving large numbers of people. What happens in these cities has important dimensions for Mexicans in the United States. Nearly ten million Mexicans live in the "zona fronteriza," a number roughly equal to the residents in the United States. Together both populations are a significant percentage of all Mexicans.

Acute labor exploitation and cultural degradation and disintegration are the principal features of the Mexican border cities which are economically linked to the United States. Women are of notable importance socially and economically. Whatever factors contribute to the existence of family stability in the rest of Mexico, they are weak in these cities. The exploitation of women in factories and in vice sustains these cities. There are nearly 500 factories along the border and thousands of prostitutes; both consist of sexual and labor exploitation. Vice is the major industry and supports a whole subconstellation of economic activity employing thousands of people. Corruption permeates the society. Working people are subject to strong lumpenizing features: alcoholism, prostitution (male and female), drug traffic and consumption. The values surrounding these activities are features of life and culture in the border cities. These aspects are not unique to these cities, but they are particularly acute and influential there, as are other features: extreme poverty, unemployment, underemployment, poor housing, and substandard education, nutrition, and health conditions. All of these features affect an unusually regionally heterogeneous uprooted population in search of the yankee dollar and material commodities. Millions of people are conditioned by these features as laborers and consumers. Rather than politicizing people, these conditions may generally depoliticize.

This judgment is supported by political and cultural features of the border cities. There is a clear relation between the upper and middle classes and vice. Not surprisingly, this border élite is very sensitive as to its "culture" and social legitimacy. Thus the ridiculous importance given to "clubes sociales y cívicos." Further educationism, "self-improvement," quackery, and spiritualism are abundant. A particularly exaggerated and limited cultural nationalism is propagated, which is a response to a weakened Mexican identity and cultural integration. They in turn are a reflection of weakened economic integration. If progressive Mexican nationalism is a set of ideas for political sovereignty, social welfare, economic justice and development in behalf of national well-being and progress, in short, nationalism as radical social change, then this nationalism is not that. It is a pathetic and ridiculous cultural nationalism propagated by the government élite and the officious local intellectuals, diffused to *all* sectors of the population. This nationalism is a catalogue of things "we have" and others don't: holidays, dress, bad art, battles, scenery, mythified and embalmed heroes, food. In short, it is a counterpoint to reality: something unique and marvelous, a holiday divorced from economic and political struggle. This nationalism is expressed within the content of an exaggerated local chauvinism which is an effective block against critical thinking. People defend what little they can claim. Identify is mythified as local chauvinism and as "folkloric" idiosyncratic style of behavior. The sense of personal identity is weak, the sense of national community is weak, a sense of the world is absent. To compensate for these, or in place of identity, culture and a world view, is an exaggerated masculinity, hollow in substance but real enough in brutal acts, and to this is added a vile consumerism, an exaggerated competitiveness and egotism. Despite the ostensible cultural nationalism, the penetration of cultural domination is facilitated and reinforced by these features.

The northern frontier is where a national identity has been forged by peculiar social and economic developments and where the national culture has sharpened itself against the daily grinding stone of the North American system. However, these historical features have been and are mitigated by the economic nature of the societies in the cities. A progressive historical relation is present but latent. Politicalization, rather than depoliticalization, is, however, possible. Hundreds of thousands of people uprooted from traditional social moorings are being brutally urbanized and industrialized. The North American system and its agents are not veiled either by "national capital" or liberal institutions: both are a palpable daily reality as a force. The agents of the system are experienced as individuals of labor exploitation and cultural degradation. Political dissent is evident by widespread hostility to the state and the ruling party. Exploitation, the centrality of women and weak integration may facilitate a different consciousness. This is not going to come about by hope, more "culture," poetry or study.

Culture and Class

Among the population of Mexican descent in the United States, culture and identity divide into three. In any public or private group situation, the three cultures and identities are operable as cultural and social divisions, but are not always discernible to the participants. One is the sector committed to United States culture and identity. This population, though of Mexican descent, has the culture or identity of the dominant culture usually along lines affected by class, education, status and region, though individuals certainly may selectively practice one trait or another of the Mexican culture, and certainly may rhetorically argue Mexican or Chicano authenticity and identity. They may also play a role in community political affairs, but they are outside the Mexican/Chicano cultural context. The second sector is the transitional group culture and identity composed of the self-denoting subgroups—Chicano, Hispano, Mexican American, Spanish American and so forth—which practice and identify with a subculture generally made up of adaptations and borrowings from the 20th century national cultures of Mexico and the United States and survivals from Mexican national culture current in the nineteenth century. This subculture is also affected by class, status, education and region. This sector is not a new nationality. Often individual bearers desperately seek to prove that it is a unique national culture, a point difficult to prove because of its amalgamated character, its brief time of existence, and because of the dynamic syncretic character of all culture. Upon inspection, what gives uniqueness and cohesion to this group vis-à-vis the culture of the United States is its Mexican content. Regional variants mask this Mexican content or are mistakenly taken for expressions of a unique national culture. This transitional culture is fluid, and at times the balance favors the dominant culture. This fluidity is noticeable in the labels used to denote it. Psychologically, as well as politically, this culture and identity is a safe-house and thus provides strategic and tactical elasticity vis-à-vis the dominant society. The third sector is the group of *Mexicano* culture and identity. It is also affected by class, status, education and region. Here the lag between new and traditional, the conflict between progressive and retrogressive, between traditionals and creators, is keenly felt. Further, as is obvious, Mexicano culture is not static nor exists in a vacuum; it too changes. In addition, its content and transmission also undergo change as change occurs within Mexico, and additionally, culture in Mexico is affected by external cultural forces. These influences and changes are carried by bearers of the culture in the United States. Though there may be three culture and identity groups, or more exactly two cultures and a subculture, the cultural poles are two: Mexicano versus Anglo United States.

In each culture or subculture the question of class is salient. In each of the cultural groups there are class divisions, values, loyalties, and consciousness. Though all too often treated as such, class is not an abstraction; it is expressed through people in a cultural context. The reverse is also true. When looking at culture, class aspects are discernible. Culture is not an abstraction; it involves individuals and it has class aspects. We cannot grossly and simply talk of "culture and identity" or "mass character" without class analysis. What is the "mass character" upheld? Is it the selfishness of the job-conscious skilled blue-collar worker, the viciousness of the lumpen? Nor can we simply say this is "developed" culture, that is "undeveloped" culture. We can make that reference in regard to an economy but not to a language. Since culture and class affect political expression and adherence, and since there is a common level of modernity to the culture due to the economy, it is not "levels" of culture, but which culture, which class. These are the meaningful questions.

The policies of cultural and economic suppression and assimilation, both in regard to class and culture, have resulted in alienation, false consciousness and internal economic and social division within the Mexican population. Each of the three groups has class divisions. There is distributed in the three groups a very small élite of high wealth, a traditional middle class of merchants and professionals, and a newer state-dependent lower middle class, and also artists, intellectuals, and workers and lumpen. Individuals in each of the cultures may have a class loyalty to a class other than the one to which they belong. Opportunism and lack of integrity are found in all classes and cultures.

Though clearly there are class divisions, domination has eschewed the general stratification patterns of bourgeoisie, petite bourgeoisie, proletariat and lumpen. Outside parts of New Mexico and Texas, the élite of high wealth is scarce. The middle-class element, which owes its origin to business, the state and education, has been historically small and in some areas absent, but since World War II is increasing. The lower middle class is recent, small, unstable, dependent and generally of working-class origin. Its political, cultural and economic instability is the result of the crisis it undergoes because of strain and conflict of the dominant economy and society.

Interestingly, elements of the middle class functioning as "colonial" mediators hold their positions, in many cases, only to the extent that they have popular support or tolerance. This class is continually pulled by the contesting forces from above and below. At this time the vast majority of the Mexican people are members of the working class, working in technologically and organizationally updated production or in urban services. There also is a large and growing lumpen. The cruelty of the job market, crime and vice fostered by the system, cultural disintegration, the schools—all increase the lumpen element. Often the lumpen historically ally with the upper and lower bourgeoisie.

Class interest and assimilation resulted in an element among the people of Mexican descent who identify with domination. Assimilation and class have a rough coincidence. Those who identify with domination are particularly numerous among the middle and upper classes, however small these may be in actual numbers. Some are forthright in their allegiance to the dominant culture and its values. Others are less forthright; a few are deceptive. On a surface level Mexican or Chicano identity is a means to bolster arguments for benefits of status and income. These persons enjoy conditional social status and relative economic privilege. They do not have full membership in domination. To place all petite bourgeoisie and salaried artists and professionals or specialized white collar elements into one cultural membership or one class loyalty would be unanalytical.

Struggle and Culture

Mexican culture in the United States is practiced within the confines of the state, an economy and a dominant culture. At the center of the "free world," the system and the values are at their strongest and most pervasive. All elements associated with commodity production and the exploitation of people and nature are at their most intense. Capitalism continually develops. Mexican culture cannot be free from this influence. All its features and expressions take place within a framework of effective control. With the greatest display of apparent liberality this control and its acceptance is strengthened as Mexican culture is practiced for its own sake. The values of the system are propagated and internalized, thereby linking the people in chains to the substructure that produced these values. In the realm of values, the control is a moral force which only a countervailing morality can defeat. Where is the dominant culture at its weakest, most diffused, most subject to critical scrutiny and negative evaluation? Where is there struggle? Struggle occurs at the junction of extreme cultural oppression and economic exploitation, at the juncture of critical consciousness and oppressive reality. Who are the people? They are Mexican workers and their children. These have allies by conviction and solidarity.

Because of the economic and political crisis of the "free world" system the Mexican community in the last ten years has undergone an intensive political process, "the movement." Concomitant with this has been a re-invigoration of material culture, intense debate on identity, conscious acts to strengthen traditional norms of culture and a creative surge in the arts. These *followed*, not preceded, the political process. This is not to deny that these cultural concerns were not present before, as a short course in history would demonstrate they were, but an undeniable aspect of the last ten years is the acceleration, scope, and intensity in these areas of culture as an *outgrowth* of political dissent. The question of cultural identity was a major aspect.

Cultural vitality is possible because culture has survived, and it has survived most strongly amongst the rural and urban working class providing the cultural base for other sectors to draw upon. The cultural strength remains generally with the working people. They have an identity consistent with their objective conditions. This sector has the cultural values and artistic themes to draw from for a progressive integration of culture consistent with the objective interests of the people; it is also the only substantive source of political power to defend the community. Witness the character and base of the initial movement organizations: the farmworkers union, the Alianza, and the early pre-1970 Crusade for Justice, followed by student organizations in California and Texas. The class and cultural character of the first three is clear. The student groups, though different in base from the first three, came into being, among other reasons, as sufficiently large numbers of working class students were able to form a critical political mass at middle class or élite universities, particularly in California and Texas. Undeniably there were class differences and class tensions within the student organizations. Amongst all these organizational sectors the question of identity varied in importance—not much worth discussing among farmworkers, and intensely discussed among the university students, though not by all.

The importance of identity increases in relation to social status, urbanization, and education, in other words, in relation to the subjection to assimilation which by the sixties had touched *all* sectors of society but with varying degrees. Cultural reaffirmation of the community as a whole may be viewed from two contrasting cultural points and divisions: 1) those who never greatly suffered cultural or identity loss and hence had preserved their culture and identity, and 2) those who consciously sought to·acquire or reacquire culture and identity. There has been a vigorous cultural vitality, conscious propagation and dissemination of cultural material for both groups.

The crisis of the system, the impact of the movement, cut across class and cultural divisions among the Mexican people. As economic and political crisis ensues and class and cultural resistance occurs, a two-fold division is present: those who unquestionably hold to their identification and participation in domination, culturally, economically and politically, and those who gradually but increasingly question domination in regard to identity and cultural allegiance. These, along with others heavily exposed to assimilation—students, artists, and highly skilled workers—develop a compelling need for overt cultural identification and paraphernalia, and conceive elaborate, often merely decorative artistic and literary forms, themes, and styles which exalt culture as transcendent. Identity, rather than struggle, is the central theme. Without class identification and political participation, this is at best neutral. At worst, it becomes deceptive, diversionary and conservative, thus supportive of the status quo. Cultural activity *qua* culture, even in groups ostensibly allied to the political movement, retains this conservative character.

However, the crisis is foremost economic and political; thus, community survival demands a response in these areas. From the point of view of culture and assimilation, politics generally involves four groups: 1) those who support domination and its culture, 2) those who vacillate, 3) those who practice culture but ally politically with domination, and 4) the individuals who join the cultural-political process of resistance. The return to culture and identity is demanded by the need to avoid social annihilation, by the need for recognition, and because of discrimination.

At a time of crisis, class resistance and cultural reaffirmation joined to politics has a number of ramifications. The system of oppression is under attack politically, economically, culturally, and ideologically. Ideological weapons which domination has monopolized and has used to intimidate are now turned against domination with irony and skill. When even a few, a tiny fraction, who were seemingly favored or indoctrinated by domination, attack oppression, it sets a temper. Other elements of this "privileged" sector are affected, influenced. Individuals are recruited, while yet others withdraw to a neutrality favorable to reaffirmation, and importantly the opposition is forced on the ideological defensive. Further, this cultural and ideological reaffirmation, with its aggressive stance, has effects on the middle-class professionals, intellectuals and artists of the oppressor causing them disorientation. Most importantly, despite the esoteric language or the stylistic idiosyncrasies of the individuals in cultural and ideological revolt, the meritorious thoughts, ideas, and facts are retranslated and absorbed by the popular class in a reflective and dynamic manner. What is the culture and identity needed for economic and political survival and liberation? ...

What Source?

When acting consciously, individuals can forge class and culture into a unity for the people. A question of class may become one of culture and vice versa. Is the predominant class the workers? Is the predominant culture

Mexicano? What are the well-springs of the vitality of the past ten years? What are the directions visible?

Class and culture have been closely interrelated in the most widespread and influential organizing efforts during the last ten years: the unionization of farmworkers, the struggle for land and language in New Mexico, the struggle for the educational rights of Mexicano parents and children and most recently the struggle for national unity and defense of the undocumented workers. These were seminal to current developments.

Numerically, in fact, the working people are the majority and potentially the most politically powerful. Generally their culture and identity is Mexicano. Historically, and in the present class, conflict and cultural reaffirmation is the pattern. Each has and can strengthen the other. However, there are primary and secondary elements of culture. There are positive and negative, reactionary and progressive elements. Those elements that are unjust, and thus debilitating and divisive, do not contribute to freedom, strength and survival, hence they are not positive. Progressive and positive elements must be reinforced or introduced consciously; people can act upon culture, thus strengthening the group. A strong community means a national culture which provides for satisfaction, progress, a critical awareness, group solidarity, values of self-sacrifice for the common good, and a world view. Art is central to this process.

The forms and ethos of one art must be broken—the art of domination; another art must be rescued and fashioned—the art of resistance. For the latter the aesthetic ethos is the result of sensibility developed through experience, identification and critical intelligence. This art emerges from the experience of struggle. It glimpses a different way of life, of organizing society, of creating more rational relations among men and more intelligent relations with nature and its resources, and minimizing conflict and the use of human intelligence for freedom. It is art that is not afraid to love or play due to its sense of history and future. It negates the exploitation of the many for the few, art as the expression of the degeneration of values for the few, the corruption of human life, the destruction of the world. At that point art is at the threshold of entering the dimension of politics. It becomes the aesthetics of politics as art—art accessible to all, practiced by all, in the full sense of the word—universal. The incompatibility of art and politics is an insidious, debilitating ploy which has been promulgated and uncritically accepted. Art can reconcile or negate. To whose ends? According to what values? These are the questions to ask when confronting art...

Notes on the Evolution of Chicano Prose Fiction

by Juan Rodríguez

Despite the important and productive efforts of such persons as Anselmo Arellano, Luis Leal, Alejandro Morales, Phillip Ortego, Raymund Paredes, and others,[1] the Chicano literary past still remains largely unknown. To date, almost all the critical attention given to Chicano literature has been limited to the literary analysis of contemporary Chicano texts. Nevertheless, there have begun to appear recently essays which contribute significantly to the indispensable task of uncovering our literary past.[2] Until substantially more of this crucial research into our literary history is carried out, any work on the subject will be far from definitive and must necessarily be read as notes that attempt to order and understand research which is far from complete. Our essay, of course, falls within this category.

Undeniably, one event, the Mexican-American War (1846-1848), principally established the conditions which resulted in the creation of the Chicano people's history and literature. It was at that historical juncture that the literary expression of the Mexican people living in the conquered territory turned from what might have developed into a regional variety of Mexican literature, a Northern Mexican variety, and became — at least in principle —

"Notes on the Evolution of Chicano Prose Fiction" by Juan Rodríguez. This article appears for the first time in this volume. It is used by permission of the author.

[1]Anselmo Arellano, ed., *Los pobladores nuevomexicanos y su poesía, 1889-1950* (Albuquerque: Pajarito Publications, 1976); Luis Leal, "Mexican American Literature: A Historical Perspective," *Revista Chicano-Riqueña*, Año I, Número I (1973), 32-44; Alejandro Morales, "Visión panorámica de la literatura mexicoamericana hasta el Boom de 1966" (Ph.D. diss., Rutgers University, 1975); Phillip Ortego, "Backgrounds of Mexican American Literatures" (Ph.D. diss., University of New Mexico, 1971); Raymund Paredes, "The Image of the Mexican in American Literature" (Ph.D. diss., University of Texas, 1973).

[2]See, for example, Doris Meyer, "Anonymous Poetry in Spanish Language Newspapers (1880-1900)," *Bilingual Review* 2 (1975), 259-275, an article that presents valuable poetry from the Chicano past, even if the interpretive part of the essay suffers from lack of insight; Raymund Paredes, "The Evolution of Chicano Literature," to be published in the *Modern Language Journal,* an interpretive, introductory essay; and Tomás Ybarra-Frausto, "The Popular and the Elite: Chicano Poetry" (paper read at the Latin American Studies Association meeting, Houston, Texas, November 2-5, 1977), an excellent example of the type of research that needs to be carried out.

a literature of resistance to Anglo cultural imperialism.[3] The roots of Chicano literature, then, are to be found in the Mexican literature published during the middle of the nineteenth century in what was then Northern Mexico but is now the American Southwest.

By far the best sources of information concerning the literature of the period are the many local and regional newspapers that flourished in the conquered territory.[4] The prose fiction that appears in these is of two types—serial novels and short tales—both of which, as far as we are able to discern, were not locally written but borrowed from Latin American (mostly Mexican) and European sources, and therefore fall within the literary movement then in vogue, romanticism. For instance, in A. A. de Orihuela's *Un cadáver sobre el trono*—a novel which is concluded in the February 28, 1854 issue of *La Crónica,* a San Francisco, California newspaper—a prince's bride is murdered, then exhumed and placed on the throne when the prince becomes king. Even more romantic are the novels of an apparently prolific writer, J. M. Ramírez, "former pupil of the Colegio San Ildefonso de México." One of his novels, *Celeste (El Nuevo Mundo,* San Francisco, California, 8 September 1865 through 22 September 1865), deals with a tragic story of unrequited love and the suffering of two brothers. Another, *Ellas y nosotros (El Nuevo Mundo,* 9 October 1865 through 17 November 1865), tells of a crass law clerk and his friend and their Werther-like love affairs. Both would seem representative of the type of novel being read by the literate people of the conquered territory.

Alongside these longer pieces the newspapers also carried shorter narratives, usually folk tales, legends, or didactic texts selected from the inventory of classic European writers. As the Anglo-American economic presence became more evident in the shutdown or takeover of Mexican American newspapers—a phenomenon that occurred toward the end of the nineteenth century—the shorter selections edged out the novels. The important point here is that, as this happened, the traditional tale was modified to reflect the immediate sociocultural environment, and consequently Mexican American literature became more patently a literature of response and resistance to Anglo-American presence in what was once Mexican territory. Research is needed to locate and examine more examples of the narrative expression which this cultural confrontation produced during the period at the turn of the century.

Although the example of the modified traditional tale which we offer

---

[3]This remains true even if, as is often the case, the literature itself does not speak of protest or resistance; its mere existence as a literature written in Spanish for a Mexican, now American, audience makes it a response to American cultural domination, an attempt to retain Mexican culture.

[4]Juan González in "The Spanish Language Press: A Part of Americana," *El Tecolote,* VII, 13 (September 1977), states that "between 1848 and 1942, approximately 380 Spanish language newspapers were reported in existence nationally." Most of these of course were found in the Southwest.

below was published several years after the turn of the century, it is very indicative of the type of modifications the traditional short narratives had been undergoing since about the 1870s. The tale, "El hombre mudo de amor" ("The Man Silenced by Love"), first appeared in *El Cronista del Valle*, Brownsville, Texas, March 29, 1925. Even though the text is presented anonymously, one can readily see that it is of local production. The tale concerns a prince who refuses to speak after being shunned by his true love, Vera Wradislava, a Russian ballerina. What can be a typically romantic tale suddenly takes a contemporary "realistic" turn when it ironically characterizes Anglos and alludes indirectly to what was happening to many Mexican American newspapers:

> The Yankees, imagining the wondrous love words they have lost because of the Prince's attitude, offer him five dollars for every line of words he can write telling of his intimate suffering. Mr. Goldwer, a great North American publisher, even offers the Prince a fabulous quantity of money for a series of lectures on his unfortunate love affair. (My translation)

By the decade of the 1920s, the realistic element in the short narratives had become quite popular, although the romantic pieces have continued to appear even to this day. Two very important writers of the period were Jorge Ulica and someone who wrote under the pseudonym of Kascabel. Both had regular columns in several newspapers in the Southwest, from Los Angeles to Brownsville. In his "Crónicas diabólicas" column, Ulica wrote about Mexican assimilation into the Anglo world, the loss of Spanish, and disintegration of the family: themes which are very relevant today.[5] A few titles will give an idea: "Por no hablar 'English'," "Touch-down extraordinario," "Cómo hacer surprise parties."[6] Kascabel was apparently more prolific. His "Crónicas festivas" column appears all over the Southwest. Using a more standard Spanish with little, if any, English blended into his work, he preferred to write about human weaknesses in general, or about social incidents affecting all sectors of society. Some of his titles are "Las mentiras," "La primera novia," "La telefomanía," "El miedo."[7]

As far as we can tell at this point, this type of writing did not develop beyond the Depression years.[8] What one must do to continue tracing the development of Chicano prose fiction is to go back in time and examine the writings of another group of Mexican Americans, a group which belonged

---

[5]Clara Lomas, a former graduate student of mine who first located several of these short narratives, and I are now preparing for publication a collection of Ulica's writings.

[6]The best place to look for Ulica's "Crónicas diabólicas" is in *El Cronista del Valle*, Brownsville, Texas, 1923-1925.

[7]Like the "Crónicas diabólicas," the "Crónicas festivas" were published in several newspapers in the Southwest. However, a good selection is found in *El Cronista del Valle*, 1923-1925.

[8]A much clearer picture of the Chicano literary scene during this period will be gotten when the writing of those Chicano writers who worked under the WPA is located and examined. This one area of research cries for attention.

to a higher social class than those writing in the newspapers, persons who had become assimilated and acculturated to a large degree. These people generally had the ways and means of breaking into the Anglo literary world. They wrote in English for an English-speaking audience and generally perpetuated the negative or unrealistic images that audience had of the Mexican. The first writer in this group is María Cristina Mena. Her skillfully written stories, thematically and linguistically presenting quaint visions of the Mexican, were published between 1913 and 1916 in *The Century Magazine*, one of the most prestigious and powerful magazines of the period.[9] The next representatives of this group appear in the 1930s. Both Robert Hernán Torres and Roberto Félix Salazar were "Discovery of the Month" writers in the pages of *Esquire*. In a hard and powerful style, not unlike that of Hemingway (who, incidentally, was also writing in *Esquire* at the time), Torres wrote adventure stories about the Mexican Revolution, apparently a favorite theme then.[10] Roberto Félix Salazar, a much less talented writer than Torres, chose themes which completely eschew a Mexican reference. Both his "Nobody Laughs in Yldes" and "She Had Good Legs"[11] are sentimental stories that lack imagination.

During the 1930s, many women writers were also published, among them Nina Otero, Josefina Escajeda, Jovita González, and Fermina Guerra.[12] All of them actually represented a step backward in the development of Chicano prose, for they returned to the quaint presentation of the Mexican and the Mexican way of life, a view very similar to and yet much simpler than that presented by María Cristina Mena some twenty years before. While the latter invented a plot along traditional short story lines, the former somewhat nostalgically remembered (or invented) tales and legends or incidents from their "Spanish" past. Insofar as they resorted to tales and legends, they

---

[9]Paredes, in his article "The Evolution of Chicano Literature," briefly discusses Mena's stories. His discussion is based on the seven stories he found in *The Century Magazine* between November, 1913, and March, 1916.

[10]Robert Hernán Torres, "Mutiny in Jalisco," *Esquire*, III, 3 (March 1935), 37ff; and "The Brothers Jiminez," *Esquire*, V, 6 (June 1936), 90ff. See Paredes article cited above for a brief discussion of Torres' stories.

[11]Roberto Félix Salazar, "She Had Good Legs," *Esquire*, VIII, 4 (October 1937), 106ff; and "Nobody Laughs in Yldes," *Esquire*, IX, 3 (March 1938), 84ff. Raymund Paredes should be credited for locating these stories.

[12]Since it is often difficult to examine first hand some of the journals and books—such as *Southwest Review, Annuals of the Texas Folklore Society*, Otero's *Old Spain in Our Southwest*, or the several books edited by J. Frank Dobie and published by the Texas Folklore Society during the 1930s *(Tone the Bell Easy, Texian Stomping Ground, Puro Mejicano*, etc.)—in which their stories were first published, I suggest that the interested person read these authors' narratives in Raymund and Américo Paredes, eds., *Mexican-American Authors* (Boston: Houghton Mifflin Co., 1972); Phillip Ortego, ed., *We Are Chicanos* (New York: Washington Square Press, 1973); and Edward Simmen, ed., *The Chicano: From Caricature to Self-Portrait* (New York: New American Library, 1971).

actually regressed to the nineteenth century, for, as we have seen, these were the forms preferred in the last century.

The 1940s, in a sense, witnessed a synthesis of the previous trends in prose fiction and a crystallization of these into something which began to take a clearly Chicano form. Josephina Niggli, a prolific writer who wrote in almost every genre,[13] combined Mena's writing skills with the thematic approaches to Mexicans that the women of the 1930s utilized—that is, she tended to present quaint images of the Mexican past. Fray Angélico Chávez, by writing about a religious world, avoided—much like Torres and Salazar in the 1930s—the specifics of the Mexican American experience.[14] One who treated the Mexican American experience, but did so rather romantically (although some scenes are quite realistic), was Luis Pérez in his autobiography *El Coyote/The Rebel*.[15] It was Mario Suárez, however, who really began to speak of the Chicano and Chicano experiences. His stories, while still seeking an Anglo audience, contain elements which only a Chicano reader can fully understand and appreciate.[16]

In the 1940s and during the 1950s, the novel again appeared as a viable genre in Chicano letters. After a somewhat truncated or arrested development following the serial novels of the last century, the novel returned in 1947 when Josephina Niggli's *Step Down Elder Brother* was published by Rinehart. Niggli's novel merits serious attention because while it basically concerns itself with the rise of the middle class in Monterrey, Mexico, and the transformation of this city into an industrial center, it also deals with American influences in Mexico, as well as with the curious question of choice of country. In a final scene, the two protagonists must decide where their child will grow up:

"What are you thinking, Domingo?"
"I can't go to the States, Márgara."
"Why not?"
"That child is a Mexican. He has the right to be a Mexican. He can't grow up in the States, or Europe, or any place else but here in the Republic."[17]

The next novel that we find is quite different. It is Fray Angélico Chávez's *La Conquistadora*,[18] a novel about the patron saint of New Mexico,

---

[13]See her stories in *Mexican Village* (Chapel Hill: University of North Carolina Press, 1945), her novel *Step Down Elder Brother* (New York: Rinehart and Co., 1947), and her play *Sunday Costs Five Pesos* in *Mexican Folk Plays*, edited by F. H. Koch (Chapel Hill: University of North Carolina Press, 1938).

[14]See his *New Mexico Triptych* (Fresno, California: Academy Guild Press, 1940), a collection of short stories.

[15]Luis Pérez, *El Coyote/The Rebel* (New York: Henry Holt and Co., 1947).

[16]Suárez published most of his stories in the *Arizona Quarterly* during the 1940s. A good selection of his stories is found in the three anthologies mentioned in note 12 above.

[17]Niggli, *Step Down Elder Brother*, p. 372.

[18]Fray Angélico Chávez, *La Conquistadora* (Paterson, N.J.: St. Anthony Guild Press, 1954).

which continues to avoid a confrontation with the social, material experiences of the Chicano. *Pocho,* (by José Antonio Villarreal) the next novel published in this decade,[19] does attempt this confrontation, even if it fails to grapple adequately with those experiences. As the title indicates, its focus is on the Mexican American experience of immigration, upward mobility, and family disintegration. Its significance lies in establishing trends which we still find in many contemporary Chicano novels, that is, the theme of the Mexican Revolution, the generational approach to family history, the protagonist as hero or anti-hero who must undergo some form of initiation. These characteristics are found also in the novel that initiates the flowering of the Chicano novel—*Chicano* (1969), by Richard Vásquez.[20] With the publication of Tomás Rivera's...*y no se lo tragó la tierra...and the earth did not part* (1971),[21] the Chicano novel and Chicano prose fiction in general reached a progressive level which contemporary Chicano novelists must maintain and ultimately supersede if the Chicano novel is to survive. Interestingly enough, the attainment of that level also marked the return of Spanish as a mode of literary expression, reversing a trend which had been established in the first decade of this century. Examples of novelists writing in Spanish today are Miguel Méndez *(Peregrinos de Aztlán,* 1974), Rolando Hinojosa *(Klail City y sus alrededores,* 1977), winner of the coveted Casa de las Américas prize given by Cuba's excellent publishing house, and Aristeo Brito *(El diablo en Texas,* 1976). Other contemporaries such as Rudolfo Anaya *(Bless Me Ultima,* 1972, and *Heart of Aztlán,* 1976), Ron Arias *(The Road to Tamazunchale,* 1975), and Oscar Zeta Acosta *(The Autobiography of a Brown Buffalo,* 1972, and *The Revolt of the Cockroach People,* 1973), still write in English and in many respects still eschew the Chicano social situation.

While the novel was attaining this new stage, the short story was not far behind. Following Mario Suárez's efforts in the 1940s to appeal to an Anglo audience while writing about typically Chicano situations in an ironical manner, the short story remained comparatively tame in the 1950s and early 1960s with writers such as Amado Muro, Arnulfo Trejo, Daniel Garza.[22] During the mid-1960s, however, as the Chicano Movement centered around the Delano farmworkers' strike began to take shape, many young writers—among them Nick Vaca, J. L. Navarro, Carlos Vélez—began turning their attention from the Anglo to the educated, English-speaking, largely urban Chicano reader.[23] When in 1969 Miguel Méndez published

[19]José Antonio Villarreal, *Pocho* (New York: Doubleday, 1959).

[20]Richard Vásquez, *Chicano* (New York: Doubleday, 1969).

[21]Tomás Rivera,...*y no se lo tragó la tierra* (Berkeley: Quinto Sol Publications, 1971).

[22]Again, the three anthologies mentioned in note 12 are the best sources for these writers' short stories. Their stories first appeared in such magazines as *Arizona Quarterly, New Mexico Quarterly,* and *Descant.*

[23]All of these writers first wrote in the early issues (1968-1969) of *El Grito,* a critical and literary journal published in Berkeley, California.

two short stories, "Tata Casehua" and "Taller de imágenes, pase,"[24] clearly aimed at a Chicano audience since they were written in Spanish, the Chicano short story marked its coming of age. In fact, with writers like Miguel Méndez, Tomás Rivera, Rolando Hinojosa, Rodrigo Palacios-Ochoa, to cite just a few of a growing number, the Chicano short story and Chicano prose fiction have reached a stage of development comparable to that of any Western literature.

This, then, in brief, is the development—as we see it today—of Chicano prose fiction. As we learn more of our literary past and as more specific texts are found to substantiate that past, we shall necessarily have to correct, change, or modify what is presented here. For the moment, however, this is the schematic history of one of the most dynamic and complex literatures being written today.

---

[24]Miguel Méndez's early stories are found in *El Grito* and in *El Espejo* (Berkeley: Quinto Sol Publications, 1969), an anthology of Chicano creative writing.

Tomás Rivera's Appropriation
of the Chicano Past

by Ralph F. Grajeda

Like two other Chicano novels—*Pocho* by José Antonio Villarreal and *Chicano* by Richard Vásquez[1]—Tomás Rivera's *"...and the earth did not part"* is the author's first published book. Unlike *Pocho* and *Chicano*, however, Rivera's book was originally written in Spanish, and it was published by a Chicano publishing house, Quinto Sol Publications[2]—two extra-literary facts that only upon reflection acquire significance. If Villarreal's and Vásquez' work can be said to mark the first attempts by Mexican American writers to give literary expression to the experience of La Raza, Rivera's book marks a progression from those initial efforts toward a literature that —in authentically rendering the Chicano experience—can be considered a literature of liberation.

"...and the earth did not part" is difficult to describe structurally. It is not a novel in the conventional sense, but then neither is it a mere collection of stories and sketches. The book contains a set of twelve thematically unified pieces—symbolic of the twelve months of the year—framed at the beginning by an introductory selection titled "The Lost Year," and at the end by a summarizing selection titled "Under the House." Preceding each of the stories except "The Lost Year" is a brief anecdote, now directed backward (echoing or commenting on the thematic concerns of the preceding story), now pointed forward (prefacing the story that follows). Sometimes the anecdote does not relate directly either to what immediately precedes or to what follows, but instead echoes or re-echoes values, motifs, themes or judgments found elsewhere in the book. The effect is incremental. Through the reinforcement, variation, and amplification provided by the twelve stories and the thirteen anecdotes, a picture of the community is gradually

"Tomás Rivera's Appropriation of the Chicano Past" (editors' title) by Ralph F. Grajeda. This article appears for the first time in this volume. It is used by permission of the author.

[1]*Pocho* (New York: Doubleday, 1959); *Chicano* (New York: Doubleday, 1970).

[2]Tomás Rivera, *"...y no se lo tragó la tierra"*—*"...and the earth did not part"* (Berkeley: Quinto Sol Publications, 1971). Rivera's book was awarded the Quinto Sol National Chicano Literary Award for 1969-70. English translation by Hermino Ríos C., "in collaboration with the author, with assistance by Octavio I. Romano-V."

filled. At the end, the entire experience is synthesized and brought to a thematic conclusion through the consciousness of the central character.

This central figure—presumably the author's alter ego—is the unnamed hero of the two frame-pieces: the one for whom, at the beginning, "that year was lost," and who at the end discovers "that he hadn't lost anything." Though it may be conjectured that this central figure is the same one who moves through some of the other selections in the book, direct and explicit identification between the characters in the stories and the central figure is of minor importance, for the overall impression created by the book is not of an individual but a communal experience. The various persons of the stories, the experiences and the landscape of these lives, belong unmistakably to the hero's past. The emphasis, however, remains on the general experience, communal and social rather than individual and personal.

In his introduction to the book, Herminio Ríos observes that "*el pueblo* becomes the central character. It is the anonymous and collective voice of the people that we hear" (p. xvi). He is correct. The voice of the people rings as clear for the reader as it does for the central figure. Structurally this figure has importance as an individual; thematically, however, this importance is de-emphasized (it is no accident that he remains nameless). The experience of the book is finally a general one. Many of the selections have an uncanny emblematic tone to them; some of them—particularly the frame-pieces—emphatically invite an allegorical or symbolic interpretation. Even in the two frame selections, at the beginning and end, the protagonist's voice is not that of an individual hero intent on discovering and expressing his own subjective reality, but that of a Mexican American in the significant process of discovering and embracing representatively his community's experience and culture. The end towards which the narrative is directed is a social identity.

The hero of the frame-pieces plays no explicitly active part in the book. He serves merely as the "rememberer," the central figure—however unrealized he may appear as a rounded character—around whom Rivera weaves his thematic tapestry. At the beginning he is confused, alone, frightened and disoriented. He is the one for whom the year is lost. The succeeding twelve stories and thirteen anecdotes compose his effort to reclaim a past. At the end of the book he has become the synthesizer and commentator, the one who discovers his lost year and who would like to have "*long enough arms,*" so that he "*could hug them all at the same time*" (p. 176).

The form of the book is thus cyclical. Though there is no attempt to shape a strict correspondence between specific months and particular stories, the twelve stories in a general sense represent the year that the protagonist seeks to recapture. The first story is set in early April; the last anecdote is set in December. This cyclical movement functions effectively to delineate the cyclical and repetitive nature of the migrant farmworkers' lives as they yearly retrace the same roads to the same fields, from Texas and cotton in the winter months to Utah, Minnesota, Iowa, and Michigan in the spring and summer. It is, therefore, appropriate that the first story treats a family working in the Texas fields, and the 'welfth story a truckful of workers journeying north to the beet-fields of Minnesota.

Throughout the book tension is created between the opposing values of resignation and rebellion as the people are shown enduring the repetitive hardships of the present, and as they anticipate their future. Usually, but not always, these differing values break down along generational lines. The older people—parents and grandparents—are usually resigned. Theirs is a stoical position learned after years of suffering, and variously expressed by the grandfather who tells his twenty-year-old grandson that he is *"very stupid"* for wanting *"the next ten years of his life to pass instantly so that he would know what had happened in his life"* (p. 87); by the older speaker who advises the young student not to even bother with going to school, for *"the downtrodden will always be downtrodden"* (p. 45); by the worker in the fields who, in fear of being fired by the *patrón*, urges his children time after time to endure their thirst "a little longer" (p. 10); and by the father, knowing little English and fearful of the schools, who is incapable of responding to his son's plea that he accompany him to the principal's office the first day of school (pp. 30-31). These are parents who through years of deprivation and colonialism have learned to stay in their place. Again and again in Rivera's book we see them encouraging their children to stay in school, in hopes that they will escape the treadmill of migratory field labor.

The children are in many instances the victims. But they are also the rebels. There is the boy in "It Was a Silvery Night" who tests the superstitions of his parents and learns that the devil does not exist. There is the boy in "...and the earth did not part" who in anger at the suffering of his family curses an uncaring God and learns, in contradiction to what his parents have taught him, that the earth does not swallow up a blasphemer. And characteristically it is the young man in "When We Arrive," who—in the middle of the night in a broken-down truck loaded with people on their way north—with assertive vehemence cries out in his heart: *"This goddamn fuckin' life. This goddamn son-of-a-bitch's life. This is the last time I travel like a goddamn animal standing up all the way. Just as soon as we arrive I'm going to Minneapolis, surely I'll find something to do there where I don't have to work like a goddamn animal"* (pp. 158-159). In the privacy of his anxiety, he then utters a threat *("One of these days I'll screw 'em all")* which, however idle it may actually be, gains its full force from its juxtaposition with the mild thoughts of a concerned wife and mother with a child in her arms, who thinks only of helping her husband in the fields when they arrive.

The affirmation in this book, however, is not dependent on any final resolution of the tension created by the two differing stances of resignation and rebellion. Rivera's work, after all, is not a transient book of protest, but an enduring *book of discovery*. The question of "proper" or "improper" responses to social conditions is a false one, inappropriate to the premises upon which the work is created. The substantial affirmation of this book rests on the reality discovered and depicted by the author. And this process of discovery is given artistic form through the use of the central character within the frame-structure of the book and the cyclical movement of the narrative.

The overall scheme is laid out in the four brief paragraphs comprising the introductory selection, "The Lost Year." There Rivera uses the language of the dream—or at least a language suggestive of a deeper reality than what is ordinarily accepted as objective fact—to suggest the sense of psychological and social disorientation in which the hero lives. The impetus is to discover the self. The origin and cause of that impetus is perhaps outside the concern of Rivera's book; it is enough to state the truism that personal and social identity is never a "problem" until it is threatened. As Frantz Fanon writes: the native's affirmation of his own culture, and his attempts at recovering a usable past, are symptomatic of the "realization of the danger that he is running in cutting his last moorings and of breaking adrift from his people." Unless the native moves culturally in the direction of his true self, "there will be serious psycho-affective injuries and the result will be individuals without an anchor, without a horizon, colorless, stateless—a race of angels."[3]

Tomás Rivera's metaphor for this felt sense of breaking adrift is "the lost year." The confusion and general disorientation brought on by the sense of "that year [that] was lost to him" began for the protagonist "when he would hear someone call him by name. He would turn around to see who was calling, always making a complete turn, always ending in the same position and facing the same way. And that was why he could never find out who it was that was calling him, nor the reason why he was being called. He would even forget the name that he had heard.

"Once he stopped himself before completing the turn, and he became afraid. He found out that he had been calling himself. That was the way the lost year began" (p. 3).

His confusion and fear have their source in the realization that it is he himself who has been "calling." The full implications of that realization, however, are not clearly understood until the end of the book. In his beginning confusion he thinks that he thinks, and determines not to think, but does nevertheless. It is the content of this "thinking"—what Rivera describes as the hero's *seeing* and *hearing*—that the twelve stories and sketches and the thirteen anecdotes reveal. The cumulative effect is a felt sense of struggle.

"Why is it that we are here on earth as though buried alive?" asks the young protagonist of the title story, upon hearing the moans of his father,

[3]Frantz Fanon, *The Wretched of the Earth* (New York: Grove Press, 1968), pp. 217-218.

who has suffered a sunstroke in the suffocating heat of the fields. This sets the tone of the book. The full-length stories, the impressionistic sketches, and the brief anecdotes that fall within the two frame pieces are quick but lasting glimpses into the lives of these characters. There is no attempt to relate them realistically and explicitly. That they are related only in time by the metaphor of "the lost year," and in space by the fields and *colonias* in Texas and the unspecified north suggests, again, Rivera's interest in the general and social, not the specific and individual reality. The same spirit informs all of the "framed" selections: a desperate clinging to life in the midst of deprivation and suffering, and the seemingly ever-present hope that if not for themselves, at least for their children, life will not exact such a heavy toll.

The suffering begins with childhood. In "The Children Were Victims," a child is accidentally shot and killed by a boss who, because he is paying the workers by the hour, does not want them "wasting" time drinking from the water tanks that he keeps for his cattle. The story is told from an objective and detached point of view, a technique common to many of the other stories and sketches. Rarely does Rivera-as-author intrude; the understanding, the judgments, and the emotions are generated out of the narrative situation itself, which is quite brief. It consists of an introductory paragraph, some dramatic dialogue between father and child; two brief paragraphs matter-of-factly describing the child drinking water and being killed; and at the end, another fragment of dialogue, between two unidentified field-workers, inhabitants of the barrio, members of what, through the book, quickly assumes the form of a *colonia* chorus—a collective Chicano voice that, standing at times at a distance, describes and judges the actions that are being enacted on the stage.

In this story the chorus discusses the fate of the boss after the killing. One speaker affirms the consequences of human guilt feelings; he wants to believe that the boss almost went insane, that he is drinking heavily now and that he tried to commit suicide. The other voice denies the boss even the dignity of remorse. He wants to say: "they are such brutes that with absolute impunity they can kill us and our children." The first speaker says: "I really think he went crazy. You've seen the state he's in nowadays. He looks like a beggar." The other voice answers, "Sure, but it's only because he doesn't have money any more," And his *compadre* says "I guess you're right."

At the end, the story refuses to affirm either position. The chorus's function is to articulate them both as part of the book's reality. Part of that reality—in all of its harshness and brutality—is expressed through the routinely dispassionate manner of presentation. The child is shot and "he didn't even jump like the deer; he just fell into the water like a dirty rag and the water became saturated with blood..." (p. 11). Such matter-of-fact tone outweighs paragraphs of "concerned" and "committed" prose describing "the lot of the underdogs." In this selection it succinctly intensifies the horror of the situation. In other selections it works similarly to bring out the stark quality of the lives of these people.

Equally bleak and despairing is the lot of the parents and children in "Little Children Burned." In hopes that one of his children will become a boxing champion and earn thousands of dollars, a father buys boxing gloves for his children and teaches them to rub alcohol on their bodies the way he saw boxers do in a movie. Alone in their shack while the parents are working in the fields, the children accidentally start a fire while playing with the boxing gloves and two of the three children are burned to death in the shack. The chorus that enters at the end provides necessary information, and dispassionately comments on the cruel irony of everything having burned — even the children — except for the boxing gloves: one speaker, in respect if not in awe of Yankee ingenuity, says "the fact is that those people know how to make things so well that not even fire will touch them" (p. 102).

In this story, the chorus speaks with convincing authority. Responding to a question about the parents' reaction, one of the speakers expresses an essentially tragic point of view, one that acknowledges the uncertainty of human existence and the profound sense in which one has little control over what will be: "They're getting over their tragedy, but I doubt if they will ever forget it. What else can one do? You never know when death will come, nor in what manner. What a tragedy. But one never knows" (p. 102). The reticent "I guess not" that ends the sketch affirms that point of view as a community reality.

"The Night of the Blackout" is a love tragedy about two young people who are temporarily separated by their families' journeys in the migrant stream and vow to be true to one another until they return to Texas where they plan to marry. Rumors reach Ramón about Juanita's "cheating" in Minnesota, and when they meet again, they quarrel; heart-broken and in despair Ramón kills himself by grabbing onto a transformer at the electric power station. Distance and objectivity are achieved here by Rivera's focus on one tangible effect of Ramón's suicide at the power station: The lights go out all over the community! And it is in reference to this manifestation that the community thereafter speaks of Ramón and Juanita: "They were very much in love, wouldn't you say?" "Yes. Of course" (p. 116).

The attempt to hide from a harsh reality becomes frantic among people who are continually forced to struggle for their self-hood and dignity. That attempt — as it is lived by a youth — is the subject of "It is Painful." A young man is expelled from school for defending himself against the physical attack of an Anglo student, and now faces the painful duty of telling his parents. The youth's experience is intensified by the shame, anger, and hatred he is made to feel by a school nurse who forces him to undress and stand naked in her presence while being inspected, and by an Anglo American student who tells him that he doesn't like Mexicans "because they steal."

The main part of this story is told by a first-person narrator thinking in the present as he walks home from school the day of his expulsion. On his way home he wrestles with the problem of telling his parents—who have high hopes that he will remain in school and become a telephone operator like the one they saw as the leading character in a movie. Brief flashbacks fill in the context of the narrator's shame and anger, and provide ironic point to his desperate desire to disbelieve the reality of his situation. "What if they didn't expel me? What if they didn't?" he thinks repeatedly throughout his walk home. Reality, however, is too severe and too sharply insistent to be denied. Ultimately he must accept it: *"Sure they did"* (p. 35).

The children in Rivera's book, like the adults, are victimized by what exists outside them—the often invisible social and economic forces that govern their lives, the institutions, and the physical environment in which they live and work. But their victimization does not stop there. For they are also prey to what lies within. As the narrator of the title story says, "either the germs eat us from the inside or the sun from the outside. Always some illness" (p. 75). Rivera traces not only the "Chicano" and the "farmworker" contours of his characters' lives, but the universally human as well. In the fields, in the barrios, in their shacks or in the trucks moving north for the summer, the young people, particularly, are shown struggling with the "problems" always inherent in the move into adulthood. Of the twelve selections, four—"His Hand in his Pocket"; "First Holy Communion"; "It Was a Silvery Night"; and "...and the earth did not part"—are "initiation stories."

Guilt and the curious mixture of good and evil in the same person are major themes in "His Hand in his Pocket," a story about a young man who suffers a debilitating guilt from his innocent role in a macabre crime. The naive first-person narrator is sent by his parents to live with don Laito and doña Boni, an elderly couple in the barrio who steal in order to sell or give away: "when they couldn't sell it to the neighbors they gave it away. They gave almost everything away" (p. 48). Understandably, the couple are well liked by the people, and have a good reputation in the community, even among the *americanos.* The narrator, however, notices the rotten teeth that surround the gold in don Laito's mouth, and begins to wonder about his hosts' goodness, for not only do they admit their stealing to him, they try to persuade him to join in it. During the boy's visit, they murder a Mexican drifter for his money and possessions, and force the boy to help them bury the body and keep their secret. At the end of the story he is given a ring that belonged to the victim and the ring becomes a symbol of his guilt. He tries to throw it away but can't. He wears it, "and the worst of it was that for a long time, whenever I saw a stranger, I put my hand in my pocket." Time compassionately repeals his "guilt," but the habit of putting his hand in his pocket, he says, "stayed with me for a long time" (p. 50).

Guilt is again a major theme of "First Holy Communion." On the morning of his first communion—after spending a restless night memorizing all his sins—the narrator, while walking to church, looks through a tailor shop window to see what is causing the noises he hears, and sees a naked man and woman having sexual intercourse. Torn between fear and the strange attraction to see more, he intently remains until discovered by the couple and told to go away. He cannot forget what he has seen, but neither is he willing to share his experience with his friends. He is bothered by the feeling of himself having "committed that sin of the flesh." He keeps his "sin," even from the confessional priest, and when, after his communion, he arrives home with his godfather for the traditional sweet bread and chocolate, "everything seemed different." He imagines his father and mother—and even the priest and the nun—naked on the floor. "I almost wasn't able to eat the sweetbread or drink the chocolate," he says, "and I remember that as soon as I finished I ran out of the house. I felt all choked up" (p. 91). Alone outside, he recalls the scene at the tailor shop and soon begins to derive some pleasure from his memory, and even forgets that he lied to the priest. Then, he says, "I felt the same way I did when I heard the missionary talk about the Grace of God." The ambiguity at the end of the story enriches its meaning. When the boy says "I had a strong desire to learn more about everything. But then I started to think that perhaps everything was the same," he expresses both the resiliency that will enable him to take his experience in stride and a propensity to put aside what is "bothersome."

Two pieces in the book that represent, on one level at least, youth's metaphysical rebellion and its testing of religious and superstitious notions that its elders accept are "It Was a Silvery Night," and "...and the earth did not part."

In "It Was a Silvery Night," after hearing his parents tell of people for whom the devil has appeared, the protagonist becomes curious and decides to see for himself. Carefully he plans his invocation and, according to the traditional formula learned from his parents and others in the community, issues his summons. Nothing happens. "No one appeared. Everything looked the same. Everything was the same. Everything peaceful. He then thought that the best thing to do would be to curse the devil. He did. He used every cuss word he knew and in varying tones of voice. He even cursed the devil's mother. But nothing happened. Absolutely nothing appeared and absolutely nothing changed" (p. 62). The devil does not exist, he thinks; but if the devil does not exist, then neither does..., and at that moment he cannot follow through with the inexorable logic of his discovery. Later on, however, as he reconsiders his experience of the evening, he accepts the implication of his discovery: "There is no devil" he thinks, "There is nothing. The only thing he had heard in the field had been his own voice" (p. 63). This brings him to the conviction that people who went insane after summoning the devil did so not because the devil appeared, but because he didn't. There is nothing but one's own voice in the dark. His logic thus forces on him a realization of his own existential solitariness, with an empty sky as premise.

The hero-narrator of "...and the earth did not part" correspondingly tests God's existence. Not in the deliberate manner in which the protagonist of the preceding story attempts to verify the devil's existence but in the full passion of hatred, he protests against and curses a God who would allow the illness and death of his aunt and uncle, the suffering of their children, the illness of his own father, and the fate of his small brothers and sisters, who seem destined to feed the earth and sun "without any hope of any kind." In the frustration he feels at his own powerlessness "to do anything," he refuses to take solace in his mother's religion, refuses to resign himself to God's will, refuses to accept the notion that there is no rest until death. He finds his humanity in the very weariness, despair, and hatred which he feels. Having been conditioned by historical and cultural forces, however, he is at first incapable of seriously accepting the absence of a transcendent and determinant final cause. After his father suffers a sunstroke in the fields, he reviles his mother for clamoring for God's mercy. "What do you gain by doing that, mother? Don't tell me that you believe that sort of thing helped my uncle and my aunt? ... God doesn't even remember us. ... God doesn't give a damn about us poor people" (pp. 75-76). But at this point his subservience and dependence—wrought out of fear—prohibit him from cursing God, let alone imagining His absence. "There must not be a God..." he begins, but cannot go on with this thought: "No, better not say it, what if father should worsen?"

The next day his nine-year-old brother has a sunstroke, and as the protagonist carries him home from the fields he cries in anger and hatred. Yet at every moment of the emotion that he feels, he draws from it a new integrity. Without knowing when, he starts to swear; and "what he said he had been wanting to say for a long time." Unthinkingly he curses God and immediately "upon doing it he felt the fear instilled in him by time and by his parents." He imagines the earth opening and swallowing him—but nothing happens! Instead, he begins to feel the solidity of the ground: "He then felt himself walking on very solid ground; *it was harder than he had ever felt it*" (p. 78). His discovery—in the context of his former despair, dependence, and sense of powerlessness—is affirmative. Recognizing the emptiness of the heavens he does not fall into the self-pity of the existential anti-hero who finds himself in the midst of a meaningless and absurd universe. Instead he embraces his freedom, and that very evening experiences a sense of peace—and detachment—"that he had never known before." The following day, as he leaves for work, he feels himself, for the first time in his life, "capable of doing and undoing whatever he chose."

Rivera has a clear eye for the cruel ironies of life. In the world his characters inhabit, people are often victimized by the very hopes they nurture, hopes that spring from the positions in life which they endure. In such a world, attempts at alleviating one's situation often serve merely to reinforce one's deprivation. In such a world even anger is preempted. This is the theme of "The Portrait," one of the better stories in Rivera's book. The door-to-door salesmen from San Antonio—those who thrive on the innocence and misfortune of the powerless—converge on the barrio like vultures when the people arrive from the north with a few dollars in their pockets. In this story it is the portrait salesman who promises Don Mateo that "for just thirty dollars," they can enlarge—and, in color, inlay—the photograph of his son, who is missing in action in the war, so that he looks "lifelike, as though he were alive."

Don Mateo and the others in the barrio who have been "sold" wait week-after-week for their portraits. As they wait, they hopefully rationalize the delay that gives them intimations of having been duped. The photographs are finally found dissolving in a tunnel leading to the dump, and Don Mateo, in full anger, goes to San Antonio to search out the salesman who took the only picture he had of his son. He finds the salesman and forces him, upon threat of violence, to do the inlaid enlargement of his son. "He had to do it all from memory," Don Mateo tells his neighbors afterwards. "I think that a person is capable of doing anything out of fear," he explains as he shows off the finished portrait of his son. Justice is done. Don Mateo receives what he paid for. "What do you think? How does my son look?" he asks the admiring *compadre:* "Well, quite frankly I don't remember what Chuy looked like anymore. But more and more he was beginning to resemble you, right?" Complacently and with some pride, Don Mateo says "Yes. I think so. That's what everyone tells me now. That Chuy resembled me more and more, and that he was beginning to look like me. There's the portrait. One might say we're one and the same" (p. 145).

In their simplicity and powerlessness, Rivera's characters live by illusions that acquire the force of necessity. "I guess it's always best to have hope," one of Rivera's characters says halfheartedly, and—in its various forms—that is the attitude informing their lives. In "When We Arrive" these hopes are emphatically represented in the thoughts of some migrants who find themselves stranded in the middle of the night in a broken-down truck going north for the season. Privately, each is encouraged by the hope that when they arrive things will be "better." There is the pathetic anticipation of the experienced, which reality has distilled down to a modest longing for *"a good bed for my wife; her kidneys are really bothering her. I hope we don't wind up in a chicken coop with a cement floor as we did last year"* (p. 160). And there is the radical resolve of youth to escape altogether the rat-trap of the dispossessed.

The impact of the book finally is cumulative. Though the sketches and stories can be read individually and out of context, it is as particular parts of a whole which is greater than the sum of its parts that Rivera's work can best be understood and appreciated. All of the experiences, the themes, and

judgments contained in the twelve selections and the thirteen anecdotes
are finally summarized and "fixed" into a context by the consciousness of
the central character of the book, who reappears in the concluding selection,
"Under the House"—the piece that in combination with the introductory
selection, "The Lost Year," constitutes the frame.

In "Under the House" the collective voice of the community is predominant, but now it speaks explicitly to and through the central character. Till
now the voices have been the developing expression of what the protagonist
brings up out of the depths of his memory; but so readily do the stories and
sketches acquire an independent life of their own that the fact that they
constitute mere elements of the protagonist's "lost year" is obscured. Here
at the end the reader is reminded of the literary device being used and,
like the main character, is brought full circle to the beginning—but now
with the layers of experience rendered by the successive voices. There is,
in other words, an analogy between the reader's experience and the
protagonist's.

For the latter, the total experience is regenerative, capped by his realization that instead of losing anything, "he had discovered something. To
discover and to rediscover and synthesize. To relate this entity with that
entity, and that entity with still another, and finally relating everything
with everything else. That was what he had to do, that was all. And he became even happier" (p. 177).

As a "book of discovery," *"...and the earth did not part"* is a variation of the *bildungsroman,* for the focus of Rivera's work is not on the forging of the individual subjective identity; it is informed by a concern for
social and collective identity. The characters in the protagonist's recoverable past—the field-worker father, the Mexican revolutionary grandfather,
the devout mother, the *gachupín* priest, the kindly Cuquita who is everyone's grandmother, the quarreling lovers, the exploitative *patrón,* as well
as all the *comadres, compadres,* and *padrinos*—all are recognizable not
through personal quirks in their particular character, but rather because
they assume—at least within the context of the Chicano experience—
archetypal dimensions.

In including *"the names of the people in town,"* Rivera's book—like
Bartolo's poems—performs the significant function of discovering and
ultimately appropriating and embracing the past in all of its sometimes-
painful authenticity. The importance of looking closely and hard at the
colonial experience of the Chicano protagonist is assumed. The first step
in his liberation must begin with an understanding of his position. Presumably it is the kind of understanding—however felt or perceived—that
leads the protagonist of Rivera's book, as well as the author himself, toward
re-identification with that which is his own, i.e. with his people. The movement in the book is inward collectively toward an understanding of the barrio experience as it is—in its pain and in all of its suffering, assuredly, but

also in its essential strength, vitality and sense of human celebration.

Besides being a significant work of art, *"...and the earth did not part"* performs a valuable function in using "the past with the intention of opening the future, as an invitation to action and a basis for hope."[4] Criticism of the work because it does not more directly perform the function of social protest is short-sighted. The reality discovered and depicted by this author contributes to the Chicano art of self-discovery in a manner more profoundly effective, aesthetically as well as socially, than much of the explicit literature of protest that is being written. The vitality of the Chicano social movement depends on the development of a deep understanding of Chicano reality. Rivera contributes notably to this end.

[4]Fanon, p. 232.

Narrative Technique and Human Experience in Tomás Rivera

by Daniel P. Testa

Tomás Rivera's *...y no se lo trago la tierra*[1] is a fascinating composite of stories and anecdotes of personal and collective true-to-life situations. The stories and anecdotes seem to fall into two structural types: those that are socially or collectively oriented, and those that focus on an individual. In the first group, the milieu of work and of daily life plays a dominant role; in the second, the character's internal drama is central. These two basic types, however, are usually not sustained in absolute or pure terms, but rather are often mixed. With a free and flexible narrative technique, the author blends abrupt exchanges of dialogue, shifts of perspective, and internal monologue into the account of an external action or series of actions. The majority of the pieces in the work, while generally tending to belong to one structural type or the other, are in fact fusions of objective and subjective experience. Thus, what purports to be an objectively narrated account ends up being subjectivized, and what purports to be a subjectively narrated account acquires the appearance of objectified fact.

The anecdotes themselves are simply brief accounts of varied aspects of Chicano life. Some are miniature short stories in that they are sufficiently unified and suggest a point. Others reflect an attitude in dialogue form or are schematic accounts of incidents and give the impression of being overheard or found. Still others are vignettes that assume importance because they are somehow connected to the "boy" of several of the longer stories who emerges, as we shall see, as the principal character of the work. As authentic flashes of everyday Chicano life, the anecdotes lend support to the more detailed portrayals of collective and individual experiences. The author has turned them to good use simply by juxtaposing them in alternation with the stories, and thus through suggestion rather than close integration, achieves a much richer pattern of relationships. In tone and feeling, the anecdotes range from the innocently playful to the most pathetically

"Narrative Technique and Human Experience in Tomás Rivera" by Daniel P. Testa. This article appears for the first time in this volume. It is used by permission of the author.

[1]Tomás Rivera, *...y no se lo tragó la tierra (...and the earth did not part)*, bilingual edition (Quinto Sol Publications: Berkeley, 1971); the translations are mine.

tragic, and between these extremes, we find situations of joy, hope, enigma, love, exaggeration, prejudice, understatement, and irony.

Among the stories, the most "collective" is the one entitled "Cuando lleguemos," which treats of a fairly routine and physically painful event in the lives of migrant workers. It is a story of some forty people riding in the back of a truck on their way from Texas to Minnesota. After traveling for more than twenty-four hours, the truck breaks down in the early morning hours in a rural area somewhere in Iowa. Here the passengers must wait until the truck can be repaired. What is interesting is the way Rivera has preferred to narrate the story. Instead of a traditional narrative, we find a series of interior monologues, which contain the private feelings, thoughts, memories, etc., of eight or ten people. The author has seemingly stepped aside, relinquishing his role as narrator, in order to let each consciousness "speak," under the cloak of darkness and early dawn. The irony in this type of novelistic technique, used by Faulkner, Juan Rulfo, and others, is that the intimate realities presented owe their formal or literary existence to an author who pretends to be absent. But here it is not merely an ironic effect that Rivera creates. He seems to be more concerned with the authentic exposure of the Chicano farmworkers. By removing himself as the external observer and spokesman, the author allows each migrant worker the opportunity to reveal himself without an intermediary and without the need for prior physical or external description. A basis of differentiation of character traits and attitudes among the various "speakers" is established as well as a basis of commonly held goals, hopes, and dreams. It is this directness that gives a vibrancy to those nameless individuals.

But if the author has technically disappeared as the visible narrator, it is the thematic and tonal structure of the monologues that subtly and slowly reveals auctorial direction and interpretation. In varying degrees of intensity, most of the "speakers" voice their irritation, frustration, and anger over the basic hardships they must endure in their lives. Although one of the "speakers" reflects on the stillness and beauty of the early dawn, the thoughts predominantly express the hectic pace, the daily anguish, and the economic precariousness of their lives. Through narrative detail, Rivera amasses a convincing body of evidence to indict a whole social, political, and economic system that exploits the farmworkers and keeps them trapped in a constant cycle of anxiety over the most rudimentary essentials of life. These personally narrated accounts are convincing, however, precisely because Rivera, instead of relying on a blatantly political statement, has incorporated those conditions of economic hardship into a total rhythm and pattern of life. There is the occasional relapse into disillusionment and feelings of defeat, as one of the monologues puts it succinctly:

> —when we arrive, when we arrive, well, the plain truth is that I'm tired of arriving. Arriving is the same thing as leaving because we're hardly there and

...the plain truth is that I'm tired of arriving. Why not say when we don't arrive because that's the plain truth. We never arrive (p. 152).

As a sympathetic insider, Rivera sees his fellow Chicanos as whole human beings, who are capable of rich variety and intensity of feeling and who, although struggling against incredible odds, push on in life by projecting and anticipating a better tomorrow. What keeps the harried migratory life active is the fragile but constant hope that is expressed in that obsessively repeated refrain "cuando lleguemos."

Rivera's narrative art is thoroughly committed to the lives of his people, but it is his nature to suggest a larger environment in which to cast the drama of his characters. In the story under discussion, we should note a poetic tendency in Rivera's art, in addition to the skillful narrative accounts that "occur" in the consciousness of several individual farmworkers. By having those normally silent thoughts of the farmworkers come alive during an involuntary interlude of a few hours, Rivera seems to suggest a contrastive structure to human existence: the externally active, everyday routine of life and the internal core of being that gives to each individual life a sense of completeness and worth. Rivera's story implies that the Chicano migrant, no less than other human beings, has the capacity for internal expansiveness and for introspective awareness. It further implies that of all the deprivations of the hard-working and exploited lower classes, the cruelest is an impoverished "soul," which is a result of a lack of time and opportunity to feel the wholeness and the oneness of the self. We might even venture to say that it is the poet in Rivera who senses that there is a deeper dimension to the quest and need for Chicano identity and self-determination.

If this story attempts to portray the collective consciousness through multiple viewpoints, a single perspective is the basis of the story entitled "Un rezo," which is a prayer spoken by a Chicano mother intimately troubled by a lack of news from her soldier son.

> Here's my heart for his. Here it is. It's here beating in my breast, tear it out if you want blood, but tear it out. I'll exchange it for my son's. Here it is. Here's my heart. ... My heart has the same blood as his...(p. 15).

In recalling the Aztec sacrificial ritual, Rivera communicates a powerful intensity in the mother's groping for understanding through such primitive beliefs. The reference to that ritual, however, is unobtrusively presented, since the belief which underlies it seems naturally to have syncretized with the woman's Christian beliefs. More in conflict with formal Christianity would be the folk belief in spirits, and undoubtedly it is for that reason that Rivera, in the anecdote which immediately precedes "El rezo," briefly and somewhat mysteriously recounts a visit to an "espiritista" by perhaps the same woman who is distressed upon hearing that her son was lost in action. Again we see the insider's point of view and the lack of extraneous or external statement that would detract from the authentic experience.

If "El rezo" is an example of a subjective experience presented "objectively," we shall find a more complicated narrative method in the majority of the other stories. In "La noche buena," for example, a traditional third-person narrative is freely mixed with dialogue and interior monologue. This story, as well as "Los niños no se aguantaron" and "Los quemaditos," again gives evidence of Rivera's sensitivity to the humble and poor Chicano family and to the hostility and prejudice of the Anglo world.

The tone, mood, and setting of the last two stories of the "collective" type illustrate, each in its way, Rivera's concern to dramatize other dimensions of life. "La noche que se apagaron las luces," a story that is almost entirely in dialogue, concerns the world of young people, and the difficulties and excesses of love that lead to the self-destruction of the principal characters. "El retrato" is, by contrast, a serious story dealing with a fraudulent salesman which is resolved satisfactorily by ingenuity and humor.

The "collective" stories serve Rivera well in providing wide perspective on Chicano life. The five "individual" stories focus sustained attention on the internal development of an adolescent Chicano boy.

Rivera's interest in evoking certain moments of crisis that affect the main character is most evident in the story whose title was given to the collection as a whole. The fact also that we find "...y no se lo tragó la tierra" placed in the center of the book indicates that the author views it as having more importance than the other stories. What makes this story so effective is the way Rivera has kept the perspective rigorously within the bounds of the mentality of the "muchacho," whose sensitivity focuses, with terrible authenticity, on the problem of injustice and human suffering. As the misfortunes of the family begin to mount, the boy's hatred and rage intensify and it is that very intensity that will impel him to question why his people have been condemned to that cruel cycle of punishing farm labor, serious sickness, and early death. His questioning slowly and painfully drains him of any respect for the traditional pattern of submission and finally leads him to revolt against his mother's faith in God. During the moments of personal rebellion, in which the youth curses God, he is shaken by fear, the fear "instilled by the years and by his parents" and the expectation of divine punishment ("he saw that the earth opened up in order to swallow him whole"). He emerges, however, from the split-second crisis feeling purged of his fear and finding the earth firmer than ever. With renewed inner strength, he purges himself of his fury by repeating his curse. The result of his rebellion is a "peace that he had never experienced before." That turning point in his internal life also seems to him to be the turning point in the fate of his family; inexplicably, both his father and brother are soon in better health.

In the evocation of this personal crisis, Rivera has again been careful not to intrude with explicit commentary on the character's realm of sensitivity and being. The account, however, has not only profound meaning with respect to the internal development of the boy, but, by implication and suggestion, it offers a basic attitude that penetrates to the very root of Chicano culture and the Chicano way of life. Rivera's commitment to his people cannot be doubted, but his militancy is not directed simply towards social or political solutions. Rivera no doubt would subscribe to Unamuno's statement that "the most effective war is the one that we contrive against ourselves, the war against the mystery of our lives and of our destinies." This stance implies no indifference, but rather it gives a deeper and more radical dimension to the Chicano struggle. It makes self-assertiveness and self-consciousness the starting point and the most potentially useful weapon against a cultural system that either cruelly exploits and oppresses a whole class of people, or ignores and even thwarts those efforts that would improve their quality of life.

Perhaps the most effective of the personal stories is "Es que duele," in which the author dwells sympathetically and convincingly on the thoughts and feelings of the boy. It succeeds less· as a story than as a thoroughly honest and delicate evocation of the Chicano experience, as lived by a boy of a migrant family, and narrated from the perspective of that boy's consciousness. In a quiet, impassive manner, the boy recalls his humiliations in the North, the prejudice against him as a Mexican, his conflicts with the Anglo boys and the fist fight that leads to his expulsion from school. Along with his objective and angerless tone, however, we note the vitality and freshness of his thought processes as he mulls over and over in his mind the central event that unifies the heterogeneous memories and the possible consequences of that event. In this story as in others, the expansiveness of the boy's consciousness is due in part to Rivera's peculiar mix of narrative modes, which consists of objective reporting and subjective self-analysis interspersed with set pieces of dialogue and monologue.

In our analysis thus far, we have examined Rivera's collection in terms of the two structural groupings to which most of the stories belong. It is evident that Rivera's esthetic thrust has been not only to record and document the social reality in which he has been a participant but also to probe the emotional and psychological realm of that world in its most intimate terms. There remain, however, the first and last stories of the collection, which raise the interesting problem of the relationship between Rivera's auctorial self and the biographical self that seems so inextricably imbedded in his Chicano past.

In the opening story, "El año perdido," noteworthy for its brevity, the narration concerns an unidentified "he" involved in a struggle to clarify his memory of a time period which is vague but which is suggested to constitute a year. Psychologically more confusing is who the "he" is:

> The whole thing would start whenever he heard that someone was calling him but when he looked back to see who it was that was calling him, he would turn completely around and end up where he was before. For that reason he was never able to figure out who was calling him or why, and later he even forgot

what name was used to call him. But he was sure that he was the person being called (p. 1).

We find here the crisis of a person who is trying to come to terms with his own identity, and with what it was that occurred during the "lost year." The "lost year" is lost to the person of the story in the sense that that is the length of time it took him to find himself. In other words, the person who lived those experiences gives in to the person who became aware, as though suddenly, of the existence of that other person. Or we might say that it is consciousness which suddenly becomes self-reflective and in doing so finds an integrative power that will rise above the confusions of life experiences. The person of the first story, while not identified, is not unlike the boy of other stories and is very much the same as the person of the last story. But we should note here that in not identifying the subject of the story, Rivera has created a deliberate ambiguity.

If our analysis is valid, it is interesting to observe the way Rivera has fused, through the fictional device of a "lost year," the process of psychological integration (the character's becoming conscious and self-reflective about his experiences) with the creative process of turning the stuff of life into stories. The term "lost year," in addition to having a double meaning, must be seen as ironic, in view of what the person/writer has gained (psychological and esthetic control). From one point of view, psychological or esthetic distancing amounts to a lessening of intensity; hence the year is "lost"; but from another point of view, nothing is lost. The experiences, rather, are pulled together and transformed, since the person has gained in psychological and existential meaning, and the writer has achieved a mastery of language and form. With its ingenious, simple complexity, the first story serves the author well because it creates an openness of form and theme and at the same time suggests a temporal framework which unifies the fragments to be presented.

The brevity and the relative clarity of language of the first story find their counterparts in the final story, "Debajo de la casa," in which the author differentiates between internal and external perspectives by placing a richly profuse monologue within a more or less realistic action. For the external plane, Rivera has chosen the familiar young boy of earlier stories to carry out the crisis of the self which was introduced in the first story. The boy responds to an inexplicable inner need to withdraw from his normal routine and spend the time reflecting on his life. One of the neighbors comments on his "strange" behavior:

> —Poor family. First the mother and now him. He must be going mad. I think he's losing his mind. He's wasting his years (p. 169).

What is happening internally to the boy, however, is quite the opposite. It is the precise moment of illumination and victory over the psychological drift and sense of incoherence that had engulfed the boy's inner life:

He suddenly felt happy because as he thought about what the woman had said he realized that in reality he had lost nothing. He had found. Found and found again and brought together. Relating this with that, other things with the remote past, everything with everything else. That's what it was. That's all it was (p. 169).

A modest triumph perhaps, but one which is indispensable for the self's struggle towards acceptance, identity, growth, and expansion. In evoking the boy's discovery of meaning and self-integration, the author seems to suggest that the youth had to overcome a real fear of being destined to inherit his mother's unstable and fragile mental condition. But whether that was indeed a contributing factor or not, it is the final outcome that matters because it lays the foundation for a healthy confrontation with the uncertainties of the future.

To parallel the external line of the story, Rivera has created a dense and powerful monologue, which expresses the inner consciousness of the youth in a seemingly uncontrolled flood of recollections. The latter are disparate bits and pieces of lived experiences which, after a sudden release of pent-up or repressed emotion, flow in a rapid succession of cascading thoughts that finally coalesce into an exhilarating whole. The cumulative evocation of the past, however, has such vitality and force that we begin to sense that the author has again fused his own joy of esthetic creation with the boy's psychological situation.

As in "El año perdido," we must sense the ambiguity—the presence of the second level—because the author avoids identifying his auctorial self by retaining the fiction that we are in the inner world of the boy. From the perspective of the boy's consciousness, the monologue evokes an authentic inner reality and expresses his joy at having integrated the fragments of his past into existential wholeness. At the same time, the monologue functions in the work as a structuring device through which the earlier fragments are repeated in summary form and expanded with additional details. The monologue is effective in this double sense since it not only unifies what had previously been isolated events but also reveals and exalts the dynamic force underlying the unifying process. In terms of technique, the monologue serves to integrate the disparate strands which are the basis of the earlier stories and anecdotes, but it also suggests, paradoxically, a circular relationship, since the final integration (the boy's victory over chaos) may be said to be the source of any of the individual parts which precede it. Thus, in sustaining the logic of the boy's perspective, the author has created a certain temporal and emotional confusion. The confusion, however, is dissipated when we realize that what the author has done is to project his own reality as writer into the monologue without identifying it. The relationship between "life" and artistic creation has been perfectly blended, and it is only through the concrete embodiment of the boy's thoughts that the author makes his presence felt. He has given shape and structure to a series of perceptions and memories but, ironically, he has carried out his craft as though he were invisible. Thus Rivera confirms the function and value of art, while at the same time giving priority to the primacy and immediacy of life. We referred earlier to Rivera's twofold purpose: to present the wide spectrum of events that make up the social reality of Chicano farmworkers, and to illuminate that social reality through subjective perspectives that evoke inner dimensions of the Chicano people. The individual stories, as esthetic constructions, are uneven in their appeal and impact. It may even be said that a few of them are somewhat contrived or at least do not have the ring of authenticity (for example, "La noche estaba plateada" and "El retrato"). Rivera, however, is at his very best in those well-sustained individual perspectives in which the language expresses the character's intimate thoughts and feelings with true-to-life naturalness and vitality. He has also discovered, in evoking the events of his Chicano past, a joyful cohesiveness in his own youthful self. In the figurative act of embracing his people, his culture, his experiences, he discovers self-liberation and independence.

Interpreting Tomás Rivera

by Joseph Sommers

I

In an introductory article in this volume,[1] I attempted to set out the assumptions and the methods of three critical approaches to Chicano literature. I have called them the formalist, the culturalist and the historical-dialectical. What follows below is an effort to test these approaches by applying each one to a given text— *...y no se lo tragó la tierra (...and the earth did not part)* by Tomas Rivera. This effort to separate the approaches will seek to avoid the merely mechanical, for we all realize that in published criticism such neatly and conveniently delimited distinctions are rare. Further, it will seek to demonstrate as objectively as possible the critical rewards which derive from each of the first two critical modes, even as it will be clear that my own preference is for the third.

What would lie at the center of a formalist approach to the text? In the first place, there would be a relatively minor concern for historical and social information, though attention would be paid to Rivera's experience in achieving the doctorate, and the extent to which he acquired familiarity with Hispanic literary traditions and with the landmark authors of Europe and North America. This type of information would be useful in examining how the writer achieved his "personal voice," so that his work might be seen in the individualized terms stressed by formalist critics.

A more important formalist concern is usually to situate the text in the larger framework of western literature. A prime critical goal is the identification of literary influences, for two reasons. On the one hand, the degree to which they are assimilated and transformed is an index of the valued quality of "originality." On the other, the presence of literary influences and indirect references to recognized authors or narrative techniques is evidence of the equally valued quality of "universality." Specifically, the formalist critic would identify traces in the text of four major authors: Faulkner, Joyce, Dos Passos and Rulfo, in order of ascending significance.

In formulating and presenting much of the narrative from the first-person perspective of an innocent boy, Rivera can be said to have had recourse to the classic narrative strategy of Faulkner in *The Sound and the Fury*. The

"Interpreting Tomás Rivera" by Joseph Sommers. An enlarged version of this study entitled "From the Critical Premise to the Product: Critical Modes and Their Applications to a Chicano Literary Text" appeared in *The New Scholar*, 5, no. 2 (1977). Reprinted by permission of *The New Scholar*.

[1]"Critical Approaches to Chicano Literature," pp. 31-40.

interior monologue which closes the book and constitutes a unifying re-examination of the experiences of the preceding chapters, may be a modest reminiscence of Joyce's technique in the ending of *Ulysses*. And the influence of Dos Passos can be identified in the central structural device of prefacing each major narrative unit with a brief passage comparable to the camera-eye segments of *Manhattan Transfer*. These serve to provide thematic resonance, introduce remembered experience, and extend in more general terms the particularized experience of the narrative unit.

But it is Juan Rulfo, the Mexican master-narrator, whose novel *Pedro Páramo* and short stories are most apparent as influences in... *y no se lo tragó la tierra*.[2] This affinity has been noted by critics, but rarely analyzed.[3] In a general way, the two authors are linked by a spareness of narrative and a focus on rural themes. More precisely, the innocent first-person narrative voice is even more closely anticipated in Rulfo's story "Macario,"[4] which has likely derivations from Faulkner, than in Faulkner s own work. The innocence of Rulfo's narrator is closer to that of Rivera's, sharing with him an iconoclastic reaction to sexuality and to the phenomena of the natural world. Like Rulfo, too, in *Pedro Páramo*, although much less radically, Rivera ruptures his narrative sequence and interposes unexplained fragments to jar the comfort of a reader accustomed to revelations of cause and effect through linear narrative sequences. Furthermore, in both Rulfo and Rivera a central fundamental irony is generated by the contrast between apparently direct,...uncomplicated folk-language and the deep thematic overtones of violence and passion which inform the lives of their characters.

At the center of the formalist approach is rigorous textual analysis. Here issues of genre, language, structure, and theme come into question. In this case the problem of genre is indeed important, for the tendency has been to see the volume as a collection of short stories. The formalist would examine the arguments for seeing the text as a novel (arguments with which I agree) and thus would adduce definitions of the novel, distinctions between realism and modernism, and especially questions of structure. Language explorations, already referred to above, would include the role of rural folk lexical terms, syntactic patterns, linguistic symbols, and English loan elements penetrating the Spanish text. Interesting distinctions could be made between the characters' language, that of the young narrator, and that of the narrator or *persona* closest to the author. An important area, as yet untouched, is critical analysis of the English version, which clearly lacks the linguistic coherence of the original Spanish.

A formalist critic would no doubt devote extensive analysis to questions

[2]References throughout the article are to the second edition (Berkeley: Editorial Justa, 1976). Page numbers will appear in the text. Translations are my own.
[3]An exception is Charles Tatum, who begins such an analysis in "Contemporary Chicano Prose Fiction: Its Ties to Mexican Literature," *Books Abroad*, 49, no. 3 (Summer, 1975), 432-38.
[4]This story is part of the collection *El llano en llamas* (Mexico City: FCE, 1953).

of structure.[5] He would note that underlying the sequence of narrative units is an understood linkage in time. Despite internal inconsistencies (for example the references to seasons are contradictory), the chapters correspond approximately to the passing of a crucial year in the boy-protagonist's life.

Structural likewise is the scheme by which each experience narrated becomes in some sense a rite of passage, displaying the delicate and complex growth by which a young boy comes of age. This scheme is also evident in the prefatory sections, which function as magnifiers extending the scope and depth of the boy's experience with the quality of typicality, so that they acquire a representative Chicano character. Lastly, there is the thematic framing provided by the introductory section, which introduces the notion of the "lost year," and the final section, which in effect recapitulates and integrates the twelve intervening units, thus impelling the reader to understand that there has been a cumulative process marked by a beginning and an end, a questioning and an answering.

Another area of formalist analysis is likely to be that of thematics, linking the literary idiosyncrasies of a text to systems of meaning within it. One such system might be psychological, involving issues of personality formation and maturation, such as the boy's self-contemplation in the early scene, his encounters with both sexuality and social taboos, and his symbolic emergence, at the end, from a womb of isolation and hiding beneath the house.[6] Another possible thematic system originates in the existentialist formulations of Octavio Paz in his essay on the dialectics of solitude.[7] Applying this, Luis Dávila identifies the crucial process in the novel as the search for the other, for in this view (closely related to early Sartrean thought), being can be defined only in relation to otherness.[8]

What is important here is that formalist criticism stresses the identification of meaning as an index of the "literariness" of the work. The goal of this criticism is not to integrate the literary experience into larger frames of cultural, social and broadly political experience, but to distinguish literature and its aesthetic from other modes of experience.

Formalist analysis, then, can tell us much about the richness, the complexity, and the generic identity of...*y no se lo tragó la tierra.* However,

---

[5]Interesting observations on structural patterns are offered by Ralph Grajeda, "Tomás Rivera's Appropriation of the Chicano Past" which appears in this volume, and by Francisco Lomeli and Donald Urioste, in their *Chicano Perspectives in Literature* (Albuquerque: Pajarito Publications, 1976), pp. 46-47. The latter critics support the argument that the text is indeed a novel.

[6]The case for the central thematic thread being that of personality formation, although not in specifically psychological terms, is argued by Frank Pino, Jr., in "The 'Outsider' and 'El Otro' in Tomás Rivera's...*y no se lé tragó la tierra,*" *Books Abroad,* 49, no. 3 (Summer, 1975), 453-58.

[7]*El laberinto de la soledad,* 3rd ed. (Mexico City: FCE, 1972), pp. 175-91.

[8]"Otherness in Chicano Literature." Paper presented at IV International Congress of Mexican Studies, Santa Monica, California, 1973.

we must understand that the formulae of this analysis are a stress on the individuality of the work and the writer, the compatibility of the text with those of established authors, and the definition of internally distinguishing structural and stylistic features which are seen to set the "literary" work apart from other modes of linguistic discourse and from the apprehension of social meaning and historical knowledge.

II

Several objectives would be apparent in the way a culturalist critic approached...*y no se lo tragó la tierra*. One would be to understand the work as a product of Chicano culture, and to see in it a reflection of this culture.

For example, the critic would present instances of expressive language which demonstrate the special capacities of Chicano speech patterns to communicate the nature and the significance of Chicano experience. One such instance is the ironic use of the negative, elliptically, to render more vehement the positive. The laconic three-word sentence, "No pos sí" which ends the narrative unit entitled "The Night the Lights Went Out", exemplifies this effect superbly. The story is recounted in part by an omniscient third-person narrator who is close to the scene, in part by conversational fragments or interior monologues of the two protagonists Ramón and Juanita, and in part by dialogue between two anonymous people of the community. What emerges is the early love between Ramón and Juanita, her momentary interest in another man during the family's migratory travels, Ramón's possessive jealousy and Juanita's insistence on independence, and finally Ramón's dramatic suicide after Juanita defies him by dancing with the other man. Once the narrator has chronicled Ramón's death (by self-electrocution at the electrical plant, inducing a power failure which stops the dance), the chapter ends with a two-line exchange between the ananymous community people, who throughout have been piecing events together and evaluating them. One voice concludes, "The fact is that they really loved each other, don't you think?" The powerful response to this is couched in a popular idiom that in its very form parallels and reinforces the narrated irony (that too much love brings about its own destruction, that what appears good can be bad, that appearance is the reverse of reality, that what may be voiced as negative can in fact signify the positive) and compresses with remarkable brevity an affirmation: "No, pos sí." (Roughly translatable as, "No, of course they did.")

A comparable example is the deployment of a similar linguistic construction, "N'hombre, sí" in the chapter, "It Really Hurts." It functions as a *motif* throughout the text, which takes the form of an interior monologue by a boy protagonist whose family had immigrated north from Texas. He meditates upon his expulsion from school, obviously for racist reasons, and the impact it will have upon his family's aspirations for him. As he feels the hurt and the injustice, he keeps hoping to fend off reality by convincing himself that perhaps it has not really happened. Each time, his relentless sense of realism brings him back to truth and pain as he tells himself that the school authorities did in fact expel him. And the story ends with this final realization, "N'hombre sí." ("No, man, they sure did.") Once again, powerful because the "sí" ironically reverses the "no," the very form of expression echoes and underlines the theme—yes, one must face the concrete reality of injustice rather than retreat to the fantasy of Utopian imagination.

The culturalist critic would affirm, based on analyses such as those cited, that the essence of the narration derives directly from distinctive cultural features, many of which are imbedded in the language itself. Furthermore, it is the migratory experience, itself a matrix of Chicano culture, which gives shape and meaning to the experience narrated in the text.

Another culturalist tendency is to examine the text for the cultural profile it generates, and to validate it if this profile is extensive and detailed. Here the critic would identify many features of Chicano traditional culture which are integral to the make-up of the characters' attitudes and behavior. For example there is both dependence upon religion and incipient critical awareness of conflict between religious orthodoxy and natural human impulse. Thus the critic would affirm that the novel spans the range of impact which Catholicism has had upon Chicano consciousness.

The critic would also stress that the novel projects a view of the Chicano world from within, and would focus on the aspects of Chicano existence which make up the narrative texture: family life, the migratory cycle, attitudes toward love, marriage, religion, school and work. These have special characteristics among Chicanos, and taken together reveal the coherent patterns of Chicano culture. Particular scenes would be singled out and identified as unique to the Chicano experience: the mother's prayerful offer to sacrifice herself to save her son fighting in Korea; the boy suffering from thirst as he and brothers and father stoop to labor in the field; the mother panicked at the prospect of venturing into the center of the strange English-speaking city to shop at the dime store; the fathers aspiring that their children be prizefighters or telephone operators; the boy being refused a haircut or insulted racially by other school children in a strange town in which his family are transients.

In singling out these scenes the critic would stress that Rivera conveys both the particularity and the coherence of Chicano culture. Since it is in culture that the critic sees what characterizes the Chicano, he is concerned with uncovering it in its "purest" form. As a consequence he gravitates logically toward its most traditional manifestations. If he is also influenced by ethnopoetics, he may argue that, because "original" Chicano culture still survives, authors like Rivera are not cut off from their roots, and can enrich their works with the authenticity of themes, characters, and language free from contamination or assimilation. By contrast, he would point out that modern Anglo culture suffers from an *ersatz* quality deriving from loss of the past, urbanization, artificial and elitist sophistication, corruption by the manipulative mass media, and a voguish stress on the mental, the imaginary, and the irrational. The Chicano may live outside the mainstream, this critic would say, but his very exclusion has permitted the retention of traditional culture.

For the culturalist critic the central unifying theme of Rivera's novel is the search for identity, a search which enables the boy to discover that he has rich cultural resources upon which to draw, resources tempered by suffering and endowed with the strength of humanism. In developing this thematic argument the critic might refer, with Ralph Grajeda, to the notions of Frantz Fanon in tracing the development of cultural awareness and the process of cultural identification by which the "colonized" *persona* throws off psychological acceptance of the mask imposed by the colonizer.[9]

In essence, then, the objective of this approach is to show that the work is distinctive because it emerges from the Chicano experience, and valid because it embodies an authentic view of Chicano culture. Its consequent difference from non-Chicano narratives will make it a healthy cultural reinforcement for Chicano readers, who will see themselves and their culture projected in the text with dignity, as compared to the degraded images packaged and transmitted daily by the mass media.

The richness of linguistic variation, the distinctive features of Chicano life style, both rural and urban, and the dramatic nature of Chicano historical experience, all serve to guarantee that embedded in most literary texts will be much material for the culturalist critic to work with. On the other hand, the limitations of culturalist criticism deserve spelling out. Here I refer to the "pure" form of this approach as outlined in the introductory essay. In placing culture (and by implication, race) at the center of Chicano experience, the critic underestimates the all-important factor of class, a factor which shapes and influences the process by which cultural expression is generated.[10] For example, the experience of the migratory cycle is fundamental to the cultural content of...*y no se lo tragó la tierra*. Because the structures of the food and textile industries in the United States require special seasonal forms of agricultural production, the migratory labor system is imposed on a large segment of the Mexican-descended population.

[9]"Tomás Rivera's Appropriation of the Chicano Past."

[10]After the present study was completed, the article by Juan Gómez Quiñones, "On Culture," was published in *Revista Chicano-Riqueña*, V, no. 2 (*primavera* (Spring), 1977), 29-47. It contains a lucid, developed analysis of questions such as theory of culture, culture and class, culture and domination, and culture and race. I believe its positions to be consistent with those expressed here. A slightly condensed version of this article, entitled, "Toward a Concept of Culture", appears in this volume.

Were this system of exploitation to disappear, new forms of cultural expression would soon manifest themselves, as has been the case when rural Chicano population has gravitated to urban areas in search of an improved life. One limitation, then, of culturalist criticism is its failure to show how cultural manifestations are part of a total system of social relations at the base of which are economic structures shaping these relations. A second limitation is the general view of culture as adaptation rather than as a complex of responses to the total set of life conditions which a people faces. The adaptive view tends to be acritical, all-inclusive, and descriptive. The latter view attempts to be critical, to see cultural expression as an area of struggle, and to distinguish between those elements of culture which are adaptive (such as the ideology of organized religion) and those (such as satirical humor) which evolve out of the need to analyze reality, to criticize oppressive institutions, to affirm a people's sense of worth, and to facilitate structural change.

III

A critic working in the third mode, concerned with a historical and dialectical approach, might well begin an analysis by situating the text.

While the narration itself is set in the 1950s, the perspective from which it was conceived reflects consciousness of the 1960s. The end of the decade—the time of composition of the novel—was an important historic juncture. In the first place, coincident with deepening official commitment to the brutal war in Viet Nam, there had been a critical questioning of national policy and of the very assumptions on which United States society was structured. This questioning had come in part from the younger generation which to an unprecedented degree resisted the war and made many tenuous attempts to forge a counter-culture.

Deeper blows to social complacency had been dealt by black people, whose demands for change, heard first during the Montgomery bus boycott, spread throughout the North, from Harlem to Watts. To the humanist ideas of Martin Luther King were added the more radical formulations of Malcolm X, Angela Davis, and The Black Panthers, which analyzed the origins and nature of racism, took account of its economic roots and connected it to the history of Western imperialism. Black consciousness, the reexamination of black history and culture, the ideas of Frantz Fanon, the works of LeRoi Jones, Richard Wright, Ralph Ellison, James Baldwin, Langston Hughes and Claude McKay—all formed part of the nation's cultural atmosphere at the turn of the decade.

A comparable social ferment was felt throughout the Southwest during the years immediately prior to the composition of Rivera's novel. Although the black movement clearly influenced the Chicano upsurge of the 1960's, this did not, as is sometimes simplistically stated, derive basically from the black movement. Rather it continued and renewed long established patterns of struggle for change and justice, whether social or economic, urban or rural. By the end of the 1960s Chicano activity was at a high point in all phases. Land seizures had occurred in northern New Mexico. Chicano urban movements were organized in Denver and Los Angeles. Chicano students initiated national meetings at Denver in 1969 and 1970 which were notable for inspiring student publications, most of them placing a heavy emphasis on cultural nationalism.

For their contribution to the literary coming of age of Tomás Rivera, two elements of the national upsurge were particularly important. The first was the movement in Crystal City, Texas, to take power from the hands of the Anglo minority and transfer it democratically to the Chicano majority. Many constituents of this majority were Chicano farmworkers who annually embarked on migratory treks to Michigan, Wisconsin, Minnesota and Illinois. Indeed, Rivera's family had resided in Crystal City in the 1940s, and had participated in the migratory cycle, traveling to the Midwest and returning. For this reason, the Chicano political movement in Crystal City in the 1960s contained a special personal meaning for him. A second important element was the organizing efforts of the farmworkers' union, renewing the struggles which had begun in the 1920s and had echoed again and again in succeeding decades. The modern union, led by César Chávez, was launched in 1965. By 1970 it had won historic victories in California and had established an organizing committee in Texas. These efforts served to focus national attention on the situation of the migratory farmworker.

While there was no unified national leadership of this many-faceted Chicano movement, there was a widely shared sense of the need to challenge established social structures, and to demand significant change. The cultural nationalism which peaked in the Plan de Aztlán of 1969 began to be supplanted by a more politically and socially based militancy stemming from the hard political realities of Crystal City, the brutalities of the Los Angeles moratorium, and the class consciousness engendered by the farmworkers' struggles against agribusiness. All this experience generated a rich diversity of cultural activity: newspapers, journals, art exhibitions, poetry festivals, and drama performances. Of key importance, a Chicano publishing house, Quinto Sol Publications, proved able to sustain a critically oriented journal, *El Grito* (launched in 1967), to provide an independent forum for Chicano writers and scholars, and to announce a literary prize based on norms respecting the language and the artistic integrity of Chicano creative authors.

The purpose of this schematic effort to situate Rivera's novel is not to arrive at a simplified equation of cause and effect assuming that the literary work is a mechanically predetermined product of given historical conditions. Rather it is to identify the issues and conflicts of the historical experience to which the author responded, and to analyze the quality and the content of the cultural atmosphere in which he was active at the time of literary productivity.

Turning from context to text, problems of structure and of narrative point of view demand attention. Here our point of departure is serious textual analysis. The formalist's arguments that there are structural and narrative patterns which justify treating the text as a novel are indispensable to this analysis. They need not be repeated but they serve to show that precisely *because* the text has novelistic scope and unity, it embodies a complex system of values and can be analyzed in terms of meaning and ideological contradictions. In brief, then, a close reading of the text uncovers an experiential process narrated across time in such a way as to refer both to the protagonist's personal life and to the common realities shared by Chicanos.

Of crucial importance is the particular *way* in which the narration reaches the reader. Whether by means of first-person passages in which the boy himself conveys his account of events, or through a third-person limited omniscient point of view, the narrative perspective remains largely that of the protagonist. The reader perceives events through the boy's eyes as he undergoes the trials of that crucial year and observes how others act and react. The larger cognitive process for the reader is shaped by a fundamental ironic movement in the narrative—the boy's change from innocence to awareness, from the idealism inherent in unformed human nature to the realism shaped by exposure to the difficult contradictions of the social condition.

The question of whether the same boy figures in each of the narrative sections is not crucial, for ambiguities in this regard are cleared up in the final section, when the central figure assumes knowledge of and responsibility for each of the scenes narrated. We can conclude that his role was that of either protagonist or witness. What is literarily more significant is that the reader in effect looks over the boy's shoulder or listens to his voice as he first encounters the realities of his cultural and social circumstances: the stifling omnipotence of an observant and demanding God; the sense of sinfulness associated with the natural arrival of puberty; the cruel racism of the educational system; the mendacity of some figures who prey upon fellow Chicanos, figures like doña Boni and the portrait salesman. Each encounter embodies elements of irony, for they reverse the hopes and expectations of the reader, who would prefer to see growth and maturation in the boy parallelled by increased education, social mobility, personal freedom, and access to the fruits of modern society.

This ironic contrast between innocence and awareness, accentuated by the reader's identification with the boy from whose point of view the story is narrated, is the basis for the critical perspective of the text, as we shall see below. Thus narrative technique is fundamental to the shaping of meaning and of ideological emphasis.

Another distinctive formal feature of *...y no se lo trago la tierra* is its extreme compression. The various narrative units have the intensity of focus of the short story with its insistence on brevity. This has the advantage, on the one hand, of creating tight endings which enrich the text because of the semi-autonomous, self-contained quality of its component parts. On the other hand, in its bare-bones narrative quality, with an almost complete absence of landscape, the text displays a lack of the texture and the detail of experience which can be novelistic virtues in fleshing out human experience. To be specific, excessive laconism contributes to ambiguities in meaning, which will be discussed below. Remarkably, the reader realizes, upon looking back, that the total narration spans no more than sixty-odd pages.

A final aspect of the text, correctly singled out by culturalist criticism, is the casting of much of the narration in popular language. The directness and expressiveness of common people's speech patterns pervade the text and endow it with deeper authenticity than could ever be attained by a distanced voice closer in tone to the Mexican or North American novel. The important critical observation here is that the expressiveness of folk language functions not merely reflectively, to provide an authentic view of traditional culture, but actively to show how people respond to each other and to the harsh realities of their existence. The total narrative process, which shows the boy finding sustenance in his cultural identity, implies the fusing of this identity with awareness of the need to change the surrounding reality. And this critical awareness, frequently expressed through language, applies not only to the larger societal structures, but also to aspects of traditional culture itself, such as orthodox religious attitudes toward sexuality and guilt.[11]

An example, conveyed in popular language, of the interaction between traditional cultural values (acceptance of social norms, hope that the children will achieve success) and a critical realism (albeit tinged with cynicism) based on actual experience, much of which has to do with social class, can be seen in this brief anonymous interchange, which serves as *introito* and thematic preface to the unit concerning the boy's education:

"Why do you go to school all the time?"
"My dad says it will prepare us. In case some day a chance comes up, he says maybe they'll give it to us."
"Hell, man. If I were you, I wouldn't even worry. The one on the bottom always stays there. We can't be more screwed over, so I don't even think about

it. The guys who really have to play it smart are the ones on top who have something to lose. They could be forced down to where we are. But us, what do we have to lose?" (p. 26)

Taken together, the formal qualities of the text—a hidden but tight novelistic structure, a narrative point of view which precipitates irony, an emphasis through language on popular culture, and an insistence (probably excessive) on narrative compression—must be seen as fundamental to its total literary nature. Indeed the novel is rich in meaning and values as it goes beyond describing the Chicano experience to interpret it. This becomes especially clear in the final section entitled, "Under the House," in which the protagonist takes shelter in a solitary hiding place in order to think over the events of his year.

This recapitulation of his thoughts, reordering and reviewing events which flow through his mind in a jumbled sequence, is meaningful in three separate but interrelated ways. In the first place, he goes through the process of interrelating discrete experiences, as he himself realizes: "He had discovered something. To discover and rediscover and connect. To relate this thing with that, and that with still another, to put it all together. That's what it was all about" (p. 127). As he realizes this and vows to repeat the effort each year, he consciously assumes the intention to grapple with his own and his people's experience, to review, relate, analyze and understand.

The second aspect of this synthesizing process is the feeling of solidarity it produces: "I'd like to see all those people together. And if my arms were big enough, I could hug them all" (p. 125). Here he identifies with all those whose lives have intersected with his during that *lehrjahr:* the people huddled in the migrants' truck, the praying mother, the children burned while their parents worked in the field, all Chicanos who have shared the details of his experience.

Finally, in his recall of events and conversations, he does more than reconstruct. In many instances there are additional fragments, extending what had earlier been narrated. These fragments indicate that the participants in the various scenes have themselves responded to experience analytically and critically, and that the boy, in singling out for recall precisely these qualities, is assimilating their critical perspective. One example occurs in "It Was a Silvery Night." The prefatory paragraph tells of a boy who is refused a haircut repeatedly and finally realizes it is because he is Chicano. The paragraph ends, "Then he understood it all and went home to get his father" (p. 37). The equivalent section at the novel's end adds only a fragment of a sentence, but it extends the scene, adding new meaning as it conveys the father's reactions upon learning of the incident: "...those bastards are going to cut your hair or I'll tear them apart" (p. 121). An analogous example can be seen in your section, "And the Earth Did Not Part," in which the boy's mother seems tolerant of misery as she tries to cushion her son's resentment at injustice. The fragment at the end of the novel, however, shows that the boy recalls her in an amplified light, in which she understands the injustice and shares her son's resentment: "...I think my old man won't be able to work in the sun any more. The boss didn't say a thing when we told him he had a sunstroke. He just shook his head. All he cared about was that the rains were coming on strong and he was losing his crop. That's the only thing that made him sad" (p. 121). Both these fragments, which show understanding of oppression and the disposition to resist it, cast light on the boy's final synthesizing process. (Other examples could be cited.) The clear indication is that "recollection" has led him to understanding and resistance.

The dominant literary features of the text, taken together, highlight the larger experiential process of the protagonist. This process is one of coming of age, of discovery, of passage to awareness. The reconstitution, at the novel's end, of the year which in the introduction had been called "the lost year," in effect signifies the beginning of recuperation of historical experience.

The boy's discovery of self in the experience and the suffering of others is the antithesis of individualism and the affirmation of the value of collective identity. Thus the novel ends as he waves his hand in symbolic confidence, openness, and friendship to the other being he thinks may be watching him. Whether this being is a part of the boy's self—a sort of *alter ego*—or an imagined representative of the outside world, the boy no longer fears him. This act contrasts dramatically and ironically with his feelings at the beginning of the year. At that point he was alone, uncertain of his words, unsure of what was real in life, and fearful that the cause of all his uncertainty might be lodged in his own imperfect self.

Furthermore, the road to critical awareness is laid out in potential for both protagonist and reader. While the boy's is only a beginning step, the critical reader can see beyond it to the sources, instruments, and techniques of exploitation, beginning with those relations of production which determine the very style and rhythm of Chicano lives. The reader, if not the boy, can see how rural agriculture promotes the use of migratory labor in the first place, and how it squeezes from men, women, and children the last drop of production before casting them back into the ever-moving stream without being obliged to pay wages out of season.

Rivera examines the facilitating institutions of oppression, ranging from the system of usury to the method of labor transport at high cost under dangerous conditions. He details the social and cultural mechanisms which function as ideological supports of the institutions of oppression. One is the racism which in school, barbershop, and shopping center isolates and marks its human target, dividing him or her from others, withholding knowledge and education, keeping a man or woman psychologically on the defensive. Another is that aspect of organized religion which inculcates a sense of guilt, sinfulness, and imperfection, upholding as virtues passivity, self-sacrifice, and respect for the authority wielded by growers, school

principals, and the omnipresent state with its power to conscript for whatever military endeavor it chooses.

This is not to imply there are n o contradictions or shortcomings in the
text. One has to do with the sense of history. The novel indeed does narrate
the protagonist's coming to grips, personally and socially, with his own
immediate history. And while the fragment concerning Bartolo, a folk poet
who names the returned migrants in his songs, suggests a form of oral
chronicling, the bulk of the narration tends to present both characters and
narrator as lacking awareness of the historical past. In the way people
speak and think, there are almost no references, direct or indirect, to earlier
experiences. Symbolically, the final collage of the boy's memories contains
a brief dialogue, extending an earlier interchange between grandfather and
grandson. The old man mournfully states: "...since I had that stroke, I
can't remember too well what I used to tell people. Then the Revolution
came and in the end we lost. Villa came out all right, but I had to come over
here, where no one knows the things I did. Sometimes I try to remember,
but to tell the truth, I really can't any more. Everything gets blurred" (p. 123).

This particular fragment, coming as it does at the story's end, tends to reinforce the effect mentioned above, suggesting that to a great extent people
have been cut off from their past, and in particular have lost touch with the
rich and complex historical heritage of the Mexican revolution. On the whole
this effect is secondary in the novel, but it does stand in contradiction to
the main narrative thrust, the coming of the boy to a stage of maturity, self-
confidence, and critical awareness.

A final limitation, also tending to counter the novel's value system as a
whole, lies in its treatment of female character. With the noteworthy exception, cited above, of critical awareness on the part of the boy's mother,
women tend to be presented either as passive prisoners of traditional culture
in its most static form, or as tempters whose charms provoke men to tragedy.
Thus one mother prays in total self-sacrifice for her son's survival, another
panics at having to confront Anglo hostility while shopping. Likewise,
dona Boni in "His Hand in his Pocket," and Juanita in "The Night the
Lights Went Out," bring tragedy to their men. Granted that Juanita is con-
strained by a male value system which places burdensome restrictions on
her young temperment, her motives in challenging the code of absolute
fidelity are frivolous, related to a need to provoke jealousy in the other
girls. As a consequence, the novel lacks the depth which might have been
created had there been more sharing by women, even on a secondary level,
of the boy's experiential process.

Two observations concerning Rivera's response to literary traditions
may serve to extend the earlier discussion on influences. A thematic cluster
found in Borges posits the inseparability of the subjective from the objective,
the difficulty of finding truth in empirical data when the causal explanation
is located in the mind of the investigator, and the vulnerability of logic

and reason to the more profound categories of the subconscious and the instinctive. This position also is the point of departure of Rivera's novel. The boy, like a character in Borges, is confronted by the mystery of self-consciousness, the origin of the thought process, and the fallibility of memory. The answers, it seems to him, are locked up in his own being, in his own incapacity to separate dream from reason and to order the past. But the process of the novel, which is the narration of experienced Chicano reality and the struggle to recover fragmented time, is Rivera's solution of the perplexities and the labyrinthine dilemma posed by Borges.

Similarly there is an assimilation from Juan Rulfo of literary qualities and techniques, as noticed earlier. But Rivera's novel, in its critical confrontation with social reality, and in its protagonist's passage to a new stage of consciousness, departs from the cosmic pessimism and despair which saturate Rulfo's narratives. Without question, Rivera's text is richer for its connections with literary traditions. Equally without question, it is a novel in which the author's sensitivity to popular culture, social issues, and historical reality enable him to avoid both imitation and derivativeness.

Clearly, then, *...y no se lo tragó la tierra* is a text which challenges the critical reader to analyze its formal characteristics and thus to decipher the cultural and historical meanings which lie beneath its surface. The work stands as a major contribution to Chicano narrative, but also must be seen simultaneously as part of North American literature and most certainly as a response to Latin American techniques and themes. Only a multi-leveled and totalizing critical approach, capable of addressing itself to both text and context, to form, meaning and values, without glossing over the considerable shortcomings of the novel, both formal and ideological, can do it the critical justice it deserves.

[11]An insightful analysis of the boy's critical encounters with religious doctrine or belief is offered by Juan Rodríguez, "Acercamiento a cuatro relatos de *...y no se lo tragó la tierra*," *Mester,* 5, no. 1 (November, 1974), 16-24.

An Introduction to Chicano Poetry

by Felipe de Ortego y Gasca

I.

"Chicano" has come to be the acceptable term for those peoples who heretofore have been identified as Mexican Americans[1] (and at times as Latin Americans, Mexicans in the United States, or Spanish Americans— I shall not enumerate the well-known pejoratives). "Chicano" functions much like "Democrat" or "Republican" or "New Yorker" or "Okie" or "Southerner" or "rebel" to name a people whose roots lie in the American Southwest or Mexico and whose antecedents were either autochthonous American peoples, Mexicans (Mestizos or Criollos), Mexican Colonials (Españoles), or some combination of the above. And it is a term used more and more by the people themselves, though they do not mean to imply by it that Chicanos are a homogeneous group. In truth, Chicanos are a heterogeneous group, and the term "Chicano" at best describes their shared experiences and history.

By the term "Chicano poetry," then, I mean poetry written by Chicanos since the Treaty of Guadalupe-Hidalgo (1848). That covers a period of roughly 130 years. This is not to say that Chicanos did not possess (or that their forebears did not write) poetry prior to 1848.[2] They did. Such poetry has generally been labeled Mexican poetry, Spanish poetry, Spanish American poetry, and so on.

But here an important consideration rears its head. In the term "American poetry," we include poetry written prior to 1976 by Colonial Americans. Most anthologies of American literature include such figures as Anne Bradstreet (1613-1672), Bejamin Thompson (1640-1714), Edward Taylor (1642-1729), Thomas Godfrey (1736-1763). Philip Freneau (1752-1832), and others. The list is extensive. Strictly speaking, these writers were English citizens, British colonials in America. Yet we include them in our chronology of American poetry. The point I want to make is that the colonial history of the United States was no more confined to the Atlantic frontier

"An Introduction to Chicano Poetry" by Felipe de Ortego y Gasca. This article appears for the first time in this volume. Used by permission of the author.

[1] Felipe de Ortego y Gasca, "What's in a Name? The Chicano and the Question of Identity," *The Prospector*, 37, No. 48 (May 14, 1971), 2-3.

[2] Cf. Felipe de Ortego y Gasca, "Backgrounds of Mexican American Literature" (Ph.D., University of New Mexico, 1971).

than its history since 1776. In the American Southwest, Spanish colonials (later Mexicans) were also making history, keeping diaries, maintaining journals, writing letters, and creating poetry.[3] The literary impulse of the Hispanic American Southwest was much like that of the Anglo-American Northeast. For Americans today, the geography of the Southwest lies as secure in our national identity as the geography of the Northeast. So, too, the *literature* and *history* of the Southwest should lie as secure in our literary and historical identity as the literature and history of the Northeast. This identity ought to include the colonial period of the Southwest in the making of America, just as it includes the colonial period of the Northeast in that saga.

I belabor the point because it is crucial to defining the American experience. Otherwise, the term "American poetry" ought to include only that poetry written after we became an independent nation. I doubt that we would agree to this. And we shouldn't. To do so would rule out a significant body of literature from the Spanish colonial and Mexican periods of the American Southwest, a body of literature that can only enrich the corpus of American literature. In sum, though the "Chicano poetry" I propose to emphasize is poetry written by Chicanos since the Treaty of Guadalupe-Hidalgo, Chicano poetry itself is much older; older, in fact, than American poetry (including the British colonial years).

There is still one more point to be made: Chicano poetry, like Black poetry, forms part of the multicolored fabric of American literature. Why distinguish it then? Because nowhere in that fabric have the strands of Chicano poetry (or Black poetry, for that matter) been recognized and valued Black poets have fared better than Chicanos in recent years. Phyllis Wheatley has made the anthologies. But in the anthologies we do not find the name of Gaspar Pérez de Villagrá, for example, poet of the first American epic memorializing the battle between the Spaniards and Pueblos at Acoma, New Mexico, a battle fought in December, 1598. This epic (entitled *Historia de la Nueva México)* was published in 1610.[4] Nowhere in the literary record do we read about Juan Rodríguez Cabrillo's voyage to California, or Antonio de Espejo's journey to New Mexico, or the Mendoza-López expedition to Texas, or Father Kino's travels in Arizona.[5] The last five centuries have produced an important literature in the American Southwest. Yet, as forgotten as its authors, that literature is still *terra incognita* on the American literary map.

Lest Chicano poetry be thought of as regional only, let me hasten to ex-

[3]Felipe de Ortego y Gasca, "Which Southwestern Literature and Culture in the English Classroom?" *Arizona English Bulletin*, 13, No. 3 (April, 1971), 15-17.

[4]Gaspar de Villagrá, *History of New Mexico*, trans. Gilberto Espinosa (Los Angeles: The Quivira Society, 1933).

[5]For these accounts see *Spanish Explorers in the Southern United States 1528-1543*, Frederick W. Hodge and Theodore H. Lewis (New York: Barnes & Noble, 1965); and *Spanish Exploration in the Southwest 1542-1706*, ed. H. E. Bolton (New York: Barnes & Noble, 1967).

plain that until World War II this may have been the case but that it is no longer. I say "may have been" because we do not yet have evidence of Chicanos writing poetry, say, in New England, the Middle Atlantic states, the Old South, the Midwest, the upper Rocky Mountain region, and the Northwest before World War II. The great migrations of Chicanos to those areas did not begin until after the immigration of Mexicans into the United States during and following the Mexican Revolution of 1910-1921. This momentous migration was to have a profound effect upon the population patterns of Chicanos.[6] The Chicago communities of Chicanos, for example, date from this time, communities which created a highly charged Chicano culture that was to stretch across the whole of the Great Lakes crescent—from Minnesota to Pennsylvania. Estimates suggest that three million Chicanos are to be found today in communities like Northfield (Minnesota), Racine (Wisconsin), Harvey (Illinois), South Bend (Indiana), Lorrain (Ohio), and Midland (Pennsylvania).[7] While a majority of Chicanos live in the five southwestern states of California, Arizona, New Mexico, Colorado, and Texas, Chicanos have established communities in every state in the union—including Hawaii and Alaska. They may be small communities, only a handful of people, or they may be communities identified, as Jewish American communities are identified, not as a physical entity but as a body of individuals sharing an ancient culture. Thus there are Chicano poets everywhere in the United States. Some, like Tino Villanueva, in Boston, are originally from the Southwest; but many more are now second-generation Bostonians.

A perusal of the *Cambridge Dictionary of American Literature* reveals no Chicano authors and none of their literary forebears. I am not speaking here about Spanish/Mexican literature, but about literary works which were written in (or pertain to) what we now consider the continental United States. And I am not suggesting that such writers as Mariano Azuela or Octavio Paz should be considered Chicano. *They* are part of that Hispanic literary heritage which Chicanos also are heirs to (as Anglos are heirs to the English tradition). What I am talking about is a distinct Chicano literature that spans five hundred years. In all that time it has been influenced (and nourished) by various sources. The works of the Spanish Colonial Period (1492-1810) were Spanish in every way. In the Mexican National Period (1810-1848), literary works of the Mexican Southwest reflected the new nationalism which severed colonial ties with the mother country. In the Period of Transition (1848-1912), Chicano literature manifested the influence of the Anglo-American presence. This influence became more pronounced during the Modern Period (1912-1960) and has achieved a rather interesting (but by no means startling) blend in the Contemporary Period (1960 to present). Perhaps in

[6] Carey McWilliams, *North From Mexico: The Spanish-Speaking People of the United States* (New York: Greenwood Press, 1968).

[7] Midwest Council of La Raza *Organizational Bulletin*, 1971.

no other genre except Chicano poetry does that blend manifest itself so dramatically, as we shall see.

In *The Well Wrought Urn*, Cleanth Brooks has responded to the question of modern poetry and what it communicates by reminding us that modern poetry "communicates whatever any other poetry communicates."[8] So, too, Chicano poetry communicates whatever any other poetry communicates. Like poetry everywhere and in all times, Chicano poetry sifts experience, preserves the continuity of a people, probes the past and ponders the future, consecrates the word in acts of language (English, Spanish, or both) to expose truths of life. Chicano poetry also strives for authenticity as it seeks to validate a Chicano perspective on the situation of its people in the larger world.[9]

In an article of some years ago I tried to trace the roots of Chicano poetry.[10] While that essay sought to shed some light on Chicano poetry, it went little beyond an exposition of how literary America had neglected Chicano writers. That was 1971—a world and a half ago, as one reckons ideological time. The intervening years have produced a host of Chicano poets whose works reflect not just the concerns of Chicano ideology but the concerns of a radical humanism whose roots stretch back to the founding fathers. The consequence is that contemporary Chicano poetry may at times be virulent in its assaults on current American mores and institutions, employing ambiguous styles in its complex revelation of existing discordancies as it pleads for liberation of the human spirit. Yet while Chicano poets like Ricardo Sánchez[11] and Sylvia Gonzales,[12] for example, share the same humanistic concerns as Robert Lowell and Sylvia Plath, as Chicano poets they are little known outside Chicano circles or coteries of Anglo aficionados. Books dealing with contemporary American poetry[13] [(A. Poulin, Jr.), the poetics of the new American poetry (Donald Allan and Warren Tallman), new voices in American poetry (David Allan Evans), the new American poetry (Donald M. Allen), and contemporary American poets (Mark Strand)] include no Chicano poets. With rare exceptions, moreover, major publishers publish little or no Chicano poetry—either in anthologies or as books by Chicano poets. Like

---

[8]Cleanth Brooks, *The Well Wrought Urn* (New York: Harcourt Brace, 1947), p. 67.

[9]Felipe de Ortego y Gasca, "Mexican American Literature," *The Nation*, 209, No. 8 (September 15, 1969), 258-59.

[10]Felipe de Ortego y Gasca, "Chicano Poetry: Roots and Writers," *Southwestern American Literature*, 2, No. 1 (Spring 1972), 8-24.

[11]Ricardo Sánchez, *Canto y Grito mi Liberación* (New York: Doubleday, 1973).

[12]Sylvia Gonzales, *La Chicana Piensa* (San Jose, Calif.: San Jose State University, 1974).

[13]A. Poulin, Jr., ed., *Contemporary American Poetry* (Boston: Houghton Mifflin, 1975); Donald Allan and Warren Tallman, eds., *Poetics of the New American Poetry* (New York: Grove Press, 1974); David Allan Evans, ed., *New Voices in American Poetry* (Cambridge, Mass: Winthrop, 1973); Donald M. Allen, ed., *The New American Poetry* (New York: Grove Press, 1960); Mark Strand, ed., *The Contemporary American Poets* (New York: World, 1972).

Sisyphus, I am back to my never-ending task: exposing the gaps in American literature.

II.

Most contemporary Chicano poetry is intensely personal. Both the acoustic and the literary relationships between the Chicano poet and his subject are intimate, fraternal. They reflect the private experiences of the poet in time and place. The metaphor of Chicano existence is woven intricately into the writing, which is to say that in order to assert a Chicano or Chicana identity, the poet marshals for us the splendor of Chicano antiquity and shows us how that antiquity bears directly on the present.

Since the Chicano Renaissance of the sixties,[14] Chicano poets have turned to pre-Columbian history for their themes. The first batch of Renaissance poets—the Quinto Sol group—drew its images and metaphors from ancient settings and origins. All things Aztec became bright and beautiful. The Aztec sun calendar became the symbol of this linkage with the past. Along with Villa and Zapata, Cuauhtemoc (Montezuma's brother and last Aztec ruler before the Spaniards) became the embodiment of ideological resistance. The loss of that world became for Chicano poets what the loss of the Golden Age became for classical Greek poets.

This seems at first in marked contrast to the thematic tradition of the older poetry. Yet much Chicano poetry of the Modern Period (1912-1960) is already marked by parallel concerns for a time long gone. "Modern" Chicano poets reveled in the glory that was Spain (in the Southwest); contemporary Chicano poets have revitalized the arcadia of the Aztecs. Both perspectives may be seen as "pastoral" but each reveals the ideological states of Chicanos across time. Before 1960 many Chicanos had conceptualized the good life as one of assimilation or one that could be revived from the ashes of the Spanish past. In 1953, for example, Aurora Lucero wrote optimistically:

> There now remains but one renaissance to be effected—the literary. With the happy accident that New Mexico possesses more traditional literary materials than any other Hispanic region it should be possible to bring about such a rebirth in the reenactment of the lovely old folk dances and in the singing of the old traditional songs.[15]

Ironically the Chicano Renaissance came into being not in relation to the traditional Spanish past (mythic as it had become) but, rather, in the wake of a growing awareness by Chicanos of their Indian identity. The Chicano

[14]Felipe de Ortego y Gasca, "The Chicano Renaissance," *Social Casework*, 52, No. 5 (May 1971), 294-307.

[15]Aurora Lucero, *Literature Folklore of the Hispanic Southwest* (San Antonio, Texas: The Naylor Company, 1953), p. 210.

Renaissance was but the manifestation—long overdue—of a people's coming of age.

The old and traditional forms of Chicano poetry were still vital: *corridos*, *coplas*, *redondillas*, all artfully wrought in the tradition of Hispanic poetry. Until 1848 the language of that poetry (in what is now the American Southwest) was Spanish. During the Period of Transition (1848-1912), Chicanos continued to write in Spanish but many like Napoleón Vallejo, for example, acquired an easy facility with the English language. By the beginning of the Modern Period (1912-1960), English had challenged Spanish as the language of Chicano poets. In 1916, one year after his death, a collection of verse entitled *Las Primicias*[16] appeared, which established Vicente Bernal (of Taos, New Mexico) as a man of "double portions." The slim volume contained poems in both Spanish and English. By and large much of the early Chicano poetry in English was imitative, in the American tradition of the time, just as Chicano poetry in Spanish was equally imitative in the Spanish tradition.

In the thirties Chicano poetry was scarce in print but both *LULAC News* and *Alianza* magazines published Chicano verse. One *ubi sunt* verse by Robert Félix Salazar (whose poems appeared in *Esquire*), is a polemic about the Hispanic pioneers of the United States.[17] These pastoral poems were meant to give Chicanos not only pride about their cultural heritage but pride in being Americans.

The most important poet of the Modern Period (1912-1960) was Fray Angélico Chávez, still a U.S. Army Chaplain when his *Eleven Lady-Lyrics and Other Poems*[18] was published in 1945. The collection is about and dedicated to "ladies" such as the Lady of Lidice, the Lady of Peace, María Stella, Mary, the Sistine Madonna, Ruth, Esther, and the Lyric-Lady of Gerard Manley Hopkins. The poetry is sharp and brittle, crackling with the articulate anxieties of a "man of God" at war. In 1948, Chávez displayed the full range of his poetic voice in *The Single Rose*.[19] In one evocative spiritual love poem he wrote:

> The love I love is not like one,
> it is, a Rose.
> Under the sun
> or over it none other grows
> More white and ruddy, roseate surer,
> more petal-felt,
> rose-attared purer,
> Nowhere, not even Eden, dwelt
> such loveliness, its essence sum

[16]Vicente Bernal, *Las Primicias* (Dubuque, Iowa: Dubuque College, 1916).

[17]Roberto Félix Salazar, "The Other Pioneers," *LULAC News*, July 1939, p. 32.

[18]Fray Angélico Chávez, *Eleven Lady-Lyrics and Other Poems* (Paterson, N. J.: St. Anthony Guild Press, 1945).

[19]Fray Angélico Chávez, *The Single Rose* (Santa Fe, New Mexico: Los Santos Bookshop, 1948).

of all delight
that spiritdom
and flesh and flower could unite.

However hard Chicano poets struggled to find their voices, many of them had no alternative but, as in this instance, to write either in a language whose code transmitted alien images or in a language considered alien in the context of their national environment.

The Chicano Renaissance of the sixties changed all that. Chicano writers came to realize that the only outlets for their works would be those they created for themselves. In the process, they cast off the sometimes meretricious identification with the Spanish literary tradition foisted on them by Anglo American society because of its preference for things European. More Chicano poets started writing in Spanish again; many switched back and forth from English to Spanish; but many, like Alberto Urista (Alurista), developed a unique combination of both English and Spanish in what may be called a binary line, that is, a line of poetry in which Spanish and English are mixed in utterances using either language's syntactic structure. For example, one of Alurista's poems reads as follows:

Mis ojos hinchados
   flooded with lágrimas
de bronce
melting on the cheek bones
of my concern
   razgos indígenas
the scars of history on my face
   and the veins of my body
that aches
   vomito sangre
y lloro libertad'
   I do not ask for freedom
I am freedom.[20]

A fundamental question in any discussion of Chicano poetry pertains to the relationship between literature and culture. This question assumes that Chicano culture produces a particular kind of literature particularized further by the demotic language of Chicanos. Thus, to comprehend Chicano poetry one must be open to language, free of preconceived notions of what is correct or standard in language usage in Spanish or English. One must be open to the frank utterances of frustration and alienation:

smile out the revolu,
burn now your anguished hurt,

crush now our desecrators,
chingue su madre the u.s.a.

[20]Alurista, "Mis ojos hinchados," in *El Espejo-The Mirror: Selected Mexican American Literature* (Berkeley, Cal: Quinto Sol Publications, 1969), p. 172.

> burn, cabrones enraviados,
> burn las calles de amerika[21]
>
> — Ricardo Sánchez

But the heart of Chicano poetry lies in the imperative cry "I shall endure, I will endure!" which Joaquin utters at the end of Rodolfo Gonzales's stirring lyric poem "I am Joaquin." As the Chicano everyman, Joaquin is

> Lost in a world of confusion,
> Caught up in a whirl of a
>   gringo society,
> Confused by the rules,
> Scorned by attitudes,
> Suppressed by manipulations,
> And destroyed by modern society.[22]

Faced with a very real existential dilemma, Joaquin must choose between "the paradox of/Victory of the spirit" or existing "in the grasp/of American social neurosis, sterilization of the soul/and a full stomach." It is, in effect, a choice between cultural apostasy or cultural loyalty. Joaquin opts for *La Raza,* becoming the enduring spirit of the Chicano soul buffeted by alien winds in the land of his fathers, where he is considered a stranger by hostile Anglos.

There is anguish and frustration in the vision of Chicano poets, but there is also a fiery determination to forge their own identity. In "Aztec Angel," for example, Luis Omar Salinas glorifies the beauty of the Aztec mother and child:

> I am an Aztec angel
> offspring
> of a woman
> who was beautiful.[23]

There is also a determination to change the hearts and minds of Anglo-Americans with an appeal for brotherhood. In the poem "The Chicano Manifesto," Delgado writes:

> there is one thing I wish
> you would do for us,
> in all your dealings with us,
> in all your institutions
> that affect our lives,
> deal with us as you openly claim you can,
> justly...with love...with dignity,

---

[21]Ricardo Sánchez, "Smile out the revolu," *Canto y Grito mi Liberación* (New York: Double-day, 1973), p. 40.

[22]Rodolfo Gonzales, *I Am Joaquin* (New York: Bantam, 1972), p. 110.

[23]Luis Omar Salinas, *Crazy Gypsy* (Orígenes: La Raza Studies, Fresno, Calif.: Fresno State College, 1970), pp. 50-51.

correct your own abuses on la raza
for your own sake and not for ours
so you can have some peace of mind.[24]

Although the spirit of contemporary Chicano poetry may be considered revolutionary, its intellectual emphasis is on reason, its theme the quest:

It is not the great plumed serpent
that we seek in the dark and lonely
niches of the street; we seek the mysteries
of who we came to be: victims
of the prison of the skin.[25]

—Felipe Campos-Méndez

This same quest, be it for identity or for the understanding of lived experience, characterizes the work of two excellent (and radically different) modern poets, Raúl Salinas and Gary Soto.

In that same essay of 1971 I suggested that Chicano poetry would soon shift away from mainstream American poetry to a distinctly new poetics embracing the politics and sociology of poetry as well as new linguistic parameters. It was all too clear then that the aim of Chicano poetry was to identify the enemy, praise the people, and promote the revolution. My view now is that Chicano poetry has probably moved past that highpoint of the decade from 1967 to 1976. Hard-hitting "movement poetry" has mined the thematic vein of ills visited upon Chicanos by Anglo-America. This is not to say that those ills are no longer with us or that the spirit of Chicano poetry is no longer revolutionary. They are; it is. But the shift is now towards artistic competence. The poetry of social protest prevalent in the sixties and early seventies has given way to a poetry of introspection and a poetry that will continue to reflect for us not just the splendor of our antiquity but the entire range of the Chicano experience. The poetic expressions of the Chicano Renaissance have given us all a better image of who we were.

I now see five critical points of departure in the organization of Chicano poetry: the nihilistic view of liberal iconoclasts, the nostalgic view of mythopoetic romantics, the canonical view of revolutionary nationalists, the Olympian view of metaphysical esthetics, and the visionary perspective of eclectic pragmatists. These are not absolute categories, of course. But most contemporary Chicano poets may be described by one or several of these categories. All contribute to our understanding of the Chicano experience. All assume that being Chicano remains a source of inestimable pride.

---

[24]Abelardo Delgado, "The Chicano Manifesto," in *25 Pieces of a Chicano Mind* (Denver: Barrio Publications, 1970), pp. 34-35.
[25]Felipe Campos-Méndez, "Hijos de la Chicangada," *Nosotros,* 1 no. 2 (February 1, 1971), 9.

Alurista's Poetics: The Oral, The Bilingual, The Pre-Columbian

by Tomás Ybarra-Frausto

I

Alurista (Alberto Urista) is a seminal figure in the contemporary florescence of Chicano poetry. During the tumultuous phase of the Chicano Movement (1965—1969) his creative participation was one of action within the struggle. Alurista helped project the role of the poet as public performer and the poem as public conscience. His experiments with bilingualism and the incorporation of indigenous themes in his work became points of departure for other poets. As a philosopher and ideologist he helped formulate the "Plan de Aztlán" and theoretical notions such as the concept of "Amerindia" which became basic to the nationalist phase of the Chicano Movement.

Alurista's early poems were published in barrio newspapers or mimeographed and passed out during the hectic round of the mid-1960s—picketing, sitting in, walking out, and organizing for community control, for student services, for justice on farmworkers' issues, and for total Chicano self-determination. A direct participant in the social upheavals of the period, Alurista was constantly surrounded by diverse groups of Chicanos, ranging from rural *campesinos* to urban *pachucos,* from recently arrived *mejicanos* to loyal regionalists such as *manitos* or *tejanos.* Each group expressed its particular experience in a particular variation of Spanish or English, or in creative combinations and transformations of these languages. The rich cadences, unique vocabularies, and other expressive resources must have attuned and inspired the poet to explore the poetic possibilities of this compelling multilingual actuality. Alurista began at this time an experiment with poetry in various bilingual modes which he and other Chicano poets would continue to develop. This overture has renovated Chicano poetry by creating fresh images and metaphors and allowing new rhythms to be heard.

In addition to technical innovations in language, Alurista has helped es-

"Alurista's Poetics: The Oral, the Bilingual, the Pre-Columbian" by Tomás Ybarra-Frausto. This article appears for the first time in this volume. It is used by permission of the author.

tablish another significant dimension of contemporary Chicano poetry: the emphasis on poetry as spoken rather than privately read. The Chicano poet writes for an audience that is not predominantly a reading audience, and on the whole has little inclination to value the printed word. This public's educational level does not predispose it to habitual reading, especially of poetry. Chicano poets assume that their audience will not ponder individual lines, savoring the formal composition by reading and rereading. A Chicano audience is more likely to hear the poem, perhaps only once, and must comprehend it as it is sung or spoken. This focus on public comprehension calls for rhythmic patterning, a strong narrative line, and frequent use of the vernacular to reinforce "orality." Such poetry represents an attempt to reverse the tradition of private poets who elaborate a personal hermetic world in their verse. Alurista by contrast stresses the communal nature of poetry with an outward social thrust.

Although it is impossible to be sure that Alurista is the first contemporary Chicano poet to compose poems from selective mixtures of Spanish, English, and "Chicanismos," he is certainly one of the pioneers in this unique form of expression. The fluid and intricate possibilities of linguistic hybridism are deftly exploited by Alurista and become a striking characteristic of his poetry. Furthermore, he moves beyond bilingual experiments with poetic form to establish a bicultural content. Forging new images and a new vocabulary from the confluence of cultures which nurtures the Chicano experience, he sings of "the radiance of our quilted heritage." In his poems, pre-Columbian images relate to barrio symbols. Culture heroes like Quetzalcoatl, Tizoc, and Zapata coexist with Pachucos, Vatos Locos, and contemporary pop culture stars like Jimi Hendrix. Verbal portraits of archetypal Chicanos from the barrio contrast with caricatures of "the man," Mr. Jones, and the sterile "gabacho" society. A constant juxtaposition of words, images, and metaphors from Anglo-American and Mexican sources which have been incorporated into Chicano life create a rich bicultural effect.

II

Alurista has so far published three books of poetry: *Floricanto en Aztlán* (1971), *Nationchild Plumaroja* (1972), and *Timespace Huracán* (1976).[1] Each is related to the particular thrust of the Chicano Movement on which it comments and to which it is bound.

Floricanto en Aztlán records a change in consciousness induced by the campesino movement led by César Chávez. In the summer of 1968, during

[1]Alurista, *Floricanto en Aztlán* (Los Angeles: University of California, 1971); *Nationchild Plumaroja* (San Diego, California: Toltecas en Aztlán Publications, 1972); *Timespace Huracán* (Albuquerque, New Mexico: Pajarito Publications, 1976).

the historic march from Delano to Sacramento, Alurista recalls standing on a hill and watching the long line of farmworkers and supporters as they trod the steaming asphalt of the highway chanting and singing, led by fluttering red and black thunderbird flags with images of the Virgen de Guadalupe held aloft:

> It was the farmworkers who brought Chicanos to the forefront of national consciousness. As I watched the pilgrimage from Delano, I said to myself, that man Chávez is either a fool, a fanatic or a truly wise man. And very soon his genius was apparent.[2]

The campesino movement, while drawing on spiritual and mythic impulses, was firmly rooted in historical and material reality. Fighting for better working conditions for farmworkers, it often incorporated religious attitudes of non-violence and universal brotherhood into its programs for social action. Its dual nature is well articulated in the *Plan de Delano*, which called for pilgrimage, penitence, and revolution.

This duality, incorporating systems of belief as well as action, was very appealing to Alurista, who at that time was immersed in the study of pre-Columbian philosophy, especially that of the Nahuas. Fascinated by a philosophic system which ran counter to many Western tenets, Alurista appropriated elements of indigenous thought into an evolving philosophy which could serve as a basis for Chicano mobilization. This linkage of indigenous thought to contemporary reality gave the Chicano Movement mythic and psychic energies that could be directed toward its political and economic goals.

Nahua concepts of poetry and art became firmly established in Alurista's poetics. Although most extant collections of pre-Columbian poetry translated into Spanish feature work of educated courtly poets,[3] Alurista chose to focus on the poetry of the people. Looking back through the millennia of aboriginal thought, he discovered in the Nahuas a collective voice:

> We should note that in contrast to European poetry written by the privileged classes and destined for the same audience, Nahuatl poetry was publicly sung, dialogued, and collectively danced as much by the nobility as by the working classes. And although much of it was written in elevated style with didactic intent, it never ceased being an object of tribal recreation and delight.[4]

From these notions, Alurista laid the framework for much contemporary Chicano poetry. Developing an idiom, collective and didactic in character, taking his vocabulary, metaphors, and allusions from pre-Columbian myth,

[2]Interview with Alurista in San Diego, California, March 24, 1977.

[3]See for example Angel María Garibay, *Historia de la Literatura Nahuatl*, 2 vols., (México: Editorial Porrúa, 1953-54), and Miguel León Portilla, *Las literaturas pre-colombinas de México* (México: Editorial Pormaca, 1964).

[4]Alurista, "La estética indígena a través del Floricanto de Nezahualcoyotl," *Revista Chicano-Riqueña*, 5, no. 2 (Spring 1977), p. 56.

experimenting with the spoken Chicano vernacular, he opened windows on
new horizons. As he began to publish in the Chicano press, to read his
poems at hundreds of rallies, and to ask for the revitalization of an indigenous Chicano world view as an antidote to the vacuous and sterile reality of
white America, he drew attention to a cultural legacy from Indo-America
which he designated as the authentic root of Chicano culture.

This root continued to nourish his imagination in his first published book,
Floricanto en Aztlán (1971). Most of the one hundred "cantos" in the collection grew out of the rich mytho-religious tradition of the Nahuatl-
speaking peoples. The linkage of Chicano actuality with indigenous
thought and culture structures the collection, which celebrates in both past
and present the regenerative force of creation itself. Just as poets perpetuate the past in the present through their songs, Chicanos are admonished
to absorb the humanitarian and spiritual values of their Indian heritage
as elements contributing, now, in the present, to a symbolic new birth. Affirmation, optimism, and joy are the dominant tones. Quetzalcoatl (god of
light and knowledge), Ometeotl (dual principle of self-creation), Tlaloc
(god of rain and vegetation), and Tonantzin (mother earth) are invoked to
underscore the emphasis on positive renewal.

Alurista's poetry is dense with figurative language through which he re-
creates a Nahua world view interpreting a metaphorical universe. What appear to be concrete details—flower and song, red tunas, quetzal feathers,
eagles and serpents, jade and precious stones—are metaphors used to express subtle abstractions based on ancient philosophical symbology. Alurista's use of parallelism also has antecedents in oral pre-Hispanic poetry
such as was recited at religious festivals. Here, for example, is a fragment
from a Nahua lyric exalting the bellicose spirit of the Aztecs:

> From where the eagles are resting,
> from where the tigers are exalted,
> the Sun is invoked.
>
> Like a shield that descends,
> so does the Sun set.
> In Mexico night is falling,
> war rages on all sides...[5]

In addition to parallel phrasing within a poem, Alurista often parallels
ideas in several poems. The following examples symbolically emphasize
the theme of survival in alien territory, through the symbols of the maguey
(cactus plant) and the seed:

...*(siembra de bronce)*	...(bronze cornfield
-perpetua Raza	—perpetual Raza
fértil abono del desierto	fertilizer of the desert

[5]Miguel León Portilla, *Pre-Columbian Literatures of Mexico* (Norman, Okla.: University of
Oklahoma Press, 1969), p. 86.

```
-crece          -grow
reproduce...    reproduce...
```

(No. 65, "to be fathers once again")

el maguey en su desierto
-even though arid-
produces tunas
let your seed turn fruit
allow the tuna of your
humanity to flourish...

(No. 18, "el maguey en el desierto")

Another device much used in Nahua compositions is the combination of two words which complement each other either because they are synonymous or because they evoke a third idea, usually a metaphor. Samples of this technique from *Floricanto en Aztlán* include *fuegopizca*, *brotafuego*, *sangrerojapiel* and *genterazabroncepiel* ("peoplerazabronzeskin").

Going beyond stylistic echoes, Alurista also evokes modern barrio manifestations of ancient themes. This fusion of contemporary life with mythical events sharpens appreciation of both the indigenous heritage and the present challenge. In the poem "los tripas y los condes," for example, he compares barrio gangs, such as *tripas* and *condes,* with ancient warrior societies to give an extended historical dimension to the idea of struggle and self-sacrifice. The implication is that a spirit of rebellion has been maintained in Chicano barrios from time immemorial:

"los tripas" y "los condes"	"Los tripas y "los condes"
"los tequilas" y "los coloraos"	"los tequilas" y "los coloraos"
today in the barrio	today in the barrio
los clanes de mi gente	the clans of my people
incarnate gangs of caciques	incarnate gangs of caciques
con plumas y navajas	with plumes and knives
caballeros águilas y tigres	eagle and tiger warriors
los pumas y los cocodrilos	the pumas and the crocodiles
los clanes de mi gente...	the clans of my people
(No. 50, "los tripas y los	
condes")	

The confluence of pre-Columbian and modern themes is not always used to spur Chicano activism. Sometimes its function is to question the modern loss of venerable customs. For instance, the poem "must be the season of the witch" uses one of the basic Mexican myths, that of "la llorona" (the weeping woman), to project a chilling loss of identity in the modern Chicano. The myth dramatizes an earth mother who wanders aimlessly in search of her children. Many of them, however, have been cut off from their heritage and can no longer draw sustenance from her:

```
   ...la llorona
   she lost her children
      and she cries
   en las barrancas of industry
      her children
   devoured by computers
   and the gears
   must be the season of the witch
   I hear huesos crack
   in pain
      y lloros...
   must be the season of the witch
   la bruja llora
   sus hijos sufren; sin ella
                    (no. 26, "must be the season of the witch")
```

As noted earlier, Alurista has been a pioneer in the alternating use of languages. Sometimes a poem is written entirely in English (No. 57, "sacred robe"), sometimes entirely in Spanish (No. 73, "cantar de ranas viejas," the chant of ancient frogs). The majority, however, exploit both languages, creating exciting possibilities as demonstrated by this fragment of the poem titled "wheat paper cucarachas":

```
   wheat paper cucarachas
   de papel trigo
   y la cosecha del sol
   winged in autumn
   de vuelo al sol
   y las alas de trigo
   a volar
   en la primavera
   spring of youthful bronze
   melting in the lava of our blood
   la cucaracha muere
   y muerde el polvo
   powder wheat
   de atole con el dedo
   and they bleed
      crushed by florsheims
```

In seemingly chaotic and random fashion, the poem unravels a series of images. The impact comes from understanding the bilingual and bicultural context to which the images are related.

wheat paper cucarachas
de papel de trigo
y la cosecha del sol   The hidden meaning here lies in understanding that
                                cucaracha does not literally refer to a cockroach. "Roach"
                                is barrio slang for a hand-rolled marijuana cigarette.

Thus the *cucaracha de papel de trigo* is marijuana wrapped in wheat paper. Swiftly, the image is extended so that *trigo* becomes wheat, a crop grown with plenty of sunlight: la cosecha del sol."

winged in autumn
de vuelo al sol
y las alas de trigo
a volar
en la primavera
spring of youthful bronze
melting in the lava of our blood   The principle in this section is the interplay of opposites. Autumn is related to the migratory flight of insects juxtaposed to the moving yet passionate blood of impetuous youth. "Lava" unites both images since it is destructive and yet powerful in its flow.

la cucaracha muere
y muerde el polvo   The key element here is the ironic commentary on the death of the cucaracha. "Muerde el polvo" is a direct translation of "bite the dust," which in itself is a euphemism for death. This brings back the initial image of the cigarette, the "roach" crushed to the ground.

powder wheat de
atole con el dedo   Powdered wheat brings to mind *atole* (a mush made from crushed wheat). However, this positive image is extended to a popular Mexican *refrán* with negative connotations: "Ya no queremos atole con el dedo" (we no longer want to be spoon fed, i.e., tokenism)

and they bleed crushed
by florsheims   Now the literal meaning of cucaracha, "a small insect often found in the ghetto," is reintroduced. Here the image of "cucaracho" also suggests young people, "los cucarachos," whose self-esteem is also crushed by consumer products such as Florsheim shoes which serve as a symbol for the dominant culture.

The image is liberated by exploring the connotative and denotative domains of two languages. This is one of the major formal contributions of Alurista's bilingual poetry.

III

Floricanto en Aztlán, published in 1971, responds mainly to the farmworkers' thrust within "El Movimiento" from 1965 to 1967. An introduction to an evolving poetics, it establishes a cultural kinship between modern

Chicano life and past indigenous values, explores and validates bilingual expression, and seeks to unite social concerns with artistic practice. By 1968, Alurista had pared down his poetic creed to one ideal: "Poetry is for the transformation of consciousness." His activism shifted from the farmworkers to focus on the Chicano Student Movement in San Diego, California.

> Those were the days when we were moving in the schools developing Chicano studies, organizing brown berets, organizing the moratorium against the war, organizing for welfare rights, establishing free clinics in the communities.[6]

It was a time of mass activity, a period when many Chicanos approached revolutionary ideals through practice. The aim was to act and then articulate. Alurista began teaching in the Chicano Studies program at San Diego State University. During the same period, student uprisings in Paris and Berkeley and the massacre of students at Tlatelolco Plaza in Mexico City fed the turbulence of Chicano student groups. Alurista, activist and artist, confronted a key question posed in moments of social agitation — how to be true to his art while meeting the social demands of the historical moment.

> Where do we begin?...with the rifle or with the pen? With the armed revolt for the popular take-over of the Yankee state or with the cultural revolution for organization of the popular revolutionary conscience of the Chicano peoples north of Mexico. The first alternative is heroic suicide. The second is protracted (long-range) insurrection.[7]

Looking back on a process of resistance by Chicanos during almost a century and a half, Alurista joined with many other writers in reaffirming the central role of the artist in social struggle. The preservation and renewal of a literary tradition were seen as insufficient; the poet must be actively involved in the battles against oppression and inequality.

A landmark contribution toward defining the ideological thrust of the Chicano Movement was the proclamation "El Plan Espiritual de Aztlán," written by Alurista during the first Chicano Youth Liberation Conference held at the Crusade for Justice in Denver, Colorado, in 1969. "El Plan Espiritual de Aztlán," which put forth the notion of a material, cultural, and psychic identity for the Chicano, stresses spiritual values derived from a return to nature. Validating cultural permanence rather than change, it focuses on traditional features as core elements of the Chicano experience. Essentially it posits a program of action that fails to respond to immediate and tangible social conditions. Nonetheless, the proclamation of "El Plan Espiritual de Aztlán" served as a catalyst for discussions on the role of the artist in "El Movimiento."

By 1971, the year of *Floricanto,* Alurista had entered a third phase center-

[6]Interview with Alurista in San Diego, California, March 24, 1977.
[7]Alurista, "The Chicano Cultural Revolution," *De Colores,* 1, no. 1 (Winter 1973), 23-33.

ing on identification with Indian experience. He aided in the organization of a center for cultural workers called "Toltecas en Aztlán" in San Diego. Its aims included study of indigenous wisdom in art, music, literature, and life, but also the provision of "cultural guerrillas," people trained to use art as a weapon in the struggle for social change. Experimenting with an indigenous lifestyle, Alurista also experimented with poetry to be sung, chanted, and danced. An important influence in his developing poetics was his participation with Juan Felipe Herrera and Mario Aguilar in a theater/music group named "Servidores del Arbol de la Vida" (Guardians of the Tree of Life). This ensemble attempted to re-create Indian chant and ritual singing and dance forms in a modern context. While maintaining a reverent attitude toward the spiritual intent of their performance, they wove a secular sociopolitical commentary into their texts. A key assumption in many of these song-poems is that spiritual and material realities must be fused:

no le aflojen a la lucha	don't give up the struggle
transformando l 'energía	transforming the energy
liberando la conciencia	liberating the consciousness
cultivando la materia	cultivating matter
no negamos la energía	we do not negate energy
ni negamos la materia	nor matter
pos las dos en su dialéctica	for it is both in their dialectic
nos entregan vida nueva...	which give us new life...

Playing the conch, a modern adaptation of a pre-Conquest instrument, and experimenting with sound, Alurista developed a style of recitation which is a cross between Gregorian chant and monotone. The intent is to locate poetry not only in the mind but also in the viscera.

IV

During the intense period of experimentation between 1968-1973, Alurista elaborated a poetic credo that reflects the social genesis of his art: "Poetry captures movimiento, conciencia y con medida." His movement was increasingly toward chanted plainsong, his consciousness was rooted in Indio-American struggles, and his rhythm was based on natural breath cadences. The *cantos* are to be read as sustained cycles, even though they are printed as individual poems in his second collection, *Nationchild Plumaroja*, appearing in 1973. This book reflects two of Alurista's perennial sources of inspiration, the spiritualism of the native people's movement in the United States and the political ideology of international socialism. The poet continues his reinterpretation of indigenous culture, shifting attention from the militaristic-theocratic society of the Nahuas to the scientific-aesthetic formulations of the Mayas.

Nationchild Plumaroja is divided into five sections, or *katuns* (five units of twenty), derived from the Mayan mathematical system. Each unit uses animal and flower symbols to signify the mood and the emotional coloration that should be assumed by the reader or interpreter of individual *katuns.* All the poems in the "Conejo" *katun,* for example, are to be read in a fast tempo, whereas the poems in the "Xochitl" or "Nopal" *katuns* are to be chanted in a more reflective, lyrical style. Each symbol taken from nature — *flores, venados, serpientes, conejos, nopales,* — denotes a particular type of *energía.* This energy is the actualization of thought as idea. Once the idea is transformed through the process of creation it has the capacity to incite concrete action. The source of this energy resides in the self:

> turn on
> to yourselves
> cause carnales, carnalas
> there just ain't
> no carga
> or righteous drug
> as the self...   ("turn on")

The shift toward introspection in many of the poems of *Nationchild Plumaroja* can be seen in such titles as "I have found my flesh," "mi mind," "i like to sleep," "i had chilaquiles," and "face your fears carnal." Their theme is that individual integration can be a path to a larger cultural wholeness and meaning. Individual consolidation must precede the more complex philosophical alignment with the indigenous inhabitants of America who share with the Chicano people a common language, a common spirit, and a living unity of the heart. In the sterile world of "robots y tragamonedas" the reader is incited to transform time into a plow, to affirm those values which negate "progress" in the sense of material gain:

> ...take the time to be born
> take time by the neck
> turn it into an arado
> cultivate el maíz de nuestra
> identidad indígena
> a la vida, a la muerte
> al nacimiento de un nopal...   ("come down my cheek raza roja")

Time and again, nature is seen as the source of ultimate strength and wisdom. Only in harmonious coexistence with it can one escape the "frigidaire of pestilence" which is life in North America, a wasteland "shrouded with green money and shiny guns of frozen death."

Bilingual exploration continues to engross Alurista in his collection. One noteworthy feature is the creation of neologisms from ordinary words whose explicit meanings are transformed. Examples would include *chili-maíz, razasol, adobecorazón*, and many others. Intensification of the link to ancestral memory is projected by images that merge elements of Mexican culture such as "a people glazed in barro," "our joys in the Quetzal pride," and "the comal of our heart warms our blood."

Steadily working to bring poetry into the area of performance, Alurista envisions many of the poems in *Nationchild Plumaroja* as near eruptions of song. Old bardic devices of chant and simple rhythmic repetition emphasize melody and syncopation, pushing language into the realm of music:

> tuning flower tones
>   guitarra sings in serenata
> the twanging, twanging, tone
>   to tablas tuned
> the thumping of a rhythm shoe
> tapping, tapping, taconeo
> y latido de la sangre
> en el corazón explota...   ("tuning flower tones")

The "sounding" of the poem acquires new emphasis, the ideal being to bring composition and performance together in a single improvised event.

The technical innovations in the collection did not dampen Alurista's central concern with writing poetry which was political, partisan, and committed. In Chicano communities this period saw the escalation of protests against the war in Vietnam and support for the Native American movement in its takeover of Alcatraz and its struggle at Wounded Knee. Culminating the activism of the time, the Chicano Moratorium against the Vietnam War in Los Angeles on August 29, 1970, ended tragically with the assassination of Rubén Salazar, a prominent Chicano journalist. Alurista responded to these events with poems in which political consciousness runs deep; yet their exhortations remain mannered and rhetorical. On only a few occasions, as in the poems "Trópico de Ceviche" and "danza leonina," are denunciatory elements fused with flights of the imagination to create felt designs of insight and emotion.

In the evolution of Alurista's poetry, *Nationchild Plumaroja* is a work of synthesis and ongoing dialectic in which he continued to experiment with bilinguality and with the linking of indigenous themes to Chicano actuality. The poet calls for collective action even while the poetic voice turns inward toward a more personal tonality as experienced in the self. Perhaps the most significant breakthrough is a decided emphasis on oral performance in the invigorating new forms of chants, songs, and incantations. This oral impulse adds new dynamism and coloration to words as articulated sound.

V

Issued in 1976, *Timespace Huracán*, Alurista's third book of poetry, offers both a synthesis of previous thematic concerns and a new departure. The new effort is to return poetry to a kind of collective articulation. Previously, the act of "sounding" the poem arose from visionary, sacramental intent, as in the performances of the "Servidores del Arbol de la Vida" (Guardians of the Tree of Life). Poetry was chanted and forays made in the use of verse as prayer and incantation. Now, in *Timespace Huracan*, the emphasis falls between the oral and the visual. Among its definable features are numerous experiments with form, including shaped poetry, serial poems, prose poems, and haiku. The dislocation of voice from written sign is expressed by the almost equal division of text between poetry meant to be read silently and that which is to be performed orally. An emphasis on "speaking," "sounding," or "singing" is evident from the nomenclature assigned to the various sections. The collection opens with fifteen "tunas alabanzas" (cactus fruit chants), progresses through three sections of meditative poems (meant to be chanted), and ends with six "songs for dawn." In these experiments with voicing or singing the poem, Alurista is again attempting, as we have seen, to revive an indigenous, tribal orality. In some poems, the written text serves merely as a guide for vocal elaboration and embellishment during performance. Many of the short haiku-like poems, for example, can be seen as vocal scores in which the text is to be declaimed with melodic variations. Some poems like "Petra/logan 74," "Corrido Proletario," "Venadito terrenal," and "What for?" are actual song lyrics. In allowing the poem to be carried by the voice, Alurista makes extensive use of rhythmic patterning and acoustic effects, as in this fragment from the poem "cuetes chispas":

> tuna
>   retoña raíz
> tuna
>   retoña rama
> raíz tuna rama tuna
>   raíz
> tuna retoña tuna
> fruto verdadero
>   rama

As a songman, Alurista recognizes the physical basis of the poem within him. The articulation of sound springs from the imagination, creating the lines of the poem in direct relation to breath patterns. This is "minimal" poetry requiring maximal involvement by the reader-recipient. The poet's techniques are not limited to verbal maneuvers, but operate also through visual signs, shapes, and images. Reaching back to a primitive graphism where the glyph had the power of the thing represented, Alurista makes some poems take the form of their content. The typographical innovations dislocate the print, enhancing the word with the same potent power ascribed to the graffiti, or *placas*, scrawled on barrio walls. Although formal experimentation takes precedence, this collection carries a vision which has infused much of Alurista's work: a Utopian vision of America in which indigenous spiritual values are to supersede the dominant reality. In the modern world the individual has become isolated:

> each
>   alone
> stands
>   lost
> reed
>   hollow
> heart

This splintered, fragmented being can only become whole, the poet says, when he begins a quest for his "raíz, vereda, y fruto" (root, path, and fruit). "Raíz" is linkage with the totality of indigenous heritage; "vereda" is a personal code of ethics and morality built on the spiritual values of Amerindia; "fruto" is personal integration and connection of the self with others and with nature. Man, situated as he is between heaven and earth, must unify with both:

corazones/rostros	hearts/faces
Amerindios	Amerindian
sueños	dreams
tiran raíces en los suelos	casting roots in the earth
tienden ramas en los cielos	spreading branches in the sky

The polarity of the earth and the sky becomes the operative dialectic in *Timespace Huracán*. Earthbound creatures must find a point of stasis, "balance terrenal con armonía celular" (terrestrial balance and cellular harmony). In conjunction, the poems chart an odyssey through different timespaces searching for this unity between man and nature. The first poem in the collection is situated in Tijuana. Next we travel to rural New Mexico and finally to Texas. In each location the landscape is foregrounded, presenting truths embedded in the "vientre orgánico" (organic matrix). The timeless landscape full of the singing, chirping, and calling voices of birds, frogs, and other four-legged creatures makes a majestic "melodía adentrada" (internalized melody) that one must decipher and learn to sing oneself. It is the song of the earth that embodies eternal truths and yields a "retoño que perdura" (an enduring bloom). The wind, water, and sun are balm to a scarred, nonproductive environment. Only by cultivating within the laws of nature can truth be harvested.

Though in *Timespace Huracán* the subject matter is the same as in Alurista's previous collections, the language is more lyrical, more lapidary, and more colorful. Explorations into visual/verbal and written/oral communication surface as an attempt to reinvent and redefine the word and the sign. The central metaphors giving form, origin, and foundation continue to flow from indigenous sources. Alurista's recovery of these sources was not an isolated phenomenon but part of a pervasive validation of pre-Columbian heritage as an integral part of the Chicano Movement. At its best, this linkage with a non-European cultural tradition provided abundant mythic and symbolic structures for artists, writers, and intellectuals. At its worst, it inspired a romantic "neo-indigenism" designed to make barrio vatos think of themselves as descendants of Aztec nobility without focusing on the basic realities of pre-Hispanic life. Furthermore, the glorification of a remote past tended to obscure the historical contradictions of Indio-Chicano relationships within the United States.

One of the articles which instigated this indigenous trend was "The Historical and Intellectual Presence of the Mexican Americans," published by Octavio Romano in 1969, in which he stated:

> symbolically, the Indian penetrates throughout, and permeates, major aspects of Mexican-American life, and hardly a barrio exists that does not have someone who is nicknamed "El Indio" or "Los Indios." ... On occasion los matachines still make their Indian appearance in churches, and Aztec legends still pictorially tell and retell their stories in barrio living rooms, in kitchens, in bars, restaurants, tortillerías and Chicano newspapers. The stern face of Don Benito Juárez still peers out of books, still surveys living rooms and still takes a place of prominence in many Sociedad Mutualista halls and in the minds of men throughout the Southwest. Small wonder then, that several hundred years after the totally indigenous existence of Mexico, reference is still made to these roots and origins in the Mexican-American community. ... The Indian is root and origin, past and present, virtually timeless in his barrio manifestations—a timeless symbol of opposition to cultural imperialism.[8]

Like Romano, other Chicano intellectuals strove to uncover and validate their authentic cultural roots, which they sensed at base to be indigenous. They turned to Mexico and the ideas of such thinkers as Alfonso Caso, Angel Garibay, Octavio Paz, and Miguel León-Portilla. From these and similar sources that researched and promoted Mexico's pre-Hispanic past, converting it into a golden age comparable to the Greco-Latin splendor of

[8]Octavio Romano, "The Historical and Intellectual Presence of Mexican Americans," *El Grito*, 2, no. 2 (Winter 1969). For other important statements of this Chicano *indigenismo* see Miguel Méndez, "Tata Casehua," *El Grito*, 2, no. 2 (Winter 1969); Andrés Segura, "Continuidad de la tradición filosófica nahuatl en las danzas de Concheros," *El Cuaderno*, 3, no 1 (Winter 1973); Ysidro Ramón Macías, "Nuestros Antepasados y el Movimiento," *Aztlán*, 5, nos. 1 and 2 (Spring and Fall 1974). In poetry, Rafael Jesús González is both a prominent investigator of pre-Columbian sources and, in his own right, a poet whose work embodies an indigenous world-view.

the Old World, Chicanos garnered aesthetic and cultural elements. Poets like Jesús Rafael González incorporated traditional mythology and themes into their poetry and avidly investigated pre-Columbian literatures. Stan Padilla and other painters featured Indian motifs and design elements from tribal sources, and *teatro* groups performed *actos* based on the rituals and legends of the Toltecs, Mayas, and Aztecs. Quetzalcoatl was often evoked as the supreme exponent of a humane philosophy of life. The exaltation of pre-Cortesian Indian culture was significant in awakening Chicano artists to explore and incorporate material from this rich patrimony.

Yet although the glories of past civilizations could provide ideals, the contemporary situation of indigenous people in Mexico and the Southwest was the result of domination, conquest, and subjugation. The integration of both currents—the validation of indigenous values and a critical evaluation of the modern role of the Indian—became, as we have seen, Alurista's major concern. His three collections of poetry all share in the exploration of an indigenous consciousness which is often formulated in terms of opposition between a decaying and corrupt Anglo-American culture and an ascending and unsullied culture of "la raza." Portrayals of "White America" are likely to be satiric. One of the harshest of them depicts the white man as a mute and lifeless scarecrow fluttering about with little dignity and no hope. "Paja" ("Straw"), describes not merely his physical exterior but also the weakness of his spirit and intellect.

> hombre de paja
> frigid in the fields
> scarecrow
> blind figurine...
>
> de paja el cerebro
> de paja su piel
> ojos de paja
> de paja el corazón
> ("Cuervo Chicano")

Such abject and pitiful figurines belong to the "klan del penny amerikkkano," a vast army of people whose supreme deity is the dollar and the things money can buy. As a counter view, *Floricanto en Aztlán, Nationchild Plumaroja*, and *Timespace Huracán* create a structure of recollection where cultural heroes, mythology, and values from the Chicano's indigenous heritage are evoked as sources of pride and identity. The poems chart a spiritual journey aimed at achieving an organic, almost pantheistic, relationship between man and nature. Like a majestic hymn to the earth, the poetry parallels the natural cycle of abundance, erosion, death, and regeneration with the historical experience of "la chicanada," endlessly repeating patterns of struggle and survival.

Alurista's role as initiator, activator, and literary model for Chicano poets and prose writers of the mid-1960s is inestimable. His commitment to art and his partisan politics helped define the dual task of poets within "El Movimiento": to participate as intellectuals in the struggles for social change in Chicano communities and to remain responsible to their art by elaborating techniques and approaches to reality that, in their aesthetic challenge, awaken, maintain, and enhance human alternatives and possibilities.

The Other Voice of Silence: Tino Villanueva

by Juan Bruce-Novoa

True art is the continual invention of new languages to reach
an as yet unexpressed truth.

JUAN GARCIA PONCE

Tino Villanueva's *Hay Otra Voz Poems (There Is Another Voice
Poems)*[1] clearly exemplifies the extent to which Chicano literature is a response to chaos. As I have stated elsewhere,[2] the thematic-structural para-
digm of Chicano literature is this: chaotic discontinuity threatens vital life
images —> recuperation of images —> continuity in literary space. In
Villanueva, death's agents, especially time, move man toward disappearance, each present instant being a crisis point requiring his personal
affirmation of being or his silent loss of it. Future and past extend from the
present; thus wasted "nows" condemn one eventually to total disappearance
with no memorable historical presence. Self-affirmation can occur through
any positive molding of the moment, but the most effective means is speech.
Silent moments slip into oblivion with their voiceless victims. Chaos is
eventual disappearance, but it attacks through steady erosion now. When
man's physical presence fades, only images not dependent on the physical
will survive to maintain that presence, as in literature, oral or written.
A simple solution might be to speak up, but one risks raising empty noise

---

"The Other Voice of Silence: Tino Villanueva" by Juan Bruce-Novoa. This article appears for
the first time in this volume. It is used by permission of the author.

[1]Tino Villanueva, *Hay Otra Voz Poems* (New York: Editorial Mensaje, 1972). All poems cited
come from this edition and page numbers will be given in the text. The book contains thirty
poems, thirteen in English, twelve in Spanish, and five in which the Spanish and English are
mixed. Thus, the first two sections are bilingual, in that the poems are in either one language
or the other, while the last section contains only one poem ("Escape") which is written only in
Spanish. The mixing of two languages I call interlingualism, because the two languages are put
into a state of tension which produces a third, an "inter" possibility of language. "Bilingual"
implies moving from one language code to another; "interlingual" implies the constant tension
of the two at once. In truth, although the first two sections of *Hay Otra Voz Poems* are technically bilingual in structure, the total experience of the reading is interlingual, but only in the
last.section does the surface of the text itself become obviously interlingual.

[2]Juan Bruce-Novoa, "Literatura chicana: la respuesta al caos," *Revista de la Universidad de
México*, 29, No. 12 (August, 1975), 20-24.

and becoming the loud oppressor. *Hay Otra Voz* is Villanueva's journey through this dilemma to discovery of art and his orientation vis-à-vis that art.

The thirty poems are divided into three sections. In the first and longest —17 poems—silence operates at all levels of human existence, from intrapersonal to extrapersonal.[3] The second is structured as a diary of a week during which the poet ponders his art, reaffirms the priorities of Section I, and assumes a social perspective. Section III fulfills the promise of II with poems on Chicanos, he expression of a voice for the silent people. The following analysis concentrates on the images utilized to convey the movement from silence to eloquent voice.

The very first poem illustrates the method.

> My certain burn
>   toward pale ashes, is told by the
>   hand that whirls the sun; each
>   driving breath beats with the quick
>   pulsing face.
>
> My falling stride
>   like sand toward decision,
>   drains heavy with fixed age; each
>   ghostly grain a step in time that
>   measures tongues.
>
> My ruddy sea
>   that streams to dryness, bares
>   bewildered its clay bone; each
>   vessel's roar at God's speed drowns
>   by force.
>
> My waking light
>   began when the fertile lips spun
>   my pulse; and I, with muted tongue,
>   was drawn destroyed from the making—
>   mouth into this mass.
>
> And held below
>   by nature, the sweeping hand now
>   turns my dust-bound youth; tell the
>   world that I was struck by the
>   sun's grave plot. (p. 8)

The first three stanzas are images of the speaker's life divided into balanced but conflicting elements of constant flow and singular moments within the flow. Verses 2 and 3 of each contain time images: the sun, draining sand,

---

[3]Juan Bruce-Novoa, "Time, Death and Silence: The Poetic Dynamics of Tino Villanueva" (chapter from unpublished manuscript, *Chicano Literature: The Response to Chaos*). The levels present are: 1) Infrapersonal: Man against time; 2) Intrapersonal: *this* man against time; 3) Interpersonal: a) love poems, b) poems with literary reference; 4) Extrapersonal: man in society.

and flowing water. The word "each" introduces images of the moment: breath, grain, vessel's roar. "Breath," an often repeated image, is a silent passage of air which could be a spoken sound if utilized differently, a sound of silence. Sand granules are points of time in the flow of an hourglass; the "measuring tongues" image can allude to the fact that the moment's value depends on expression. The roar occurs at "God's speed," eternity, an in-human non-time equivalent to death, within which drown belated expressions of existence.

While the first three stanzas focus on the present tense, 4 is in the past, and 5 swings back through the present to an implied future, this arrangement offering a structural image of Villanueva's temporal vision: The present determines the past and future.

The "waking light" birth image in 4 is undermined by its tie to day and sun, both time's agents, and by "spun," "pulse," "muted tongue," and "drawn destroyed," which recall time images from above. At the same time life originates in the mouth of the Creator, who is seen here (in the terms of Genesis) both as the Speaker whose "fertile lips" breathe life into man and as the Potter whose "sweeping hand" has shaped him from dust and "spun" him on the wheel. The mouth is also the source of speech, equating man to speech. Yet the victim's tongue is muted by time. Images from 1 echo again in 5, and the would-be voice surrenders to silence, while asking us to tell his tale, which projects the poem into a future dependent upon an alien voice for existence. The last two verses demonstrate Villanueva's penchant for irony. Has the "I" been struck down into a grave, a "plot" of ground, or overcome by time's "plot" against us all? Both at once; and obviously the book begins with a silenced being conscious of the menace to its existence and the need to achieve expression.

Another key poem from Section I is "This the Place."

> This the place where the world
> wears away; you and I, baptized
> in destiny's life stream.
> With dazzled eyes, only our
> dumb veins gush to shrink the
> quickened strain.
>
> This the place where each breath
> a turning point; life span madly
> spins and drips our moans.
> With skin and marrow, only our
> gasps tell of consuming drama
> stalking still.
>
> This the place where life's fit
> gives avid rage; time's fine grain
> filters through each wrinkle.
> And the lid that shuts our strain

gives last glimpse of burning
paradox re-told.

And so...each tick of sun has squeezed,
has hushed our liquid grain the sperm;
only marble on stuffed faces tells our
stiff.   (p. 21)

Present tense again rules three stanzas; in the last there is a shift to past,
then to present-futrue implied. Other motifs are obvious. Time-space is
fixed through repetition of "this," while images of the flow—"wearing
away," "Life-stream," "filters"—counterpoint. "Each breath" hints at the
possibility of "turning" life around with speech; but man's veins, through
which should flow his personal rhythm, are strained, by exterior pressure,
and dumb. Clock images appear in 2 and 3, while "moans" and "gasps" are
two more sounds of silence, now with painful connotations. The hourglass
reappears, with the skin as the filtering point, an intense mixed metaphor
of life flowing in singular units from and into undifferentiated mass on
either side. Man can control the crucial channel or be used by it, as here.
The conflict is universalized with "burning (another life-consuming image)
paradox re-told," implying constant repetition, like the spinning of clocks
or the turning of an hourglass.

In stanza 4 time's grip stifles man's fertility, but the verb "hushes" clearly
equates sperm to sound, linking biological creativity to speech—the future
depends on both, and both are strangled. Hope is limited to a projection into the future, again dependent on another, in the last two verses. "Marble
faces" is clarified through "Forest Lawn Cemetery" (p. 25) in which tomb-
stones are last traces of the individual, his last face; but they too wear away,
thus negating the promise of the verb "tell." "Stiff" is another key ironic
word. The noun means cadaver, a person's dead body. However, as Maurice
Blanchot explains,[4] a cadaver is also an impersonal bridge between life and
death, a surface upon which invisible death manifests itself in the world. No
longer *this* person, a cadaver is an anonymous body, revealing in its particularity death's awesome impersonalizing power. Like a moment, a body
can be man's personal presence in time, or one more nameless point in time's
flow, or the fleeting space of both at once.

These examples display Villanueva's poetic method and the type of images
employed. Throughout this section such sounds of silence as breaths, vague
echoes, sighs, groans, moans, gasps, hush, rustle, soliloquy, and *resuellos*
are attributed to man. The last two seem to be words of speech but ironically
signify sounds of silence. Soliloquies are monologues usually addressed to
oneself when alone, often employed in theatre to give the illusion of overheard thought—eloquent silence. *Resuello* derives from a verb meaning to

---

[4]Maurice Blanchot, "La semejanza cadavérica," in *El espacio literario* (Buenos Aires: Sud-
Americana, 1969), 246-49.

breathe, sometimes audibly, from fatigue. When it refers to speech, it is used either negatively—"he didn't breathe a word"—or as a first word uttered after a period of silence. Both words tend toward silence. The silent victims are constantly gripped, squeezed, spun, drawn, spewed, turned, drowned and drowned out, chilled, burnt, and more. A key image is that of the oppressor squeezing the silent victim as time flows by. Timing devices are crucial, especially the hourglass, as explained above, and the wristwatch in "Antes de acostarme" ("Before Bed") (p. 24). The wristwatch grips the wrist where the pulse beats, pitting life's inner, personal rhythm against exterior, mechanical time. Like the body, the hourglass's center, a moment, or the skin, the wrist wavers between personal and impersonal space. Villanueva designates these areas battle zones, to be won by eloquence or lost in silence. It may be superfluous to add that the mouth and the tongue are similar points. Even language—the word—can be meaningless, noisy but vacuous ("Peace Talks"), or, perhaps, someday, the enunciation of an as yet unexpressed truth.

Battle lines drawn, Villanueva pauses to take stock: "Pausas de ayer y hoy" ("Pauses, Yesterday and Today"), Section II. He shifts from the general human vision of Section I to a consciously poetic voice, beginning here with a poem on writing poetry. In this section he questions the poet's role. The pondering and the results are a step toward the eloquent voice the text has been searching for.

In the first day of the week of poems, "The Process of Myself," Villanueva discovers a means of *becoming*, which is highly significant after seventeen poems of negation. The means: poetry to lose himself in the "duration" of images, in the alternative order of literary space, outside of worldly time. However, "Myself" and "I" frame the poem, hinting at possible egoistic escapism. "Sentir" ("To feel"), poem two, restates the conflict. A blind man's wristwatch still tells time, implying that one cannot be blind to the essential problem. Time is: one feels it and carries it with him.

"Autolaberinto" ironically lends itself to escapist interpretation, while alluding to the impossibility of escape. A jailed man requests a dictionary and Borges' stories. Some claim Borges is an escapist, but in Villanueva's context this is erroneous (as it is in Borges'). In *The New Refutation of Time* Borges abolishes chronological time through logical discourse, counterposing an atemporal ideal world. However, Borges ends his essay with his famous refutation of the refutation. "*And yet, and yet....*Time is the substance I am made of. Time is a river which sweeps me along, but I am the river; it is a tiger which destroys me, but I am the tiger; it is a fire which consumes me, but I am the fire. The world, unfortunately, is real; I, unfortunately, am Borges."[5] Echoes of the closing lines of "Sentir"! The al-

[5]Jorge Luis Borges, "*The New Refutation of Time,*" trans. James E. Irby, in *Labyrinths. Selected Stories and Other Writing*, eds. Donald A. Yates and James E. Irby (New York: New Directions, 1964), 233-34.

lusion to Borges is an ironic reaffirmation of the book's intent, a strategic, ironic evoking of the poet who, more than any other in our time, has explored the possibilities and impossibilities of literary space.

"Wednesday" finds the poet waiting ("Espera") in a predawn fog, which engulfs both man's modern towers of Babel, the skyscrapers, and the poet's fingertips. The dawn will bring the sun, time's agent, and the struggle will begin; and in "The Space of Death" it does with a vengeance.

> Let's imagine in our own space,
> and how we go dying
> at every
> instant.
> With time, Death becomes so boring.
> But it's the shock of each moment,
> the anonymous screams
> that go undying—
> only to brace ourselves again.   (p. 30)

Steady death is drawn to infinity with "every," and in time's flow it is not fearful, but boring. To the infinite "every" is opposed the particular "each," and horror overtakes us. The "vessel's roar" image is transformed into "anonymous screams" of belated protest. Villanueva's theme is firmly reestablished.

In "Nevada (snowing) en Buffalo, Nueva York" words are displayed across the page like falling snow, opening a space for snow's beauty and conserving it from the sun which will come to melt it. This seemingly escapist nature poem ironically demonstrates the lesson: Poetry cannot deny death, but it can create a space for life to manifest its beauty.

"Of Age" heralds the poet's emergence from the meditative pause, like a prophet from the desert, clinging to his "unspoken silence," because silence signifies the oppressed with whom he identifies; yet "unspoken" implies the possibility of "spoken silence," prefiguring his poetic voice. The personal and the social seem to compete for his attention, but the fact that he refers to the griefs of the howling wind, an oppressive image in context, and that he steps into the world instead of remaining within the meditative mood indicate the acceptance of a social responsibility, or perhaps the intention to turn his personal life into a social project. Section III supports this interpretation.

Six poems on Chicano experience comprise this section. "Que hay otra voz" ("That There is Another Voice") and "Day-long Day" are poems about farmworkers, showing the laborers as victims of seasonal circuits, "third generation timetable," school systems, and poverty. Little hope is held for the "other voice" to break its silence. Only César Chávez's union elicits enough strength to produce a "brave shout" from the depths of silence. The images have changed to fit this ambience, but the configurations remain the same. Two *pachuco* poems follow which dignify this Chicano myth figure, while denouncing the school system's role in silencing the Chicano. *Pachucos* resisted the system with the eloquence of their dress and mannerisms, displayed in the poems. In opposition we hear the angry, hateful, and thus empty shouts from the high school principal. Silent eloquence confronts loud oppression. In "Aquellos Vatos" ("Those Guys") school experience attempts to substitute a vicarious manner of living for the Chicano's direct involvement in life. Here Villanueva enumerates a list of *pachucos*, with their animal nicknames, retrieving each image from obscurity. The poem is a spoken response to a question about the *pachucos,* and its speaker is revealed to be one by his intimate knowledge of their ways. Furthermore, in the poem's center a *pachuco* is quoted, and this brings his voice directly to us, though ironically it appears only through the other voice of the poem, itself a quoted voice. Noting that one *pachuco* who has dated Anglo girls is almost forgotten, the poem implies that flirting with assimilation can lead to exclusion from the communal memory. The poem then ends ironically, with the *pachucos'* children trying to "comprehend culture and identity by reading 'See Spot,'" (p. 43) and going to the zoo on a Greyhound bus with Miss Foxx. School imposes what is actually a less vital animal order, ignoring the *pachuco's* animal order, the signifier here for their particular culture and, by extension, the Chicano's. Like the farmworker poems, these poems use new images for the same theme of deadly silence imposed on the victims of life.

The image of the school is central here, because the farmworkers see education as a way out for their children yet the *pachucos* are excluded from it. School joins the list of time's agents as a rigidly structured, temporal procession imposing mass conformity to ensure a steady, peaceful social succession. The individual voice is restrained. When the *pachuco* resists this system, he is excluded, but his apparently futile acts become heroic in literary space, displaying their special beauty, like the snow in "Nevada en Buffalo."

The last two poems focus on victorious though dead heroes in the struggle against the Dead-Time conspiracy. "Escape" is an eloquent elegy to Villanueva's grandfather, a watch repairman, who worked all his life in the jaws of the enemy, adjusting clock springs to his own pulse. When he dies his wrists are visible, signifying personal control over the space designated a prime battle zone in "Antes de acostarme." The grandfather is not a victim, but a victor. His only words are "¿qué hora es?" (what time is it?), punctually asked, demonstrating his total mastery of the enemy, for time depends on his inquiry for its existence in his space. Yet, and yet—he was time itself and had to die, victorious but mortal, now immortalized in the space of literature by his grandson's voice, or perhaps the grandfather's other voice.

"Chicano Is an Act of Defiance" pays tribute to Rubén Salazar, a Chicano reporter killed by police during the antiwar Moratorium in Los Angeles, 1971. Chicanos had begun to *resollar,* that barely audible expression explained above, and were severely repressed. Salazar had dared even more, to speak out on mass media, and was killed. Yet, because he had enunciated his views publicly, his words remain, and Villanueva transforms them into poetry. The Chicano has found a voice, and though he can still be killed, he leaves a memorable historical presence.

Villanueva has brought us from mute-tongued, silent victims to eloquent Chicano heroes. Their death, however, makes it necessary for the poet to save them by becoming their voice in life. Victims in the first two examples asked others to tell their story, and Villanueva becomes that someone; in truth, from the very start he has fulfilled their request. This poetry becomes the people's other voice which wants to speak, thus constituting a response to the Dead-Time threat even while that threat is being portrayed in the earliest poems. At the same time, Villanueva has faithfully reflected the silences of his people in the hushed, soft tone of his writing. Harshness is eliminated, except when attributed to the enemy; irony veils the attack. Images show the struggle instead of explaining it: the poet's lens closes down to thin layers of skin separating the pulse from the watch, or the wrinkle on a face. Even more significant, silence itself becomes the zone of struggle. Will it be a sign of passive surrender, or that of self-assured being? For, as Villanueva understands, we are who we are partly because of our silences; and though speech may be necessary for survival, it must not divorce itself from the silent center. Villanueva's necessary betrayal of silence proves his loyalty and love; he turns the book's white pages into the space and surface of silence, eloquently visible and audible in the world — beauty on display.

Thus the structure of the whole assumes an hourglass shape. The personal, though general, Section I narrows into the compressed space of Section II, draining through individual temporal units, highly magnified under the poetic lens, and then bursts out into Section III on La Raza. Section II is the battleground, and like the cadaver, the poet can represent a single personal body, or the impersonal surface of totality. He chooses to be both at once and seeks to maintain the state of tension between them. His writing will be, on the one hand, an impersonal space, so that his people can speak through him. Hence the language becomes interlingual in Section III, while in prior sections the usage is bilingual (see footnote 1). Hence, too, quoted speech — the words of other speakers — appears more and more often in III, underlining the poet's effort to become a more than personal voice, even to the extent of completely yielding "Aquellos Vatos" to a pachuco's voice, which then quotes still another pachuco. On the other hand, the writing remains his own particular voice, so that a carrier for the other voices can be assured. In this extremely precarious equilibrium between the personal and the communal, between the particular and the universal, between the I and anonymity, between silence and the word, Villanueva carves out his position as the other voice of silence.

Judy Lucero and Bernice Zamora:
Two Dialectical Statements in Chicana Poetry

by Marta E. Sánchez

I

One of the fundamental dangers facing Chicano critics is that most of us have been educated to respect the dominant intellectual and cultural values of mainstream criticism. We hence tend at times to mechanically apply traditional criteria to Chicano literature, and consequently we not only perpetuate but also authenticate those values, which we should examine critically for their cultural, psychological, and social implications. Indeed, we might benefit by thinking of minority literatures here in the United States as areas of study where categories in literary scholarship and research are yet to be defined. We can think of ourselves as critics who at present are undertaking to formulate theoretical and applicable criteria leading toward such a definition. The opportunity remains therefore to approach Chicano literature as a field challenging us to think in fresh terms. This present attempt to study and evaluate two Chicana poets should not be interpreted as an assault on everything "old" and a welcoming of anything "new", but instead should be read as an effort to locate and construct formal as well as ideological categories that may prove productive in studying Chicano narrative and poetry.

This essay focuses on specific poems by Judy Lucero[1] and Bernice Zamora,[2] two poets of radically different preparations and backgrounds. Judy Lucero, a *pinta* (a woman prison inmate) and a *tecata* (a female heroin user), died at twenty-eight of a brain hemorrhage brought on by severe beatings which had previously caused her to lose two children. When only eleven years old, she had been introduced to drugs by one of her stepfathers, and she had been in a methadone program near the time of her death.[3] Bernice Zamora has taught English expository writing at the Uni-

"Judy Lucero and Bernice Zanora: Two Dialectical Statements in Chicana Poetry" by Marta E. Sánchez. This article appears for the first time in this volume. It is used by permission of the author.

[1]"Memoriam: Poems of Judy A. Lucero," *De Colores* 1, no. 1 (Winter 1973), 51-59.

[2]Bernice Zamora, *Restless Serpents* (Menlo Park, Calif.: Diseños Literarios, 1976).

[3]*De Colores,* p. 51.

versity of California, Berkeley, and creative writing in poetry for Chicanos at Stanford University. At this writing, she is in the final stages of a Ph.D. degree at Stanford in English and American Literature.

A first reading of these poets could tempt us to distinguish them diametrically. Lucero's poetry might too hastily be explained as "simple," Zamora's as "complex." Conventional literary norms program us to associate Lucero's poetry with social issues, therefore prompting us to qualify it as "topical," limited in value, and directed to a limited audience. Zamora's poems we might tend to associate with the symbolic and universal, implying that they speak to all men and women. Evaluated from this perspective, Lucero's use of language seems ordinary, the message clear and overt. Zamora's language, in contrast, is intricate and three-dimensional, the message hidden and subtle. Such facile discriminations perpetuate literary orthodoxies which define a concern with material and social (outer) phenomena as inferior to a concern with imaginative and meditative (inner) phenomena, or as a temporary stage in a people's cultural evolution to be succeeded by a second, more perfect stage.

I would here like to argue that we should not force the poetry of these Chicanas into such exclusive categories. We should instead attempt to see, in spite of certain very real differences in their poetry, how in both cases it resists narrow definitions. The poems of Judy Lucero, which might on a casual glance be dismissed as "social," "unsophisticated," "simple," "limited and particular," contain much that is actually philosophical, and those of Bernice Zamora, the poet who conversely might be extolled as "universal," "sophisticated," "complex," "symbolic and eclectic," contain much that is social. Their work shows a considerable continuity.

II

Judy Lucero's best poems express a succession of tensions between the desire for a personal human identity and the reality of a categorized bureaucratic nonidentity, between the spiritual and the material aspects of individual experience, and between the individual and society. An example of the tension between desire for personal identity and the reality of a categorical nonidentity occurs in the tacit contrast that Lucero makes between the way each poem is signed and its content. The signature she uses is her prison number "#21918," and her use of it implies an acceptance of the nonidentity society has thrust upon her. Yet we must judge this acceptance against the desperate struggle made in each poem to define a personal human identity, even if that identity be the fragmentary one of "I speak in an illusion" (It's me and it's not/ I hear and I don't," p. 56). There is thus a continuing tension between the number an impersonal system uses to codify a human subject and the subjective, individual consciousness that struggles to define itself in each poem. The three specific poems chosen for commentary here capture the interdependent relationship between the speaker's material situation—the prison house—and her desire for a life of the spirit. The prison house in Lucero's work is either the actual jail or the metaphoric prison home of drugs, or both.

The poetic voice in "Comfort" also occupies itself with the opposition between public and private being, in this case expressed in analogies between the rain and the addressee of the poem, and between the window pane and the speaker.

> Just listening to the rain
> Reminds me so much of U
> The way it runs in rivers down the pane
> The way it glistens, and eventually leaves a stain
>
> At times I'm certain I've gone mad
> just missing U,
> But those times don't compare to when I see U
> And we can't touch...
> Only smile to fill in the space
>
> Possibly madness now
> Only saves our "other" sanity for tomorrow
> For then we won't just stare at each
> other with hope.
>
> Hope will be repacked
> by its Desire fulfilled...
>
> When I get to see your face
> it reflects an image of the free world
> even now...
> It must be because you're so alive and a part
> of a "real" world
>
> Even these walls can't touch its radiance
>
> I must not fret my present madness. It is
> a Sanctuary for the lonely hours and so
> very comforting to the Soul.   #21918

The relationship between the rain, the sign of the outside world, and the window pane is analogous to that between the addressee and the speaker. Just as the rain "runs in rivers" and leaves its stain on the window glass, so the addressee makes a deep impression on the speaker, primarily because he mirrors ("glistens") images of the free world. Like the rain he can both move and listen; the prison walls cannot diminish the "radiance" of his face. The common element equating the window pane to the speaker, on the other hand, is that both are fixed, receptive as opposed to active. Since the rain's fluidity is linked to the addressee's freedom to participate in the real world, as stated in stanza 5, we must recognize that the speaker occupies a nonfluid situation, participating in an unreal or illusory world.

The speaker wants to bridge the physical space separating and isolating her from the outside world. She can gesture ("smile") but she cannot establish physical contact ("touch"). She cannot neutralize the polarity between society ("U") and herself, between reality and illusion, between desire and fact. She cannot "fill in the space" because she cannot annihilate the material prison. What drives her outward toward society only ends up driving her inward toward madness. "At times I'm certain I've gone mad/ just missing U." Hence the paradox of the poem. The pull outward recoils in a pull inward; yet the pull inward, "madness," keeps her "sane" until her desire to become a free participant in a real world shall be satisfied:

> Possibly madness now
> only saves our "other" sanity for tomorrow
> for then we won't just stare at each
> other with hope.
>
> Hope will be repacked
> by its Desire fulfilled...

The counterpoint between material and metaphysical experience is more directly described in "I speak in an illusion." Now the voice equates the illusion with the emotional condition of being placeless or, if you will, in a "space" which is neither here nor there. "I speak but only in an illusion/ For I see and I don't/ It's me and it's not/ I hear and I don't." The illusion is a "space" of fragmented and disconnected perceptions and emotions that represent the speaker's consciousness.

> I speak but only in an illusion
> For I see and I don't
>
> It's me and it's not
> I hear and I don't
>
> These illusions belong to me —
> I stole them from another
>
> Care to spend a day in my House of Death?
> Look at my garden...are U amazed?
> No trees, no flowers, no grass...no gardens...
>
> I love and I don't
> I hate and I don't
> I sing and I don't
> I live and I don't
>
> For I'm in a room of clouded smoke
> And a perfumed odor
>
> Nowhere can I go and break these bonds
> Which have me in an illusion
>
> But the bonds are real   #21918

With an ironical twist, Lucero transforms the usual landscape of fulfillment, specifically a garden full of trees, flowers, grass. Instead:

> Care to spend a day in my House of Death?
> Look at my garden...are U amazed?
> No trees, no flowers, no grass...no gardens...

By superimposing her own stark and grim reality on the pastoral illusion, the poet requires the reader to confront the contradiction. The illusion is her reality, which is no illusion. Her garden is either the prison institution or drugs, or both: "For I'm in a room of clouded smoke/ And a perfumed odor." Her landscape is not only hazed with the smoke of drugs but perfumed with synthetic odors. Her senses are stupefied by olfactory and visual messages to the point of breakdown. Paradoxically, her "bonds" are definite and precise.

> Nowhere can I go and break these bonds
> Which have me in an illusion
> But the bonds are real.

The central paradox of the poem is that the well-defined constrictions, the "bonds," of her material situation also generate her fragmented, tenuously defined spiritual existence.

The dialectic between matter and spirit, body and mind is further explored in one of Lucero's most effective poems, "Jail—Life Walk."

> Walk in the day...Walk in the night
> Count off the time...One to Ten
> Then you'll be free...Free again
>
> Walk without pain...Walk without care...
>
> Walk til you see...See the sign
> Look at the sign...Walk in Line!
>
> Then walk in hate
> Walk without the world
> Walk in fear...
> See the anger
> In their eye
> just walking by...
>
> The only thing free
> is your mind
> Free to count
> As U walk in Line   #21918

The poem's meaning is summed up in the title: her life is a walk in jail, represented in the first lines by the monotonous walk and the counting of time. The first stanza, in fact, articulates the jail experience as an unbroken routine "walk," beginning on the count of one and ending on the count of ten. "Then you'll be free...Free again." The "again" here suggests she was "free" once before, namely at the moment of reaching the count of ten in the previous "walk." Then the walk begins anew. The prison sign gives the imperative: "Walk in line." Her mind oscillates between a desire to "walk without pain...Walk without care..." and an actual walking in hate and fear of the hostile eyes of prison guards. Her body is therefore restricted to obeying the imperative but her mind is "Free to count/ As U walk in Line."

The "line" metaphor marks her struggle to maintain a fine line between sanity and rage: either walking without pain or walking in hate. The line is thus a point of relationship. It serves also to mark the tenuous balance between the body's imprisonment and the desperate attempt made by the spirit to assert freedom: thus her flight to assert freedom is inseparably bound to her material condition. With each count her "free" mind acknowledges her physical imprisonment. The paradox of the poem lies in knowing that her freedom lies in knowing she is not free.

This scrutiny of some of the poems in *De Colores* should help us understand that Lucero's preoccupation with spiritual and philosophical considerations ("illusion," "madness," "mind") emerges from the personal dependence which her material situation thrusts upon her. Her introspection is inseparable from the outward context in which it occurs. Torn between the extreme poles of body-mind, sanity-madness, separation-community, illusion-reality, the physical prison house precipitates a vision of the transcendental. This is the significant lesson we might draw from Judy Lucero's poetry: that even when pitted against the overwhelming odds of material oppression, the life of the spirit goes on.

III

When we turn to Bernice Zamora's *Restless Serpents*, we again find poems based on struggle. But here the struggle is not so much to affirm the spirit, as in Lucero's poetry, but to efface those rules of conventional society that establish artificial divisions among social groups.

The specific polarities in Zamora's poems fall normally into three sets: abortion/anti-abortion; masculinity/femininity; Anglo literature/Chicano literature. "¿A qué hora venderemos todo?" (p. 9) represents her attempt to break out of the doctrinaire definition that she feels too much structures social attitudes toward abortion. The poem "California" (p. 21) forces the reader who aims to understand it to judge it in the context of Robinson Jeffer's *Roan Stallion*, thus setting up a reference to both Anglo and Chicano literatures. Since the first two lines of "California" are the last two lines of the *Roan Stallion*, it must be read as its continuation. We might say that the Zamora poem begins where the Jeffers poem ends. In "Sonnet, Freely Adapted" (p. 47) Zamora adheres closely to the form of Shakespeare's Sonnet CXVI, but she freely adapts this classical English form to fit her own modern ideas concerning male and female roles.

It is in "Gata Poem" (p.16), however, that Zamora presents her most concrete case for the destruction of social barriers. Through a series of conversations between a man and a woman, "Gata Poem" attacks the myth of traditional masculine superiority and defends woman's assertion of her independence. Read within a Chicano context, "Gata Poem" demystifies the notion of the Chicano male as a bronze god, as it progressively deflates stanza by stanza the myth of *machismo* in traditional Chicano culture.

Desde la cima me llamó
Un hombre perfecto, un chicano
Con cuerpo desnudo y tan moreno que
He glistened in the sun like a bronze god.

—*Ven, mujer.*
Ven conmigo.
Se me empezó a morir como una gata
   en la noche.
Y yo misma era gata vestida de negro.

—*¿Qué quieres, señor?*
   ¿Qué quieres conmigo?

—*Quiero cantar eternamente contigo*
   lejos de la tristeza.
Quiero enseñarte un sol tan brillante
   que debemos verlo con alma escudada.

Quiero vivir contigo por los nueve mundos.

—*Ven, gatita.*
Ven conmigo.
   Y me fui.

From the summit he called me
A perfect man, a chicano
Naked, and so brown that
He glistened in the sun like a bronze god.

—Come, woman.
Come with me.
He began to die on me like a cat
   in the night.
And I too was a cat dressed in black.

—What do you want, sir?
What do you want with me?

—I want to sing with you eternally
   somewhere far away from sadness
I want to show you a sun so brilliant
that we must see it with a guarded soul.

I want to live with you in nine worlds.

—Come, kitten.
Come with me.
And I went.

The masculine/feminine polarities framing "Gata Poem" are presented within a sexual context. Its initial line, "Desde la cima me llamó," establishes a hierarchical relationship between man and woman. The man is on some sort of "summit," and the woman is below. Active choice is attributed to him: *he* calls *her*. Sexual rivalry is accentuated when the man, "Un hombre perfecto, un chicano/ Con cuerpo desnudo y tan moreno que/ *He glistened in the sun like a bronze god,*" utters his abrupt imperative:

   —Ven, mujer
   Ven conmigo.

A change in the relationship occurs in stanza three.

   Se me empezó a morir como una gata
      en la noche.
   Y yo misma era gata vestida de negro.

The action"morir" refers to the Chicano on the summit, synonymous with "un hombre perfecto," with the "he" glistening in the sun, and with the bronze god. Does this visual image represent the woman's view of this Chicano, or the view the Chicano has of himself, or the woman's idea of the image he has of himself? In stanza 1 we do not really know which perspective to adopt. What we do know by stanza 2 is that the image or the dream begins to die "como una gata en la noche." Here the word "gata" from the title is used for the first time. What does it mean?

Gata, as opposed to *gato*, is first of all a feminine principle. Its denotative meaning is a female cat. In a Chicano and Mexican context, associations link it to a stray female cat that wanders the streets and indiscriminately copulates with any male cat. When attributed to a woman, it suggests a flirtatious coquette "purring," so to speak, to attract the man. The word insinuates an image of women that takes into account only their sexual qualities. Extensions of the image may go so far as to suggest "prostitute" or its equivalent in Spanish, *puta*.

Line 7 defines a metaphoric relationship between man and "gata": he "dies" as does a cat in the night. If we insist on the associations of "gata" with loose woman or prostitute, then the next question is: how does a prostitute 'die' in the night? Here we may think of the effacement of identity the prostitute undergoes, the sexual commodity she must become to please the male. The image of the Chicano "glistening in the sun" changes in stanza 3 to that of a black cat against a black night because in line 8 the woman-speaker attributes the identity of a "gata vestida de negro" to herself: "I too was a cat dressed in black." The "I too" ("y yo misma") implies an antecedent event; someone else before her must be seen as a cat "dressed" in black.

The objective of line 7 is to deflate the romantic image in the first stanza. The male now occupies no higher standing than the woman, who supposedly embodies the characteristics of "gata." Male and female are now both "gatas." When the woman assumes the identity of "gata", she consolidates the equality of their positions. The male ego collapses.

We may argue now that the image of stanza 1 was the woman's because in line 8 she is garbed in widow's dress ("vestida de negro"). Thus she admits complicity in the image. But as the result of the developments in stanza 3, she can no longer entertain this image. Therefore, the use of the *tú* form in the next stanza is logical. She considers herself his equal. The choice of "señor" is made not to demonstrate respect, for this would be inconsistent with the preceding lines, but to establish distance between him and her. She poses her questions to him as concisely and tersely as he did to her. Her questioning also indicates that she is not going to respond to his beck and call without some reflection.

In the next stanza the man, feeling threatened by her hesitancy, desperately begins to promise, deploying the clichés men traditionally use to seduce women: "eternal songs," "brilliant suns," endless existences together, suggested here by the proverb of the cat with nine lives. His promises culminate in another command, only this time uttered in a more tempered, endearing tone.

> — *Ven, gatita.*
> *Ven conmigo.*

The noun he chooses is now not "mujer" but "gatita," the diminutive of "gata," which demonstrates that he sees only a flirting coquette. Thus he confirms that the transformation has taken place in her, not in him. The poem's last line, "Y me fui," has two possible meanings: either the woman goes with the man or she goes her own way. The transformation traced above throws doubt on the first possibility and supports the second. By means of process and progression, "Gata Poem" has described the transformation of women's perspective on *machismo* from uncritical to critical.

The problem "Gata Poem" forces women to confront is release from male dominance so that they may define their own identity. "Gata Poem" terminates in a midpoint between two extremes, in this case male and female. Its dialectic is expressed in the paradox that to attain an equality (a midpoint) between man and woman, a breach must first occur: the man and woman at the poem's end are not reconciled in a harmonious union. The disharmony evident between them *within* the poem reminds us forcibly of the comparable inequality *outside* the poem.

The social problems addressed in the poems of these Chicanas can only be solved in the concrete historical situation of struggle. Lucero's insistence on fighting for a life of the spirit is as much a statement of social conflict as Bernice Zamora's critique of the *machismo* myth. The poetry of both women, it seems to me, can be effectively analyzed and interpreted in the light of the dialectical approach to literary criticism proposed in the beginning of this essay.

Linguistic Structures in José Montoya's "El Louie"

by Ignacio Orlando Trujillo

"Confrontación dialéctica permanente a través de la palabra."

CARLOS FUENTES

A literature that through its language radically scrutinizes the social reality from which it arises is bound to alter the consciousness of its readership. Contemporary Chicano literature's renovative ingenuity resides precisely in its language configurations, particularly in those of its poetry. Its inherent bilingualism and multidialectalism enable it to offer a dynamic confrontation of attitudes. Bilingual expression is not employed by the Chicano as a conceit or device but rather is part of the Chicano's normal language. Not, of course, that bilingualism in poetry is new: the Arab-Hispanic *jarchas* and *muwashahas* of the eleventh and twelfth centuries exploited its possibilities, as in America Pound, Eliot, and others have often done since. But, this has been a poetry of the élite. In the case of the Chicano, it springs from the vernacular of the working class.

José Montoya (born in 1932) is a "poeta veterano" who raises disturbing social questions. Although he insists that the language of his poetry be transparent for the conveyance of his argument, he makes use of Chicano vernacular to reflect the modern Chicano psyche. Having himself been a *campesino, barrio vato,* Korean war serviceman, and artist on the Berkeley "Beat" fringe, he encompasses the experience and language of the villages of New Mexico, the rural agricultural migrants, and the Chicanos in California's urban centers. He has witnessed and empathized with the Chicano's move from a schizophrenia forced on him by his economic status to defense of his culture and language as a way of self-determination and liberation inside the larger struggle of a displaced population within the United States. His poetry reflexts the collision of two cultures: Anglo-Saxon and Indo-Hispanic.

"Linguistic Structures in José Montoya's 'El Louie'" by Ignacio Orlando Trujillo. This article appears for the first time in this volume. It is used by permission of the author.

150

Montoya's earliest published poetry portrays a stifled rebelliousness ("Lazy Skin")[1] and self-denigration ("In a Pink Bubble-Gum World")[2] conducive to despair and a sense of ineptitude ("From 67 to 71").[3] The lack of access to any constructive outlet leads to a feeling of inferiority, to self-perversion and getting "drunk a lot." The collusive oppression that he sees coming down from the Church and the landowners—"the growers...fair with blond hair"—is depicted in poems such as "Irish Priests and Chicano Sinners."[4] The dead end he has seen farmworkers ushered to in their migratory flow through California is graphically reiterated in the dirgelike "Gabby took the 99."[5] The physical and psychological maiming effects of various wars on Chicano G.I.s are bitterly evoked in the onomatopoetic staccato at the close of "tecato tattoo taps." These soliders have faced disproportional atrocities in U.S. wars of aggression leading to their death in battle or by drugs.

One surviving casualty of war is the Pachuco protagonist of the poem, "El Louie." "El Louie," along with other poems of the late 1960s such as Corky Gonzales's "Yo soy Joaquín" and Raúl Salinas's "A Trip Through the Mind Jail," is a key composition in the revival of mass interest in Chicano poetry and the resurgence of its writers. Not only has it been anthologized in various collections,[6] but it has also been recited and dramatized because of its popular oral and visual quality. The Teatro Campesino expanded the performance of the poem by inserting *boleros* and *corridos.* This piece incorporates many of Montoya's early themes and language experiments in dealing with a significant historical moment for the contemporary Chicano.

Pachucos were Chicano youth in their teens and twenties casually organized in barrio clubs according to the area they felt to be their "turf." Because of their manner of dressing, Anglo-Americans called them zoot suiters. Their language was *caló*[7] and a mixture of English and Spanish.

[1]This poem can be found in the anthology of Chicano literature edited by Octavio Ignacio Romano-V., *El Espejo—The Mirror* (Berkeley: Quinto Sol, 1969), p. 183.

[2]*Ibid.,* p. 184.

[3]José Montoya, *El Sol y los de abajo* (San Francisco: Pocho-Che, 1972), p. 10.

[4]*Ibid.,* p. 16.

[5]*Ibid.,* p. 3.

[6]"El Louie" first appeared in the journal *Rascatripas,* Vol. II (Oakland, California, 1970). The following anthologies in which "El Louie" has been reprinted are among the most accessible. Antonia Castañeda Shular, Joseph Sommers and Tomás Ybarra-Frausto; eds., *Literatura Chicana: texto y contexto* (Englewood Cliffs, N.J.: Prentice-Hall, 1972), pp. 173-76; Luis Valdez and Stan Steiner, *Aztlán: An Anthology of Mexican-American Literature* (New York: Random House, 1972), pp. 333-37. Since space does not allow for a full reprinting of "El Louie" in this study, please refer to the anthologies indicated.

[7]The term *caló* originally referred to the gypsies' speech in Spain. It has been extended to signify the syntax and vocabulary of *pachuco* jargon. For an investigation of this dialect consult George Carpenter Baker's *Pauchuco: An American-Spanish Argot* (Tucson: University of Arizona Press, 1950).

Like other neighborhood gangs, they had their occasional "rumbles," but were less an insurrectionary group than victims of the prejudices and insults of the larger society. During the Second World War the *pachuco* became the target of racial xenophobia.[8] In June of 1943 full-scale battles broke out between *pachucos* and American servicemen in what was misnamed the zoot suit riots of Los Angeles. The newspapers of the period stated one side. The investigations of lawyer-journalist Carey McWilliams and his Commission later brought out the injustices perpetrated on the *pachuco*.[9]

Louie is a member of one of these groups. He's not really from the "big time"—"Los" (for Los Angeles)—but among his peers he is as good as they come. The poem starts off with the announcement of his burial. "Hoy enterraron al Louie." The affection of the poet-narrator wells up in some highly emotional invective—"And San Pedro o sanpinche are in for it." He recounts, dramatically, the salient features of Louie's life and the world he lived in. At the end he returns to the tragic yet ambiguous circumstances of Louie's death and accords him significant homage in the style of a personal epitaph—"Vato de atolle, el Louie Rodríguez,"—*atolle* being a contraction meaning "a todo dar" or "a toda madre" (a really heavy dude).

> Hoy enterraron al Louie
>
> And San Pedro o sanpinche
> are in for it. And those
> times of the forties'
> and the early fifties
> lost un vato de atolle.

The standard Spanish of the first line includes a double *r* sound and single *r*, which necessitate a slow pace when read aloud, and a number of somber vowels *(o,e,a)* to reinforce the serious tone. But within this line is already announced the emotive language of the subsequent segment through the strident vowel sound in the last syllable of Louie's name. The second line speeds up through alliteration ("*San P*edro o *sanp*inche") and the two high-pitched vocalic sounds at the end in "sanp*i*nche" (both vowels pronounced alike and rhymed with the *ie* of Lou*ie*). The code switch (or shift from one language to another) is appropriate because of the change in the emotive situation, further emphasized by word play: "San Pedro" (city and saint) versus "sanpinche" (saint son-of-a-bitch). The contrast (blas-

[8]The mass deportations of Mexican Americans—citizens, documented and undocumented people—during the Great Depression of the 1930s and the internment of citizens of Japanese descent in concentration camps within the U.S. during the Second World War are also examples of the Anglo-American's fear of the "alien" during this period.

[9]Carey McWilliams, *North from Mexico* (New York: Greenwood Press, 1968), pp. 227-58, and Rodolfo Acuña, *Occupied America: The Chicano's Struggle Toward Liberation* (San Francisco: Canfield Press, 1972), pp. 199-208. A more recent in-depth study of the *pachuco* is Arturo Madrid-Barela's "In Search of the Authentic Pachuco: An Interpretive Essay," *Aztlán*, 4, no. 1 (Spring 1973), 31-62.

phemous, if you will) intensifies the expressive aspect. Yet the line is balanced: "And San Pedro" (four syllables in English-Spanish), then a further code switch, "o sanpinche" (four syllables in standard Spanish-*pachuco*). In other words, within the same verse, a figure of sound is repeated in three different linguistic systems.

The English, Spanish, and patois of Spanish used in this stanza convey the poet's anger and inconsolability. Linguistic choices dramatize his psychological state. Considerations of the intellect tend to take form in the standard diction of either language, while the emotions speak tellingly through the Chicano and English argot.

> Kind of slim and drawn,
> there toward the end,
> aging fast from too much
> booze y la vida dura. But
> class to the end.

Here, the poet-narrator recedes somewhat from the immediate circumstances. Having released his anger in the first stanza, he is able now to summarize Louie's career without losing the taut language that maintains suspense and gives the effect of potential violence in the present.

> En Sanjo you'd see him
> sporting a dark topcoat
> playing in his fantasy
> the role of Bogard, Cagney
> or Raft.

The first line of the third stanza uses code switching, but this does not occur at random.[10] Lanugage alternation has its grammatical constraints and in this poem is also regulated by esthetic considerations. To begin with, "En Sanjo" (In San Jose) is a prepositional phrase with an adverbial function indicating place. This cohesion of the unit must be maintained before a switch can be made. The use of the colloquial term here suggests the protagonist's (as well as the poet's) close identification with his environment. Esthetically speaking, the three syllables in Spanish are counterbalanced by the three syllables in English. Both phonetic systems are contrasted, the Spanish component being foregrounded.[11] At the end of the stanza we have

[10]See Uriel Weinreich's *Languages in Contact* (Paris: Mouton, 1968), and Rosaura Sánchez's "Nuestra circunstancia lingüística," *Voices* ed. Octavio Romano (Berkeley: Quinto Sol, 1973), pp. 420-49. Eduardo Hernández-Chávez's *El Lenguaje de los Chicanos* (Arlington, Va.: Center for Applied Linguistics, 1975) also has articles on this phenomenon.

[11]The concept of foregrounding was formulated by Jan Mukarowsky of the Prague Linguistic Circle. He claimed that foregrounding tends to push communication into the background in order to maximize the speech act. It serves to de-automatize verbal expression by creating a rich differentiation within its elements. See "Standard Language and Poetic Language," in Paul L. Garvin's *A Prague School Reader on Esthetics, Literary Structure and Style* (Washington: Washington Linguistic Club, 1955), pp. 19-35.

a sequence of repeated sound measures:[12] "The/role of/Bogard/Cagney/ or Raft."

> Era de Fowler el vato,
> carnal del Candi y el
> Ponchi—Los Rodríguez—
> The Westside knew 'em
> and Selma, even Gilroy.

Stanza 4 starts off with a block in Spanish emphasizing the strong fraternal ties, the values of origin ("Era de Fowler") and the family within the Chicano culture. "Los Rodríguez" is highlighted against the background of two language systems. Throughout the poem, the phonetic quality of nicknames brings special attention to the word itself: Louie, Candi, Ponchi, Jimmy, Primo. There is a trait of endearment in each of them.

> 48 Fleetline, two-tone—
> buenas garras and always
> rucas—como la Mary y
> la Helen...siempre con
> liras bien afinadas
> cantando La Palma, la
> que andaba en el florero.
> Louie hit on the idea in
> those days for tailor-made
> drapes, unique idea—porque
> Fowler no era nada como
> Los, o'l E.P.T. Fresno's
> Westside was as close as
> we ever got to the big time.

The poet goes on to mention the three principal possessions of any respectable *pachuco:* car, clothes, and women. The phrase "buenas garras and always/ rucas" is yet another phonetically and metrically pleasing sequence: the alliteration of the double *r*'s (In Spanish an *r* at the beginning of a word, as in "rucas," is pronounced as a double *r*), the repetition of the vowel *a,* and the symmetry of syllables (four and four). El Louie is driven by the appeal of good-looking cars, attractive girls, stylish clothes. He is the one with the "unique idea" in fashion—"tailor-made drapes"—which breaks with the esthetic norm. His guitars—"liras bien afinadas"—and his singing can only be referred to in Spanish; the songs and the emotion are Spanish.

> But we had Louie and the
> Palomar, el boogie, los
> mambos y cuatro suspiros

---

[12]This notion is outlined by Roman Jakobson in "Linguistics and Poetics," in *The Structuralists: From Marx to Lévi-Strauss,* ed. Richard De Geroge (New York: Anchor, 1972), pp. 96-98.

del alma—y nunca faltaba
the gut-shrinking love-
splitting, ass-hole-up
tight-bad news—
      Trucha, esos! Va 'ber
pedo!
Abusau, ese!
Get Louie

No llores, Carmen, we can
handle 'em.
      Ese, 'on tal Jimmy?
Hórale, Louie
Where's Primo?
Va 'ber catos!

Although Fowler was not "Los, o'l E.P.T." (Los Angeles; El Paso, Texas), it was still a center of activity for the *pachuco*.[13] The Palomar is not only a place to "boogie" (rhyming internally with "Louie"), mambo, and romance the girls but also the proving ground of the macho. Octavio Paz in his analysis of Mexican culture says that the fiesta is a ritual that turns into a Black Mass, where life-giving orgy turns into sacrifice—a fiesta of bullets.[14] Although this did happen in the dances of the *pachuco* era (and still does to some extent today), it should not be seen as an ethnic idiosyncrasy but must be studied in its socioeconomic context.

The poem started with a solemn pace; now at the center, love, life, and violence converge. The phrases grow elliptical. "Va 'ber pedo!" is an abridgment of "Va a haber pedo!" (There's gonna be a rumble!); "Ese, 'on tal Jimmy?" is short for "Ese, donde esta el Jimmy?" (Hey man, where's Jimmy?); and "Va 'ber catos" abbreviates "Va a haber chingazos" (There's gonna be some blows thrown). The jive speech structure here serves to communicate an extra-linguistic situation: an impending clash.

The jive speech structure is also alive with connotations: "Abusau" is a shortened form of the past participial adjective *abusado*. *Abusado* means "abused" but what the *pachuco* wants to say here is "beware," "be alert," "be sharp," "be forewarned." The two past participles that have this meaning and sound closest to *abusado* are *aguzado* (sharp) and *avisado* (forewarned, alert). Other variants are *agusau* and *avisau*, along with *agüisau*, which is a change in the point of articulation of the labiodental *v* in *avisau* to the easier point of articulation on the velar. It is believed that *vato* comes from *vate*, meaning "bard." In a sense the particular language created by the *vatos* of this time did relate them to the maker of poetry. *Catos*, which comes from *chingazos*, means "blows" or "punches." This word is just one

[13]Fowler and Selma are small towns in the vast semirural area of Central California traversed by highway 99.
[14]*El laberinto de la soledad* (México: Fondo de Cultura Económica, 1959), pp. 42-48.

derivative of the many which originate from the popular Mexican curse verb, *chingar,* meaning "to violate," sexually or in any other manner. In the dialogues, Montoya uses sound and rhythm to produce an upbeat —"Hórale,/Trais filero?/Simón!/Nel!/Chale, ese!" (Hey,/Got a shiv?/ Yeah!/Nope!/Negative, man!)—and then a downbeat—"Oooooh, este vato!" (Awwwww, man!)[15] Here the ideation of language is suppressed and the emotive elements of speech are placed in the forefront.

> And Louie would come through—
> melodramatic music, like in the
> mono—tan tan tarán!—Cruz
> Diablo, El Charro Negro! Bogard
> smile (his smile as deadly as
> his vaisas!) He dug roles, man,
> and names—like blackie, little
> Louie...

In the next few lines Louie's fantasies are concretized in cultural and make-believe heroes of the time, reiterating the idea already announced in the reference to Bogart, Cagney, and Raft that he lived life as if it were a drama to act out. First the Anglo heroes, then the Mexican heroes reinforce what is happening in the language of the poem, the convergence of two cultures. Montoya insists too on phonological effects. When he speaks of melodramatic music, he actualizes it in onomatopoetic nonce words—"tan tan tarán"—taking the childlike joy that presumably Louie took in associating meaning with acoustic pleasure.

Louie resists discovery of his innermost identity. When someone calls him by his name, "Ese Louie...," he rejects the name and insists on being called "Diamonds." He negates one self in order to take on others that will help disguise his true condition. He refuses to open up, since that would render vulnerable the intimate and essential being who lies concealed behind the masks of *machismo.* "Diamonds" is a fitting term for the impregnable and multifaceted exterior that he assumes. That Louie was a hero and renegade not only in his fantasies but also in actual wartime emerges in the subsequent stanza:

> Y en Korea fue soldado de
> levita con huevos and all the
> paradoxes del soldado raso—
> heroism and the stockade!

"And in Korea he had been a draftee with balls (literally: eggs) and all the paradoxes of the buck private (literally: smooth, level, flat, plain soldier) —heroism and the stockade!" There is a suggestion of psychological castration from the military and war experiences. On the one hand, potency and

[15]This phenomenon resembles the concept referred to by Roman Jakobson as "variation of verse instance," "Linguistics and Poetics," pp. 102-107.

virility are cited, but on the other, helplessness and castration. The adjective *raso* derives from the verb *rasar,* meaning "to level off, graze, skim, clear." This juxtaposition is further accentuated by its parallel in "herosim and the stockade." Emasculation is a theme which underlies much of Montoya's poetry; in an interview he discusses the dehumanizing effect the larger society has had on the Chicano farmworker and how this determines his expression:

> Certain images and words needed to stay in...like there is a difference between short cotton and tall cotton...you can't just say that you are picking cotton cuando piscas la bola...the father of the family is forced to go to la bola and they also sent other men...it was a system to castrate...la bola was like yanking your own balls out...loss of self...castration of the spirit.[16]

The phonological laws of Chicano speech often make one or both languages adapt. The most explicit example in Montoya's poem is the word *shainadas,* meaning "shined." Spanish does not have the final consonantal sound grouping *-nd.* Therefore, Montoya takes the English past participial adjective and adapts it to the Spanish equivalent of the same part of speech. By inserting the *a* between the *-nd* sound group and changing the spelling to adjust more closely to Spanish orthography, the poet introduces a new lexical and phonological item. Moreover, the syntax is ordered to correspond to Spanish. The normal position of the adjective in English would be before "jump boots," but "shainadas jump boots" would be an unusual utterance in the Chicano grammatical system.

Léon Robel states that "phonological deafness leads to an ideological deafness—a non-perception of a certain segment of the cultural personality"[17] when one hears a foreign language. This statement is in line with the hypothesis that language structure determines thought processes. Phonetic and syntactic patterns cause the speaker or auditor to think in terms determined by grammar. This means that different grammar expresses different ideas. The central figure of our poem, for example, is "el Louie," not just Louie. The definite article placed before the proper noun individualizes and does honor to the protagonist. The Spanish article confers on him the air of a Don, which the English article cannot do.

Language in this poem also functions as an indicator of generations. "Wow, is that el Louie" is obviously voiced by a teenager. The use of standard Spanish in the following stanza signalizes two women more closely tied to Mexican culture. Louie has the admiration not only of his peer group, but also of his elders, who see him as the son of Lola. "Comadre" is evidence of how language is formed by cultural requirements. The relationship of *comadres* (and *compadres*) is that between the natural parents and

---

[16]This statement was recorded in an interview with Tomás Ybarra-Frausto in the fall of 1976.

[17]In his "Polivanov et le Concept de Surdité Phonologique," in *Le Cercle de Prague* (Paris: Seuil, 1969), p. 115.

the spiritual parents of the child (godparents or *padrinos*) established through baptism. They are *compadres* (co-parents). This relationship between the adults is one which does not exist in the larger American society, since in English there is no one term that designates this tie.

The pace of the poem starts slowing down as the poet brings the reader back to the present through the use of the *leitmotiv,* "Hoy enterraron al Louie," now charged with more meaning than in the previous context. The poet gives one last glance to Louie's environs before he again repeats the inevitable truth—"Hoy enterraron al Louie"—like the significant thrice-sounded funeral bell giving more precision to an emotive image. Repetition also serves here to exhaust the grief that cannot be dissipated in just one voicing.

In Spanish, the poet vents his final disgust that Louie's "death was an insult": "porque no murió en acción—/no lo mataron los vatos,/ni los gooks en Korea" (because he didn't die in combat—/the dudes didn't kill him,/nor the gooks in Korea). The use of "gooks" by Montoya, a pejorative word for Orientals (in particular Koreans and Vietnamese), conveys a stark and lucid irony: one excluded group, the *pachucos,* an alienated internal colony of the larger Anglo society, finds another group to discriminate against. This is not a cultural characteristic but a universal human response; here its roots can be found in the sociopsychological conditions of the *pachuco.* "Gooks," an English slang term, criticizes the dominant group through its own racist epithet. The word reflects and judges the attitudes of Anglo-American society.

In English the poet makes a final philosophical understatement about the significance of the protagonist's life: "The end was a cruel hoax./But his life had been/remarkable!" He ends by assigning to Louie (for the first time his entire name is given, his full identity revealed in death), to the whole Pachuco era, and to the poem the most honorable and fitting epitaph: "Vato de atolle, el Louie Rodríguez."

"El Louie" is a circular poem of frustration enclosed almost entirely within the lines, "Hoy enterraron al Louie." A rebel without a (defined) cause, his life and death represent a solitary insurrection. He is deprived of the tragic hero's death because "no murió en acción" (he didn't die in combat). He probably overdosed on booze or drugs, imitating an illusion in death as in life ("He died alone in a rented/room—perhaps like a/Bogard movie"). But the intensity and realism of Louie's courage are immediately undercut by the inevitability of his defeat: "Vato de atolle" and "class" are contrasted to "too much booze y la vida dura (hard living)." The "cruel hoax" is a collaboration of the self-destructive forces within and the oppressive social condition without. His tragic flaw is his vehement rejection of a melting pot conformity and not knowing how to respond to the challenge that confronts him. The thrust of his thwarted virility and courage is ironically and ultimately turned on himself.

When one places Louie's struggle in historical perspective, one sees that this individual type of revolt was doomed to self-defeat, although it was one of the seeds of the present Chicano Movement. A tragic view of life can obscure the dialectical process of history and the capacity to endure and eventually overcome the apparently insurmountable. Montoya realizes this and, instead of dwelling on the human frailties and suffering which lead to a poetry of pity and lament and finally to self-indulgent sentiment, explores a new form and language in which to express the power of the Chicano mass movement toward self-affirmation and determination.

A new sense of freshness and vigor begins to articulate itself in the penultimate section of *El Sol y los de abajo,* entitled "El corrido de mi jefe." Up until that point, the tone of the collection is determined mostly by a vocabulary of tribulation with such expressions as "no tener y no Saber" (not having and not Knowing); "hopelessness...ineffective," "empty, putrid cowardly words," and "pain...llanto (moan)." Through the protagonist's voice, the poet indicates a way out of his previous defeatism through self-recognition and clarity of vision. A new era of positive confrontation takes shape in the persona's aggressive search for self-identity. In contrast to el Louie, this individual does not hide behind elusive masks. Instead, he first defines himself and accepts reality on its own terms. He will then be able to change his situation later.

In his most recent poetry, José Montoya has further developed his use of the traditional borderland *corrido*[18] to affirm the existence and collective struggle of the Chicano. This popular narrative mode has a formulaic oral quality and surface simplicity of language that encourage its dissemination among the community, which can transform it into social action.

José Montoya has given testimony to the abject circumstances of yesterday's *pachuco* in the poem "El Louie." By recognizing the significance of that period and relating it to the contemporary events recorded in his poetry, he frames a historical perspective in which to view the Chicano's survival. Louie's struggle was doomed on account of his alienation. Meaning is given to a people's destiny only through collective effort. In contrast to Montoya's earlier circular poetry, his present work enhances the dignity of the common man and of united action. The central role he and other Chicano bards have had in multilingual versification has allowed them to capture the complex heterogeneous reality of the Chicano.

---

[18]This is the popular form of the Texas-Mexican ballad that takes its name from *correr,* which means "to run" or "to flow," for the *corrido* tells a story simply and swiftly, without embellishments. For their extensive study read Américo Paredes's *With a Pistol in His Hand* (Austin: University of Texas Press, 1958) and *A Texas-Mexican Cancionero* (Chicago: University of Illinois Press, 1976).

The Development of Chicano Drama and Luis Valdez's *Actos*

by Carlota Cárdenas de Dwyer

I

The current flowering of Chicano literature began in the fields of Delano, California, with Luis Valdez's formation of the Teatro Campesino (Farmworkers Theater). In a move that eventually had a decisive effect on all other areas of Chicano creative expression, Valdez focused on the needs and interests of the *campesino* (farmworker) audience and designed a unique form of theater. Since then, the term "Chicano drama" has become synonymous with Valdez and his Teatro Campesino. To a certain extent, no other Chicano writer or art form illustrates more clearly the depth and complexity of the Chicano heritage than do Luis Valdez and the Teatro Campesino. To appreciate fully the interplay of forces in his career, one must review the development of his Teatro Campesino and then examine the expansion of his aesthetic and philosophical base.

In an article which appeared in the *Latin American Theatre Review*, before serving as introduction to his collection, *Actos*,[1] Valdez claims for his theater a myriad of dramatic sources ranging from Old Comedy and *commedia dell'arte* to Brecht and agitprop. In addition, he invokes the ritualistic theater of Japan and the religious drama of the pre-Hispanic people of Latin America.[2]

Many of these antecedents, plus the Spanish American religious dramas of the colonial period, have been mentioned by critics.[3] Before the close of the

"The Development of Chicano Drama and Luis Valdez's *Actos*" by Carlota Cárdenas de Dwyer. This article appears for the first time in this volume. It is used by permission of the author.

[1]Luis Valdez, *Actos: El Teatro Campesino* (San Juan Bautista, Calif.: La Cucaracha Press, 1971). In this study all references to the *actos* contained in this collection will be from the Cucaracha Press edition, 1971. Succeeding references will be given within parentheses in the text.

[2]*Actos*, pp. 1-2; also in "Teatro Chicano: Two Reports, Notes on Chicano Theater," *Latin American Theatre Review*, 4 (1971), 52-55.

[3]Tomás Ybarra-Frausto, "Punto de Partida," in "Teatro Chicano: Two Reports," *Latin American Theatre Review*, 4 (1971), 51-52; David Copeland, "Chicano Theatre," *Drama Review*, 17, no. 4 (1973), 73-89; Francisco Jiménez, "Dramatic Principles of the Teatro Campesino," *Bi-*

sixteenth century, Mexican colonists led by Juan de Oñate performed mystical drama, beginning a tradition of Spanish language theater in the United States. This rich and varied tradition eventually expanded to include secular drama, *carpas*, and folk drama enacted by both local and traveling groups.[4] In the most thorough discussion so far of Valdez's theatrical origins, Jorge Huerta cites influences as varied as the Roman stage, the *auto sacramental* of the Spanish Middle ages, the *Rabinal Achi* of the Maya, and the *carpas* of modern Mexico in the New World.[5]

Valdez's exuberant and improvised comic satire is often attributed to influence from either the Italian *commedia dell'arte* of the sixteenth century or possibly the more contemporary and local *carpas* of Mexican theater. Certainly the influence of both is likely, since Valdez is probably as familiar with one as with the other, and the relationship of the two is so close that they may be considered elements within an encompassing whole. Indeed, it may be argued that the Mexican *carpas* themselves originate from the sixteenth-century *pasos* of Lope de Rueda of Spain, who is said to have come into contact with Italian *commedia dell'arte* players touring the Iberian peninsula.[6] Octavio Paz notes with emphasis the impact of the entire Italian Renaissance on the early Spanish traditions in art and poetry and to the words of a writer asserting that "'the earliest American poetry may be regarded as an offshoot or continuation of the school of Seville,'" Paz responds, "might we not...claim that the Seville school itself is a branch of the Italian tree?'"[7]

In addition, Valdez undoubtedly owes much to the agitprop theater which appeared in the United States during the twenties and thirties. His first *actos* were performed almost exactly forty years after the seminal *Strike!* by Mike Gold was published and exactly thirty years after *Waiting for Lefty* was performed in New York.[8] Mike Gold's short play, *Strike!: A Mass Recitation*, contains the same assortment of semi-allegorical characters and the same blend of music, chorus, and dialogue sometimes found in Valdez's *actos*.[9] Clifford Odets's *Waiting for Lefty* is as deeply embroiled in the New York taxi drivers' strike of 1934 as Valdez was originally in the

lingual Review/Revista Bilingüe, 2, nos. 1 and 2 (1975), 99-110; and Roberto J. Garza, "Historical Antecedents to Chicano Theatre," in *Contemporary Chicano Theatre*, ed. Robert J. Garza (Notre Dame, Ind.: University of Notre Dame Press, 1976), pp. 1-5.

[4]See, for example, John W. Brokaw's "A Mexican American Acting Company 1849-1924," *Educational Theatre Journal*, 27 (1975), 23-30, and Nicolás Kanellos's "Chicano Theatre to Date," *Tejidos*, 2 (Winter 1975), 40-46.

[5]Jorge A. Huerta, "Chicano Teatro: A Background," *Aztlán*, 2, no. 2 (1971), 63-66.

[6]J. E. Varey, "Spain," *Oxford Companion to the Theatre*, 3rd ed., ed. Phyllis Hartnoll (London: Oxford University Press, 1967), p. 902.

[7]Octavio Paz, ed., *Anthology of Mexican Poetry*, trans. Samuel Beckett (Bloomington: Indiana University Press, 1958), p. 24.

[8]Myron Matlaw, "Agitprop," in *Modern World Drama: An Encyclopedia*, ed. Myron Matlaw, (New York: Dutton, 1972), p. 13.

[9]*Strike!: A Mass Recitation, New Masses*, 1, no. 3 (1926), 19-21.

strike of the farmworkers.[10] As John O'Connor of *The Wall Street Journal* puts it, "There's nothing very unusual in using the theatre as a soapbox: it's still only the quality that counts, from Ibsen to Shaw to Bertolt Brecht and Arthur Miller."[11]

II

Teatro Campesino came to life suddenly in 1965 when César Chávez gave the twenty-five-year-old drama student an opportunity to present some of his own theater to farmworkers to strengthen the union's organizing efforts. Valdez had spent most of his life preparing for that moment. His fascination with theater began during his first year of elementary school in Stanford, California, when he took part in preparations for a school play at Christmas. He missed the actual performance because his family of migrant farmworkers was forced to move on to harvest another crop. Shortly after, he began organizing his own plays at school and, later, puppet shows in the family garage. In spite of his family's frequent moving, Valdez concentrated on his studies and won a scholarship to San Jose State University, where he continued his work in drama. During his last year at San Jose State, he brought his cultural background into fertile contact with his dramatic interests in *The Shrunken Head of Pancho Villa,* a play which was later produced on campus at a regional drama conference.

Like his campesino characters, who feel uneasy in middle-class urban life, Valdez sensed at about this time a need to return to his cultural roots in the Salinas Valley. During the spring of 1965, he began to consider the possibilities of a theater which would appeal to the farmworkers, not only in subject and content but in form and style as well. That summer he joined the San Francisco Mime Troupe and there discovered a type of theater which he thought ideally suited to a campesino audience. Later that fall, he became involved in what he now considers the first major theatrical event of *la huelga* (the strike).[12] On September 26, 1965, he was one of twelve hundred people who marched at Delano under the banner of the Virgin of Guadalupe. The following spring, in March, when Chávez mobilized his supporters for a three-hundred-mile march to Sacramento, Valdez's teatro performed at nightly rallies and developed most of the materials and methods which distinguish teatro performances today. Since then, additional groups, modeled after the Valdez troupe, have surfaced throughout the Southwest. All of these groups direct their efforts to a specifically barrio or Chicano audience. In addition, they continue to conform to Valdez's early

[10]Matlaw, p. 803.

[11]"The Theatre: Shades of the Thirties," *Wall Street Journal,* 24 (July 1967), p. 12.

[12]Beth Bagdy, "El Teatro Campesino: Interviews with Luis Valdez," *Tulane Drama Review,* 11 (Summer 1967), 74.

patterns of style and content, even to the point of reenacting many of Valdez's own *actos* or sketches.

The *acto* is an original Valdez creation and is still the basic form of the teatro performance. In his first efforts at Delano he began by outlining improvisational scenes about the strike experience and recruiting actors from his audience of farmworkers. Like early Greek drama, the *actos* were performed outdoors, contained elements of song and dance, relied little on stage efforts or props, and featured the use of masks. These elements, along with an intensely social or political purpose, are still characteristic of Teatro presentations today. Almost anywhere Chicano teatro is performed, it is a startlingly dynamic pastiche of Chicano words and rhythms joined together into an uninhibited display of cultural affirmation and social commitment. Although changes have occurred in Valdez's concept of teatro as drama and in the issues he considers relevant and significant, these aspects of the form remain consistent to the present.

During the early days of his Teatro, Valdez was concerned only with the campesino and the huelga. In 1966, he wrote in *Ramparts* that his "most important aim is to reach the farmworkers. All the actors are farmworkers and our single topic is the huelga."[13] Later in 1967, in an interview which appeared in the *Tulane Drama Review,* Valdez completely disavowed any artistic aspirations and spoke only of the political purposes of the Teatro. He explained, "We don't think in terms of art, but of our political purpose in putting across certain points. ... I'm talking politics, not art. ..."[14] However, in a subsequent *Newsweek* interview, he revealed that he had changed his thinking both on the scope of the Teatro's focus and on his conception of its form. He spoke of the expansion of the Teatro's concern to include other issues, such as the controversy then surrounding U. S. involvement in Vietnam. Most importantly, Valdez expressed a developing awareness of the implications of his Teatro's success. He asserted, "I've found an audience that needs an art that speaks to their way of life."[15] From then on, Valdez upheld the essentially aesthetic nature of the Teatro Campesino without apology or qualification. Valdez was one of the first Chicano literary artists to devise and define an art form on his own terms. With it and from it flowed an outpouring of poetry and prose. His "Chicano drama" truly heralded a new wave of American literary expression.

III

Although Valdez's changing interpretation of the nature of his drama is not readily apparent in the actual text of his presentations during those

---

[13]Luis Valdez, "El Teatro Campesino," *Ramparts* (July 1966), p. 55.

[14]*Tulane Drama Review,* 78.

[15]"New Grapes," *Newsweek* (31 July 1967), p. 79.

years, the widening of his interests to include issues other than the strike appears clearly in his 1971 publication, *Actos: El Teatro Campesino*, a collection of nine *actos*. Here, early works from the mid-sixties depict the plight of the farmworker and the strike. Later works deal with discrimination in the schools, Chicano militancy, and the Vietnam war. The nine *actos* document the shift of Valdez's concern from the needs of a strictly campesino to those of a more generalized barrio or Chicano audience. *La huelga* became for Valdez, as well as for most Chicanos, only one aspect of *la causa*.

The first two selections in *Actos*, dated 1965 and 1966, are situated in the fields and portray the campesinos and the hardships they suffer. The last two *actos*, dated 1970 and 1971, present the impact of war on families in the barrio. These changes reflect a change in the formal relationship between the Farmworkers Union and the Teatro Campesino, for in 1971, the Teatro disengaged itself from the union and moved sixty miles away. Although the campesino is still one of the Teatro's major concerns, it is no longer the only concern. Legislative changes and political accommodations are reflected in the most recent *actos*, which emphasize unity between the U.S. migrant laborer and undocumented workers from Mexico.

In *Las dos caras del patroncito ("The Two Faces of the Owner")*,[16] the first of the nine selections contained in *Actos*, there are only two major characters. Each is representative of his race and class. The farmworker, like his employer, has no individualizing characteristics. When the farmworker dons the piglike mask of the owner, they reverse roles completely. The farmworker-now-*patrón* rejects the elaborate material wealth symbolized by the owner's mansion and luxury car, and is content with only his cigar. The audience grasps a relatively simple piece of propaganda: Anglo-American employers are inherently exploitative, self-serving, and hard-hearted; Chicano farmworkers are unjustly exploited but fundamentally selfless and good-hearted. The idea as well as the characterization is simplistic. The comedy and satire are equally simplistic. At one point the owner confesses to the farmworker that at times, sitting in his air-conditioned office, he thinks to himself, "I wish I was a Mexican." He elaborates:

> Just one of my own boys. Riding in the truck, hair flying in the wind, feeling all that freedom, coming out here to the field, working under the green vines, smoking a cigarette, my hands in the cool, soft earth, underneath the blue skies, with white clouds drifting by, looking at the mountains, listening to the birdies sing. (14)

This and other comparably rhapsodic descriptions of the workers' situation contrast markedly with the owner's assessment after roles have been reversed. At the end, the owner-now-worker concludes: "You know, that

[16]This title, as well as others, shows Valdez's customary merging of the Spanish language with conventions of capitalization from the English language.

damn César Chávez is right. You can't do this work for less than two dollars an hour" (18).

The first *acto* depicts the union's struggle for higher wages. Another dimension of the worker's life is presented in the second acto, *Quinta temporada*. Here the farm labor contractor, *el contratista* Don Coyote, is singled out as an equally exploitative force. In the end, the solution to the injustices of the labor contracting system lies in the union hiring hall. This time, however, the despised *contratista* is not a part of the monolithic system portrayed in the first *acto* in which both race and class are identified. Don Coyote is neither an Anglo capitalist nor an exploited farmworker: he is a Chicano, greedy and exploitative himself. The facile moral dichotomy implied formerly has been abandoned.

In the third play, *Los vendidos (The Sellouts)*, Valdez's characters reveal an almost geometrical increase in the sophistication with which they are portrayed. The scene opens at Honest Sancho's Used Mexican Lot and Curio Shop. A state employee, Miss Jiménez, who pronounces her name with an unmistakable Anglo intonation as "JIM-enez," has arrived to buy a token "Mexican type" for the governor's office. Honest Sancho introduces four models, each representing a familiar stereotype: the Farmworker, Johnny Pachuco, the Revolucionario, and finally, the assimilated Mexican American. The four are robotlike figures turned on and off with a switch by Honest Sancho. The surprise comes when Honest Sancho is revealed to be a robot himself, controlled by the four "models." They manipulate Sancho and apparently everyone else through Sancho, rather than the contrary.

As an *acto, Los vendidos* successfully blends comedy and satire as well as the elements of English and Spanish. A kind of bilingual wordplay occurs at the beginning when Miss Jiménez describes the "Mexican type" she seeks. Sancho follows her Anglicized pronunciation of such words as "suave" and "debonair" with their Spanish counterparts, rendering the latter as *de bien aire*. His English speech is crammed with clichés about Mexicans, especially when he presents the farmworker model. He refers to the grease the farmworker secretes which enables him "to slip and slide right through the crop with no trouble" (38). He calls the farmworker the "Volkswagen of Mexicans," explaining that maintenance and upkeep costs are very low. He cites housing as an example, saying, "You can put him in old barns, old cars, river banks. You can even leave him out in the fields overnight with no worry" (38). The farmworker, however, is unacceptable because he cannot speak English.

When Miss Jiménez learns that the *pachuco* is bilingual she is interested, so Sancho immediately snaps his fingers and orders "Johnny, give us some English." Johnny responds with a loud "Fuck you!" which supposedly shocks the proper young secretary. She exclaims "Oh! I've never been so insulted in all my life!" Sancho quickly retorts, "Well, he learned it in your school" (40). When Johnny Pachuco attempts to snatch her purse, she dismisses him, saying, "We can't have any *more* thieves in the state administration"(42).

Turning to the Revolucionario, Sancho emphasizes his character as a "macho" or "Latin lover." Boasting, Sancho proclaims, "there is one outstanding feature about this model I KNOW the ladies are going to love: he's a genuine antique! He was made in Mexico in 1910!" He then adds that the Revolucionario was also "made" in Tijuana, Guadalajara, and California (44). When Miss Jiménez rejects him, insisting on an "American-made" product, Sancho presents the newly arrived "Mexican-American" "built exactly like our Anglo models except that he comes in a variety of darker shades: Naugahyde, leather, or leatherette. He is bilingual, college educated, and ambitious. Say the word 'acculturate' and he accelerates" (45). The satire of the Anglo world is conveyed in broad and bold strokes easily adapted by nonprofessional groups in an improvised or makeshift setting.

IV

Los vendidos and other Valdez works have an appeal to the Chicano audience because of their relevance to contemporary Chicano experience and barrio culture. Chicano audiences readily understand the social and emotional overtones of the bilingual dialogue. Sancho's "acculturation" syndrome and his remark about color as the only differentiating quality between the Anglo and the assimilated Mexican American exemplify dimensions of Chicano life all too well known throughout the Southwest. For this reason, satellite teatro groups in the barrios of California and Texas have been able to adapt Valdez's *actos* to their local areas without major revisions. When original scripts are composed in these places, they are usually variations on character types and incidents presented earlier in Valdez's works.

In these *actos* and many that followed, Valdex acknowledges, and sometimes focuses on, the complicity of certain Chicanos with the oppressive forces. In the fourth *acto, La conquista de México* (1968), the Axtec leader Moctezuma II and his supporters are shown to be cruel and demanding imperialists. This *acto* bears witness also to Valdez's growing interest in indigenous ritual and myth as a basis for his Teatro, so that within less than a decade his Teatro had exhibited strong influences from almost every form of dramatic entertainment known to mankind. This unprecedented and incongruous adaptation of forms may be considered the hallmark of the Chicano artist. As heir to not one but clusters of legacies from several continents, he is free to select his own most worthy progenitors and from them to enrich his fund of creative images.

Brecht and Chicano Theater

by Barclay Goldsmith

I

Chicano theater, in existence for well over a decade, is rooted firmly in the popular culture of the barrio and campo. It has also drawn heavily upon many international forms and styles. It is most often compared with Brechtian theater and the Brechtian theater movement, since this also has a popular base. If the mid and late seventies are a time for reflection, as some say, then perhaps now is the time to examine and define the influence of the German writer and theoretician on Chicano theater.

The question, Is Chicano theater Brechtian?, is important for us beyond mere schematic comparison of acting styles, play structures, and themes. The question requires us to analyze the methods by which popular culture is shaped into "high art" forms. It forces us to account for the parallel manner in which two similar theatrical movements emerged in two separate cultures, in two separate historical movements—with apparently very little contact between performers, writers, or other theater artists.

II

Bertolt Brecht was highly influenced by forms of entertainment known as "popular presentational." Early Chicano theater falls into this same category. Presentational theater drops all pretense at achieving "slice of life" naturalism and attempts to eliminate what is called the "fourth wall" dividing actor and audience. It is a theater often employing masks, asides, large mimetic gesture, and a device known as "breakouts." In this latter technique, the actor drops his or her character and addresses the audience as performer. Presentational theater is the basis for such high art forms as late Renaissance *commedia dell 'arte* (Molière), German expressionism, and the Brechtian epic.

"Brecht and Chicano Theater" by Barclay Goldsmith. This article appears for the first time in this volume. It is used by permission of the author.

There is much confusion about the term "popular presentational" when the "popular" is added. Most simply stated, it refers to a working class, peasant, or *campesino* audience who can identify with the subject matter presented through song, topicality of humor, and immediately identifiable archetypal characters. The confusion arises because the mass audiences at which presentational theater aims differ as history changes economic relationships. What might have been lively and popular a decade earlier becomes suddenly irrelevant.[1]

"Popular presentational" theater has always flourished during times of social upheaval. Morality plays, a late medieval development, were performed in small towns at the same time that secular control was being wrested from the Church. Commedia troups performed in plazas and squares especially in the sixteenth century, when a new merchant class was challenging the authority of the feudal aristocracy. The Germany of the 1920s and early 1930s was ripe for the rise of a popular presentational theatrical form. The crumbling economy and rending of the social fabric had promoted a new political consciousness within the working class.

One of the popular theatrical forms which emerged in Germany at this time was agitprop. The German Workers' Theater League estimated that over 500 such groups were performing in 1931.[2] The agitprop play is a short theatrical piece which usually has as its aim the education of the audience either to reflect upon or to redress a particular immediate social grievance. The form first developed in the Soviet Union with cultural worker cadres which traveled by train through the country, urging workers and peasants to wrest control of the land. The term "agitprop" was early defined as follows:

Agitation: the putting across of one idea to many people.

Propaganda: the putting across of many more complex ideas to relatively fewer people.

Agitation is generally a call to action around a single idea—better wages, for example. Propaganda takes into account the social or cultural ramifications of an idea and usually calls upon the audience for further reflection. Thus, political theater varies from being immediate and agitational to long-range and propagandistic. (There is strong distaste for the word "propaganda" in our culture because we associate it with a manipulative disortion of truth or because many audiences are not moved by the simplistic characterizations of much agitprop theater.[3])

The original European agitprop theater piece is usually highly visual,

---

[1]An extensive analysis of popular culture may be found in Stanley Aronowitz's *False Promises: The Shaping of American Working Class Consciousness* (New York: McGraw Hill, 1973).

[2]"Nature and Development of Presentational Political Theater" (unpublished paper by Richard Seyd, former member of Red Ladder Theater, London, p. 2.) On file with Teatro Libertad, Tucson, Arizona.

[3]*Ibid*, p. 3.

using one central metaphor to explain a complicated issue. For example, in a contemporary piece developed by England's Red Ladder Theater, bakers slice large pieces of bread from a giant loaf. The knives are the means of production and the loaf represents raw material. The slices of bread are then brought back by the workers, who must eat, although leftover slices are accumulated up the side of a ladder by the company owner. When this profit becomes "excess accumulation," the workers are put out of work but must borrow money in order to eat the stockpiled pieces of bread. The owner of the factory has interlocking ownership with the bank, etc. The metaphor can be expanded into an enlarged lesson in economics. Though the visual metaphor is highly theatrical, agitprop characterizations are one-dimensional and cartoonlike. Rarely has an agitprop piece survived beyond the immediate moment of some rally or mass meeting for which it was intended.

It was upon this agitprop form that Brecht based his short plays of the 1930s, the years of his newly found political commitment. Known as *Lehrstuecke*, they differ from agitprop because character development is stronger and the issues turn from the immediate to the general or long-range. For example, in *The Mother*, Pelagea Vlassova, the protagonist, becomes a committed union agitator, nd the play takes us through the stages of her changing personality from a scared, self-effacing woman to a strong leader. The play uses archetypal characters but their development is far more complex than in agitprop. Thus the contradictions are much more subtle.

In addition to agitprop. Brecht admired the Berlin cabarets. He was a devotee of many folk comedians, particularly the Bavarian clown Karl Valentin. Brecht's friend, the director Bernard Reich, states that sketches which Valentin wrote and appeared in demonstrated "that a simple and one-dimensional plot can get across an extremely complicated generalization to an audience and that a small scene can stand for a big problem."[4]

Cabaret shows contained large mimetic gestures, grotesque but still archetypal characters, and subtle breakouts. The actor Valentin always seemed to be commenting upon the characters he was playing. It is possible that by watching these cabaret shows and Valentin in particular, Brecht learned to distance his audience from the action on stage. This distancing is one of the main attributes of Brechtian acting.

Brecht was interested in a scientific theater—a theater which led to reflection on the part of the audience. Reflection, it was hoped, would lead to action, whereas the traditional European theater, he believed, had always led to emotional catharsis and passive observation on the part of the spectator. The German playwright introduced the concept of *Gestus* in acting in order to distance audiences from the emotional impact of the play. Briefly, this device is a physical or vocal gesture which illuminates social relationships. The *Gestus* is not unlike a series of rapidly evolving still photos.

[4]Dennis Calandra, "Karl Valentin and Bertolt Brecht," *The Drama Review*, 18, No. 1 (March, 1974), 86.

An example of a *Gestus* occurs in the following line in an acting exercise based on *Romeo and Juliet* and prepared by Brecht for his actors; "But we will be without shelter, Sir," says an old tenant angrily to Romeo who is about to dislodge him.[5] A *Gestus* occurs in the word "Sir." The actor in rehearsal must search for the right body and vocal gesture which will reflect an angry recoiling away from the first part of the line. The use of *Gestus* reinforces our concept of men and women as capable of change. Our conventional physical and vocal gestures are often masks which we shed and change as social relationships change. The concept of *Gestus* allows for masks, freezes, slow motion and other presentational theatrical devices as long as they illuminate social reality.[6]

Brecht moved away from the agitprop-influenced *Lehrstuecke* form to epic theater after World War II. In doing this, he moved from a popular presentational form to a high Art form in which the psychology of the characters is more complex and more reality is illuminated than in his earlier shorter plays. In the epic form, the scope of scenes may span several decades, moving back and forth in time. Epic plays are thus non-Aristoletian, since they forsake unity of time and place. A contemporary social problem is often framed in another time period. For example, the distribution of wealth is a contemporary problem explored in *The Caucasian Chalk Circle,* yet the play is set in the twelfth century. Each scene in the epic form poses one single contradiction or illuminates one problem in such a way that it can be lifted from the main body of the work to stand alone with its own statement. Thus, epic scenes echo the simplicity of the early cabaret acts which had influenced Brecht, and they retain the didactic flavor of agitprop.

III

If we begin our analysis with a comparison between conditions for the Chicano in this country in the 1960s and conditions for the average worker in Germany during the 1920s and early 1930s, we discover vast differences. Until recently, a large proportion of the Chicano population has been rural farmworker rather than (as in Germany) urban industrial. Furthermore, the Chicano has had to confront the problems of a colonized minority within a larger dominant culture. Finally, popular Chicano culture itself has its roots in the historic tensions of three cultures—the Pre-Columbian, Spanish Catholic, and Anglo-American. Chicano theater clearly reflects these realities and differences.

One of the early dramatic forms developed by the Chicano theater move-

[5]"B. B's Rehearsal Scenes," in *Brecht,* ed. Erika Munk (New York: Bantam Drama Book, 1972), p. 121.
[6]An extensive analysis of Brechtian acting can be found in John Willet's *The Theater of Bertolt Brecht* (London: Methuen, 1960).

ment was the *acto*. Performed at first to support the United Farmworker Organizing Committee, *actos* were presented at meetings and in picket lines throughout the West by the Teatro Campesino under Luis Valdez's direction. It was the Teatro Campesino which perfected the *acto* form and inspired several dozen other groups to do likewise.

The *acto* is often called agitprop in the press, but though it shows some similarity to that form, its emphasis on character and cultural identity and lack of emphasis on economic metaphor make it decidedly different. However, in one early *acto*, *La quinta temporada*, *(The Fifth Season)*,[7] economic relationships between the farmworker, contractor, and boss do in fact receive thematic emphasis. We see a chain functioning whereby the farmworker picks money from a tree and Don Coyote (labor contractor) takes the money from the farmworker's pocket, stuffing some into his own and passing the rest to El Patrón (The Boss). This chain process is repeated over the four seasons until the Boss accumulates a wad of bills. The fifth season is the coming to awareness, the worker's realization that he must break the chain.

The *acto* is rich in theatricality, deriving from the coloring of its characters. Don Coyote is rendered both as animal-like, by way of rural imagery, and as specifically human, through his slyness and his easily recognizable vocal and bodily gestures.

The *acto* form has now flourished for over a decade, reflecting many aspects of Chicano life. It has urged audiences to redress grievances other than the farmworkers' plight, but it has also evoked the richness of Chicano culture for its own sake. Some of the more traditional characters, like La Calavera (Death) and El Diablo (The Devil), derive from medieval morality plays. While they retain their old symbolic force, their modern reference is ironically striking. Other popular cultural traditions which are decidedly Mexican have been incorporated into the *acto: el corrido*, a long narrative song, and *la carpa*, the Mexican traveling circus, which also has its own tradition. Many *acto* characters are decidedly contemporary and are both urban and rural. One of the most satirized is the Chicano professional who does not return to serve in the community *(Los vendidos)*.

Variety of language *(Gestus)* is emphasized in Brechtian epic. In Chicano theater, variety of language is used primarily to mirror cultural identity. *Actos* are often written and performed in *caló*—a mixture of English and Spanish. An example is "traite los kids" (bring the kids). Sometimes English words are given Spanish pronunciation: "wáchale" (watch out), or "dame un raite" (give me a ride). *Caló* is a language of survival and its use on stage in and of itself has political implications.

Very broadly speaking, the acting styles of early Chicano *actos* and those of Brechtian theater show affinity. Both are based on popular cultural traditions and are indebted to agitprop, but both have developed characters

---

[7]*La quinta temporada* and other early short theater pieces by the Teatro Campesino can be found in *Actos: El Teatro Campesino* (San Juan Bautista, Calif.: Cucaracha Press, 1971).

more fully than the agitprop form, although for different reasons. Both Brechtian theater and Chicano theater have characters who are capable of perceiving, growing, and changing. To show this, both use large mimetic gestures, archetypal characters, and masks. Chicano theater does not show so constant a concern with *Gestus* to denote contradictions within a character. Conversely, early Chicano theater is more exuberant, requiring a higher energy level from its actors. The most fully developed Chicano theater piece, Teatro Campesino's *La gran carpa de la familia Rascuachi*, uses the popular traditions of *el corrido* and *la carpa* in a whirlwind of sound and movement. The nuances of Brechtian acting would have slowed down the forward movement of this piece, altering its effectiveness.

Two *actos* which most precisely reflect the Brechtian acting style are the Teatro Campesino's *Soldado raso* and *Vietnam campesino*. These short pieces portray quieter, conflicting moods and more subtle, restrained character involvement. In the former play, a young Chicano is taken to war by La Muerte (Death) and eventually killed. In the latter, parallels between the lives and struggles of Vietnamese peasants and North American campesinos are explored. Valdez all but states this in an interview with Françoise Kourilsky: "In *Soldado*, I wanted to create a feeling from within the audience, that feeling of two forces, the duality of life that is a reality."[8]

In comparing Brechtian theater with Chicano theater, we must realize that Brechtian theater was developed by one person (with some collaboration from composers and actors), while Chicano theater springs from a movement which reflects differences of class, cultural makeup, and political orientation within the Chicano community. Recently, many theaters have broken with the *acto* form and taken up new styles and structural forms, some little relationship to either Brechtian epic or the popular presentational form.

One theater piece which evolved in the early 1970s and is decidedly epic is Teatro Campesino's *La gran carpa de la familia Rascuachi*. The play unfolds a series of episodic events in the life of a family headed by Jesús and María Pelado Rascuachi. Although this short piece, set to the music of a *corrido*, uses the cartoonlike characters of popular entertainment, both husband and wife experience the full gamut of contradictory feelings and torn identities. They are Brechtian not simply because they are complex, but because their specific class, regional, and racial backgrounds show them to be representatives as well as individuals. Their gestures and bodily bearing make quick, illuminating statements about their situation as recently arrived Mexican workers, without visas, experiencing American society, working in the fields, raising a family, moving to the city, and finally going on welfare. When Jesús grabs his hat and emits a *grito* (yell) of joy for having successfully crossed the Rio Grande, the shout, the upward thrust of

[8]Quoted in Francoise Kourilsky, "Approaching Quetzalcoatl: the Evolution of El Teatro Campesino." *Performance*, 2 (Fall, 1973), 37-46. This article appeared originally in French in *Travail Théatral*, 7 (April-June, 1972), 59-70.

head and stretching of limbs, make for a memorable moment in the theater. It is his gesture of hope-universally appropriate for a campesino, yet firmly rooted in the spychology of the individual character.

Another example of the epic form can be found in Teatro de la Esperanza's *La víctima,* a portrait of three generations of a Chicano family in the United States painfully achieving, against odds, a degree of upward economic mobility. In this play, collectively written and directed by the group's members, several actors assume multiple roles. This has the same effect as Brechtian acting style, which allows one character to assume many social stances. The sweep of scenes over several generations in a short theatrical time span and the use of such distancing devices as signs make this piece decidedly epic in the Brechtian sense.

A more questionable example is Teatro de la Gentle's *El hombre que se convirtió en perro, (The Man Who Became a Dog).* This is based on a play of the same name by the Argentine writer Oswaldo Dragún. The protagonist, a factory security guard, turns into a dog because his superiors treat him like one. Though used in expressionistic theater, most notably in Eugene O'Neill's *The Hairy Ape* and Elmer Rice's *The Adding Machine,* such transformations run counter to one of Brecht's main tenets, which is that the central character be a reasonable person, manipulated perhaps by outside forces but never helpless. At the same time, though decidedly un-Brechtian in this respect, the play employs many popular presentational devices. Power figures are archetypal, gesture is broad, and there are numerous instances when the audience is directly addressed.

IV

To answer the question, Is Chicano theater Brechtian?, one has to consider, then, what period, what theatrical form, and even what theater company one is referring to, Luis Valdez has stated on several occasions that he is "somewhere between Cantinflas and Brecht." This statement seems correct. His Teatro Campesino has broadly used the popular presentational style, even though there are dissimilarities, and there is of course an affinity with Cantinflas, since the latter's Mexican films represent the great masses, the underemployed, and the cast-offs, searching for identity. The predicaments he explores are similar to those that interest Valdez.

Chicano theater cannot be Brechtian in any stricter sense than this for several reasons. As has already been stated, Brechtian character development is more realistic and complex. Furthermore, Chicano theater lacks the dialectical analysis found in Brechtian epic. True, there has been some contact with Brecht's work at Chicano theater festivals. The San Francisco Mime Troupe's *The Mother* stirred considerable interest at the 1974 Chicano Theater Festival in Mexico City. The Teatro Experimental de Cali uses the

Brechtian epic form to a considerable extent and has performed widely in
the United States. Chicano theater has actually had a considerable influence
on Latin American popular theaters, most notably on TEC, which has produced several works of the Teatro Campesino. Los Mascarones in Cuernavaca, Mexico, has evolved a *carpa* style in its traveling productions, prob-
able inspired by *La gran carpa*. But apart from these instances, it is safe to
say there has been little direct contact with the Brecht tradition. Félix and
Lilly Alvarez—who played Jesús and María in the Teatro Campesino's
production of *La carpa* for several years—said that an ex-Berliner Ensemble actor told them after a performance that they were "very Brechtian,"
yet both actors state they never studied Brecht during rehearsals for that
play.

   Chicano theater is Brechtian, then, more in spirit than in specifics. Like
Brechtian theater it is based on popular culture and stresses the dialectics
of change. But if it aimed to be Brechtian to the letter, it would become a
"hothouse plant." German popular culture has grown out of an entirely
different set of historical circumstances from that of the Chicano, and the
resultant forms must therefore vary.

   Brecht wrote, moreover, with a broad Marxist perspective, and very few
teatros, if any, are Marxist in concept, at least in the way Brecht intended,
with his merciless exposé of contradictions within a bourgeois value system.
On this account, some critics dismiss altogether the possibility of comparing
Brecht with the teatros. There are, however, two positions here. One is the
viewpoint of critical realism, which argues that we are the sum total of all
cultural products, and hence all literature which accurately shows the social
tensions of a given historical period has value. This is the view taken by
Enrique Buenaventura, TEC's director, in defending the Teatro Campesino's
Catholic/Pre-Columbian ending of *La carpa* at the 1974 festival. The Teatro
Campesino, he argues, understands the religious convictions of the campesino and to deny them is to deny him his right to a cosmology of his own.
It is as if the Soviet Union were to deny Tolstoy simply because he chose to
write of religious peasant life. The other position is less conciliatory. It
argues that only a given style and content are acceptable for socialist theater
(e.g., Brecht and epic or Gorki and socialist realism). Brecht himself said
he did not "give a whit" for Tolstoy, and would have paid to have some
German classics not published.

   The right relationship between popular art and the struggle for cultural
identity remains as yet unsettled. What happens to the social fabric upon
which Chicano culture is based as more Chicanos move to the cities? Is there
now a Chicano urban culture? Does urbanization rob the Chicano of the
basis of popular culture? Can popular theater be urban or only rural? These
have become urgent questions now that the last stronghold, the barrios,
seem increasingly to be doomed. "From one end of the Southwest to the
other," says Ernesto Galarza, writing of Barrio Pascua in Tucson, "they,

like the colonias, stand in the path of Anglo progress. I am not speaking here of points of friction but points of attrition, at which the destructive power of the dominant society is at work."[9]

Thus the struggle for cultural identity is related in intricate ways to the survival of popular culture. While it is dangerous to take a narrow view and say that only the popular presentational style should be valued in Chicano theater, it is equally dangerous to become international and eclectic, searching for styles and forms which have lost their class and cultural roots. During the formative years of their development both Brechtian and Chicano theater were concerned with agitation. Both drew heavily on their own popular culture and both borrowed from the popular forms of other cultures. In this way both could remain culturally authentic while becoming international.

Because of its popular roots, Chicano theater is alive and well. If it has evolved a Brechtian flavor, this is because it has based itself on the needs of the people and has served their cause.

[9]Edward H. Spicer and Raymond H. Thompson, *Plural Society of the Southwest,* (Albuquerque: University of New Mexico Press, 1972).

From *acto* to *mito:* A Critical Appraisal of the Teatro Campesino

by Yvonne Yarbro-Bejarano

The Teatro Campesino's twelve-year history has been marked by constant experimentation and evolution. This process of growth and change has been accompanied by criticism as well as praise. The most heated controversy surrounding the group has stemmed from their concentration on the mythical and religious aspects of Chicano culture, marking a shift away from the more socially oriented theater which characterized their first five years. Before discussing this polemic, it might be helpful to review briefly the course of the Teatro Campesino from its beginnings up to the time the controversy arose.

The Teatro Campesino began as people's theater in the service of social struggle. Born in the farmworkers' strike at Delano in 1965, it was made up of farmworkers and was directed toward an audience of farmworkers; its function was to educate the people about the fundamental issues and help organize them to strike. The appeal of good theater, always of paramount importance to the Teatro Campesino, is here seen in a clear relationship to the needs of a working-class audience which is both culturally and politically oppressed. As late as the summer of 1970, Luis Valdez affirmed:

> The nature of Chicanismo calls for a revolutionary turn in the arts as well as in society. Chicano theater must be revolutionary in technique as well as content. It must be popular, subject to no other critics except the pueblo itself; but it must also educate the pueblo toward an appreciation of *social change*, on and off the stage.[1]

In 1967, the group entered a second phase of its development by breaking away from Delano and broadening its base to include other issues besides the strike, appealing to urban as well as rural Chicano audiences. *No saco nada de la escuela (I Don't Get Anything out of School)* focuses on problems

"From *acto* to *mito*: A Critical Appraisal of the Teatro Campesino" by Yvonne Yarbro-Bejarano. This article appears for the first time in this volume. It is used by permission of the author.

[1]"Notes on Chicano Theater," in *Actos: El Teatro Campesino* (San Juan Bautista, Calif.: Cucaracha Press, 1971), p. 2. Translations of passages originally appearing in Spanish are my own.

in the educational system, while *Vietnam campesino* explores the relationship between agribusiness and the military, stressing international solidarity between Vietnamese and Chicano peasants. These later *actos,* ranging from 1967 to 1971, draw upon the same dramatic techniques employed in early ones such as *Las dos caras del patroncito (The Two Faces of the Boss)* and *La quinta temporada (The Fifth Season).* They communicate directly and clearly to a working-class Chicano audience, focusing still upon social change.

Around the time *Actos* was published (1970-1971), the group began experimenting with another form, the *mito,* which differs sharply from the *acto.* Whereas the *acto* concentrates on political issues expressed in the cultural terms of its audience, the *mito* attempts to explore the content of culture itself. According to Valdez, such theater represents the recovery and validation of the culture of a colonized people, and in the introductory pieces to *Actos,* p. 3, he lays out the need for it:

> Beyond the mass struggle of La Raza in the fields and barrios of America, there is an internal struggle in the very corazón of our people. That struggle, too, calls for revolutionary change. Our belief in God, the church, the social role of women — these must be subject to examination and redefinition on some kind of public forum. And that again means teatro. Not a teatro composed of actos or agitprop but a teatro of.ritual, of music, of beauty and spiritual sensitivity. A teatro of legends and myths. A teatro of religious strength. This type of theater will require real dedication; it may, indeed, require a couple of generations of Chicanos devoted to the use of theater as an instrument in the evolution of our people.

In a treatise called *Pensamiento serpentino*[2] *(Serpentine Thought),* Valdez sets out what he sees as the fundamental concepts of pre-Hispanic philosophy, its tie-in with Christianity, and the general function of religion in life. This prose poem is the philosophical or theoretical base on which the *mitos* rest. Valdez has spoken of the *acto* and the *mito* as dramatic twins, *cuates,* implying that the *mito* is not intended to replace, but to coexist with, the *acto:*

> The two forms...complement and balance each other as day goes into night, el sol la sombra, la vida la muerte, el pájaro la serpiente. Our rejection of white Western European (gavacho) proscenium theater makes the birth of new Chicano forms necessary — thus, los actos y los mitos; one through the eyes of man; the other, through the eyes of God.   *(Actos,* 5)

Acto and *mito* were mixed in the group's production *La gran carpa de los Rascuachis,* first performed with this title in March of 1973 at the University of California, Santa Cruz. The work in its original form is divided into three parts. The middle section, an *acto,* dramatizes the story of Jesús Pelado Rascuachi, who is forced by poverty across the border to work as a farmworker, where he suffers exploitation and discrimination and eventu-

[2](San Juan Bautista, Calif.: Cucaracha Publications, 1973).

ally the disintegration of his family This *acto* is framed by two *mitos* which combine Christian and indigenous figures: Jesus Christ and Quetzalcoatl alongside the Virgin of Guadalupe, herself a blend of Christian Mary and indigenous Tonantzín. *La carpa* has stirred the most fruitful polemic in Chicano theater to date. Through it, many fundamental questions have been raised about the nature and function of Chicano drama.

One of the first critics to react to *La carpa* was Raúl Ruiz, after seeing Teatro performances in Los Angeles on September 27 and October 1 and 2 of 1973.[3] Ruiz applauds the origins of the Teatro Campesino, the first two phases of their development, and their polished professionalism and infectious enthusiasm. He praises the *acto*, or middle part, of *La carpa*, but condemns the two *mitos*, parts one and three, as irrelevant to the middle section, or essence of the play. Although the *acto* skillfully and realistically depicts the hostile socioeconomic forces which underlie the problems of Chicanos, the *mitos* displace the possibility of confronting those problems from the sphere of human action to a supernatural plane. For Ruiz, it makes no difference whether the supernatural figure who solves the people's problems for them is Christian or Indian. It is not the ethnic origin of God which should be questioned, but the role of religion in the history of the people. Valdez himself affirmed the necessity of examining traditional belief in God and the Church in the quotation cited above, but in *La carpa* this critical role is assigned to the *acto,* not the *mito.* In the *acto* a bishop appears with the name "St. Boss Church" emblazoned on his vestment and the symbol of the dollar sign instead of the cross. In the *mito,* the vision of religion is more hospitable. Ruiz objects to Quetzalcoatl as a symbol of metaphysical consciousness or all-encompassing love: "All the love in the world is not going to raise your salary, create unions, and protect your rights."

Ruiz does not condemn cultural content which is religious in general, but rather criticizes the specific use which the Teatro makes of it. He accepts the appearance of the Virgin to one of the characters in the *acto* when he is violating the principles of good which she represents: "This doesn't mean that a 'Virgin Mary' actually exists, but it does show the tremendous impact which religion has on the Chicano psyche."

Ruiz also suggests that in turning toward Indian myths and symbols, Valdez has turned away from the present reality of Chicanos: if the Teatro's intention is to return theater to the people, it should reflect their actual experience in terms they can relate to. He sees in the new direction of the Teatro the "imposition of the mind of the playwright on the created material and the audience." While recognizing the Teatro's importance, he recommends that it go back to the people's struggle for its inspiration, recognizing "that only the people can solve the problems that are caused by the material conditions that suppress them."

[3]"Teatro Campesino: A Critical Analysis," *La Raza: News and Political Thought of the Chicano Struggle,* 2 (February 1974), 12-14.

The dispute was carried to an international arena during the Fifth Festival of Chicano Theater Groups, First Latin American Encounter, held in Mexico City from June 24 to July 7 of 1974, in which 30 Chicano and 28 Latin American theater groups took part. The emphasis of the Festival was on unity, its motto "Un continente, una cultura." But from the publications which came out of the Festival, it is clear that the basis of the unity is more than a common culture—it is the realization of a common enemy as well: Yankee imperialism. Thus, there is a political dimension to the search for indigenous roots—to redeem them from the effects of colonialism. *La Carpa* provoked much discussion of the importance of understanding indigenous culture within a sociohistorical context. Two dramatists of international fame, Augusto Boal (Brazil), Enrique Buenaventura (Columbia), participated in these debates during the Festival and later published their conclusions.

Augusto Boal is a tireless worker in people's theater. Drawing from his experience, he has written *Teatro del oprimido y otras poéticas políticas*[4] *(Theater of the Oppressed and Other Political Poetics)* and *Teatro popular de Nuestra América*[5] *(Popular Theater of Our America)*. One of the founders of the Teatro Arena in Brazil, he was forced to leave after the military coup. He has since worked with theater groups in such diverse places as Argentina and New York, putting into practice his theory that the function of people's theater is the liberation of the oppressed class on an international scale. In an unpublished piece reporting on the Festival entitled "Hay muchas formas de hacer teatro popular: yo prefiero todas!" ("There are many kinds of popular theater: I prefer them all!"), Boal recognizes the search for identity through indigenous roots as a unifying endeavor as well as a means of combating the imposition of values by a dominant culture. On this ground he quotes approvingly from Valdez's *Pensamiento serpentino:* "Jesucristo is Quetzalcoatl/ the colonization is over./ La Virgen de Guadalupe is Tonantzin/ The suffering is over./ The Universe is Aztlán/ The revolution is now."[6] But when it comes to Chicanos converting themselves into "neo-Mayas." Boal warns against the danger of idealizing and romanticizing the past, rendering the search for roots "an a-historical fiction." We would search vainly in history, he asserts, for the Mayas of Valdez! He disagrees with the latter's poetic statement: "Así es que the Christian/ concept of Love Thy Neighbor/ as Thyself was engrained into/ their daily behavior/ They wouldn't think of/ acting any other way."[7] Boal reminds us that in fact the indigenous forefathers of whom Valdez speaks here practiced human sacrifice, at times for ends more political than religious. At the inauguration of a new temple in Tenochtitlán in 1487, he states, the Aztecs sacrificed 20,000 prisoners of war to the God Huitzilopochtli. In

---

[4](Buenos Aires: Ediciones de la Flor, 1974).
[5](Cuernavaca: Cuadernos del Pueblo, Ediciones Mascarones, 1976).
[6]"Hay muchas formas...," p. 4. Translations are mine.
[7]*Ibid.,* p. 4.

a historical perspective, therefore, the editorial statement of the Teatro's magazine rings false: "the Indian pre-Hispanic spirit, a spirit free from egoism, full of equality and struggle. It is a culture of love, of brotherhood, of support." In reality, such "equality" was limited to the ruling class: Mayan cities were governed hereditarily by chiefs with the aid of counselor-priests; the tribes subdued by the Aztecs were forced to pay tribute and to offer victims for sacrifice. The provocative question that Boal raises is: what place would Chicanos of today have occupied in pre-Hispanic societies? Following this line of thinking, we could ask ourselves why the Teatro Campesino overlooks the pre-Hispanic oppressed groups, choosing to align itself with the philosophy of the élite.

The Teatro's tendency at present to idealize indigenous civilizations contrasts with a puppet show which it performed in 1968, *La conquista de México (The Conquest of Mexico)*. The humor which characterizes this piece, as well as the lively use of Chicano Spanish mixed with English, dispels any hint of romanticization. The puppets voice a historical lesson which is pertinent to the Chicanos' situation today:

> *Cuauhtemoc:* We Mexicans of antiquity lost because we were not united with our brothers and because we believed that those white men were powerful gods.... Let's hope it's not still that way! Right, sun?
>
> *Stone:* Right on! Get it together, raza.   (*Actos*, 65.)

This critical view and the suggestion that religion can work against the best interests of the people are missing in *El baile de los gigantes (The Giants' Dance)*, a recreation of the theatrical rites of the Chorti Indians of Yucatan performed at the Festival in an attempt to recapture the spirit of pre-Hispanic culture.[8]

Boal and others have also been critical of mythical elements in *La carpa*. Boal, like Ruiz before him, censures the intervention of the Virgin, who miraculously saves the hero from the Devil. This is to rob the characters of self-determination, Boal maintains, preventing them from acting to transform their circumstances. He quotes Brecht on what he believes to be the obligation of people's theater: to show that "man is the destiny of man." This "transforming" perspective is the true principle of popular drama.[9] Like Ruiz, he accepts the other appearance of the Virgin, where she operates as a moral and cultural force which allows the character to make his own decisions. Boal points out what he considers to be "ideological confusion" in the Teatro's attempts to reconcile politics and folklore through the figure of the Devil, who is made to serve both repressive and revolutionary ends.

In a pamphlet called *Tía Cleta*, Boal makes other interesting observa-

---

[8]For a detailed description, see Theodore Shank's article on the Festival, "A Return to Mayan and Aztec Roots," *The Drama Review*, Indigenous Theatre Issue, 18 (December 1974), 56-70.

[9]"Categorías de teatro popular," in *Teatro popular*, p. 7.

tions about the Teatro's concentration on the myths of Aztlán. He cautions against separating the struggle for greater understanding of Aztec culture from the "very superior battle," which is the liberation of all oppressed classes. Internal division for cultural or national reasons isolates one group from the rest, imperiling the strength gained through international solidarity in the face of a powerful dominant culture and political structure.[10] A drama based on cultural myths must be placed in a historical framework. For the search for indigenous roots is only valid "when the purpose of this return to the past is to come back to the present with clarity and with greater strength, when it serves to demystify the myth. Yes, the analysis of the past interests us, this is definitive—whenever it serves to clarify the present."[11]

Boal's view is warmly seconded by the Teatro Ambulante of Puebla.[12] This is made up of Indian street vendors who act out their experience of police brutality and insist that the primary purpose of any people's theater is accessibility to the masses:

> They speak of myth...but...they should present a theater which is clear, which focuses more on the problems of the people. We don't understand what myth is and if we...don't understand it, those who are in the fields will understand it less. Therefore we think that their theater should be more real, more concrete and encompass more the problems of the people.[13]

If the people do not understand, one is tempted to ask, for whom is this mythical theater being made? The answer that seems to suggest itself is that the Teatro Campesino is making this theater, consciously or unconsciously, for itself. In 1971, the group withdrew to San Juan Bautista, a little rural town 85 miles south of San Francisco, purchased 40 acres of land, and established a communal way of life combining farming and theater based on the philosophic principles of their Mayan ancestors. The members attempt to act out in daily life the spirit which they see operating in the world—yesterday and today.[14] This inward-turning trend, contrasting markedly with more outward-directed participation in the movement, is seen by Valdez

[10]"The Debates on the Festival. The Chicano: A Search for Cultural Roots or an Encounter with the Class Struggle?" *Tía Cleta*, 4 (1974), 4. Translations of all quotes from *Tía Cleta* are mine. Thanks to Tomás Ybarra for making this material available to me.

[11]"Analysis of the Festival," *Tía Cleta*, 9 (1974), 4.

[12]Other groups voice similar opinions; for example, the director of the group from the University of Zulia (Venezuela): "in such a convulsed politico-social reality where repression, hunger and injustice exist, this mystical tendency proves evasive and distracts attention from the essential problems," *Tía Cleta*, 5 (1974), 8; Teatro Triángulo (Venezuela): "the mythical position, inclined towards a re-encounter with the past as a solution to problems...seems a bit romantic...divorced from reality...the liberation of the Chicano people is not going to be brought about through a re-encounter with the idiosyncrasy of the Chicano people, or with its culture which ultimately is suctioned within another, more powerful, since it is the dominant culture," *Tía Cleta*, 5 (1974), 21.

[13]*Tía Cleta*, 7 (1974), 5.

[14]For a more detailed description of life in San Juan Bautista, see Carlos Morton's "La Serpiente Sheds Its Skin: The Teatro Campesino," *The Drama Review*, Indigenous Theatre Issue, 18 (December 1974), 71-75.

as a reaction: "We'll be getting deeper and deeper into ourselves because the Sixties was a time of outward explosion, while the Seventies is a time of inward explosion" (75).

Enrique Buenaventura, in his "Open Letter to Luis Valdez: The Search for Identity,"[15] gently questions whether the troupe "is dwelling too much on its own identity." He suggests that the opposition of one's own cultural values to those imposed by the dominant culture can lead to a dangerous satisfaction and even a mystification "of what is ours." Buenaventura calls attention to the subtle trap of substituting supposedly eternal and absolute values for others which may prove to be equally "eternal" and "absolute." Ambiguity about these matters actually plays into the hands of the enemy, since it offers no real threat to the system:

> The oppressor wants identity to escape in the past (the more remote, the better for him), to remain in myths....He doesn't like it when identity rises from the roots and flowers in Zapata, in Sandino, in Martí....This continuous and live identity is dangerous for the system, it is too logical, too real, too concrete.

Buenaventura exhorts the Teatro to identify once again with the oppressed people of the world, as it did in the beginning. Without this unity, which transcends national and cultural boundaries, "all other identities become pure illusion and pure fantasy."

We must not, however, be hasty in condemning the Teatro. It is easy to accuse its members of having turned their backs on people suffering in the fields and barrios, of escaping history in a flight to myth and spiritualism, of making theater which propagates a cultural dependence on religion, and of presenting philosophical ideas and symbols which the people themselves do not understand. Too easy: before we rush to judgment, we must look carefully at the group's continuing evolution. As noticed earlier, the *acto* and the *mito* are *cuates*, intended to exist side by side; there is no question of substituting one for the other. The troupe's dualism, which at first seemed schizoid, is reflected consciously in the several issues of the Festival's publication, *Tía Cleta*. In No. 4, for example, Valdez counters the concerned objections of other theater groups with "universal concepts" drawn from Christianity and Mayan culture, and explicates the meaning of Quetzalcoatl, Christ, the Virgin and Mother Tonantzin, the land, the tree of life, and the sun as spiritual father. In No. 9, p. 9, he continues to define the Teatro's function in terms of international social struggle:

> Our greatest task is to mobilize the people to take conscious action....Not only in the reality of interior politics but in the exterior as well....The responsibility of art is to make concrete the reality of today, of yesterday, of tomorrow. The enemy is the imperialist system.

[15]"Carta abierta a Luis Valdez: La búsqueda de la identidad," *Sí Se Puede* (August 15, 1975), 9. All translations are mine.

Rather than suppose these statements irresponsible or insincere, we should recognize them as part of an evolving redefinition.

The Teatro is not unwilling to incorporate criticism from without into its own process of metamorphosis. Let us take *La gran carpa de los Rascuachis* as an example. The main criticisms aimed at the original 1973 version were the lack of a meaningful relationship between the *acto* and the mythical frame, the unclear symbolism of the figure Quetzalcoatl/Jesus Christ,[16] and above all, the resort to supernatural intervention to solve the character's problem. By the time *La carpa* reached the Festival in the summer of 1974, some attempts had already been made to deal with these criticisms. In the 1974 version, the first *mito* opens with the Virgin and an indigenous figure from pre-Hispanic times. In the ensuing "Colonization March," she leads him through the various popular movements in Mexican history, up to the time the story of Jesús Pelado Rascuachi begins. The closing *mito* no longer presents Quetzalcoatl as an Aztec god in full costume, but rather as an outgrowth of the Chicano character developed in the *acto,* who verbally identifies himself with the returned Quetzalcoatl.[17] These changes reflect an awareness of the need to merge the religious and mythical figures of the previous version more organically with the historical action of the *acto.*

That the troupe continued to seek an artistic reconciliation of the *mito* and *acto* is seen in the version of *La carpa* which was toured in August through October of 1976. The *acto* is still flanked by *mitos.* The first is similar to the '74 version, with minor variations intended to emphasize the continuity between pre-Hispanic Indian and present-day Chicano, Aztec deities and Christian figures. It begins with *campesinos* working in the fields singing the *corrido* "de la unidad" (of unity). These are gradually displaced by an indigenous dance, in which the participants parallel the work of the campesinos, planting corn. Out of the dance a female figure emerges, first dressed as the *milpa,* or corn, then as the Virgin, who, as in '74, delivers the same message of struggle and leads the people through the "Colonization March." The closing *mito* is significantly different. Jesús Rascuachi dies. The Sun, in indigenous costume, brings him back to life. Jesús asks whether this is the end of his *corrido,* to which the Sun replies, "¿Que dices tú?" (What do you say?). Jesús cries out "No!" and the scene flashes back to the point in his life when he had to decide whether to go with the union or the growers. Before, he had thrown in his lot with the grower; now, he picks the union, fights against the grower, and is reunited with his family. He becomes part of a struggle larger than himself, symbolized by the United Farmworkers Union and the historical struggle of the people under the banner of the Virgin.[18]

[16]See also Françoise Kourilsky, "Approaching Quetzalcoatl: The Evolution of El Teatro Campesino," trans. Gloria Orenstein, *Performance*, 2 (Fall 1973), 37-46.

[17]Thanks to José Delgado, a member of the Teatro Campesino, for this information.

[18]Thanks again to Jóse Delgado.

The version of *La carpa* which was aired on public television in the spring of 1977 seems to respond even more earnestly to the urgings of Boal and others to place cultural and mythical content in the social and historical context of Chicanos today.[19] The new direction taken is indicated by a new title: *El corrido de los Rascuachis.* Besides the shift to a *corrido* theme and form, the work also differs from previous versions in the exploitation of a different medium—television—making possible certain effects, scene changes, and elaboration of scenarios impracticable or impossible on an improvised stage.

The *acto* still tells the story of Jesús Rascuachi and his family struggling for survival in the United States. Within the *acto*, the Teatro uses folkloric figures of Death and the Devil to enhance the action, at no cost to the historical veracity of the story. They play different parts throughout the *acto* —the corrupt border patrolman, the labor contractor, the grower, the welfare official, and so on. The ideological confusion surrounding the Devil in the earlier version has been straightened out, and certain philosophical ideas which stem from indigenous cultures and permeate Mexican/Chicano culture today are presented simply and clearly.[20] For example, when María Rascuachi is in labor, Death enters and approaches her supine body. From a conventional Western perspective, one would expect the death of the child or the mother; but after the successful birth of the child it becomes clear that Death is to be understood as the "midwife" of life. It is not a hostile and tragic menace hovering ready to strike, but a friend, a *novia*. In this instance, the Teatro expresses theatrically the same vision of life and death expressed in indigenous art in the skull fashioned out of crystal—the symbol of life. The meaning is conveyed in a straightforward and unpretentious way. Other symbols function equally clearly—for example, the everpresent rope, which through its continuous transformations (border, wedding ring, etc.) becomes a symbol of the characters' oppression.

More important than this overall recasting of symbols is the way in which the solution to the cycle of poverty and exploitation in the *acto* is returned to the hands of the people. The Teatro now roots itself in the present, projecting the solution toward a historically possible future. The two *mitos* with their religious elements have been eliminated in favor of another kind of structural frame. The work now opens in the interior of a truck, which is carrying farmworkers to a new job in the fields. Various character types are presented, the main ones being a young urban Chicano and an old Mexican. The old man decides to pass the time by singing a *corrido*, which tells the

[19]Although aired in the spring of 1977, this version was filmed in November of 1975, according to José Delgado.
[20]The first productions of the *mito El fin del mundo* in the spring of 1975 were characterized by ponderous explications by a narrator of obtuse symbolism of color, the four directions, the elements, etc. The *Carpa* needs no such help. See the review of the Sixth Festival of Chicano Theater Groups which took place in San Antonio, Texas, in July, by Marcos Lizárraga in *Sí Se Puede* (August 15, 1975), 9-10.

story of Jesús Rascuachi and his family. As he sings, the scene changes to a stage with a colorful backdrop on which the story of Jesús Rascuachi is played out, with few props but much mime, spontaneity, and improvisation. The old man then passes on his guitar to the young Chicano, telling him that now the *corrido* of the Rascuachi family is his, to end as he sees fit. The Chicano protests, insisting that he doesn't know the end. At this point, the truck arrives at its destination and is greeted by an angry group of strikers, who plead with the people inside the truck not to provide scab labor, but to join their struggle for a better life. The group hesitates, afraid of the grower's power and in desperate need of work. Finally it is the young Chicano who joins the strikers, carrying the whole group with him. To celebrate the event, the striking farmworkers ask the Chicano to play them a *corrido* on the guitar he is holding. He starts to refuse, then suddenly grasps the guitar and strikes up the *corrido* of the Rascuachis. This time we know that it will not end with cyclical frustration, or with the miraculous aid of the Virgin, but with the possibility that people can change their situation through organized struggle.

The Teatro enacts this class-conscious message without sacrificing its belief in the importance of culture. The use of the *corrido* to convey the meaning of the work underlines the significance of maintaining the culture alive within the dominant society. But the vision of culture is now dynamic—the *corrido* is not accepted as "good" because it is Mexican. Many *corridos* perpetuate attitudes and values which need to be questioned or reexamined, such as the relationship between the sexes in "Rosita Alvírez" or the celebration of exaggerated *machismo* in "Juan Charrasqueado." The *corrido* in the television version of *La carpa* is seen as an essential part of a culture which is subject to change, and must change to reflect the transformations of present and future. The Teatro now shows how culture can be used as a tool in the struggle for liberation, rather than serving as a memorial to traditional values.

From this analysis we can see that the Teatro is not stagnating, that it continues to change and grow, and that criticism has played an important role in that evolution. The group has not abandoned the *mito*, just as they have not abandoned the indigenous principles by which they are structuring their lives in San Juan Bautista. Perhaps after this process of daily internalization of collective work experience, the *mito* will be able to speak to the people as clearly as the *acto*. One way of testing this hypothesis will be to see whether *El fin del mundo* will pass through as great a transformation as *La gran carpa de los Rascuachis*.

Notes on the Editors and Contributors

JOSEPH SOMMERS is Professor of Latin American Literature at the University of California, San Diego. Author of *After the Storm: Landmarks of the Modern Mexican Novel*, and co-editor of *Chicano Literature: Text and Context* (1972), he has published or edited books in Mexico on Juan Rulfo and Francisco Rojas González. His articles have appeared in many journals in the United States and Latin America. He has worked with Chicano students since 1967, and is presently researching the area of border culture and the undocumented worker.

TOMÁS YBARRA-FRAUSTO is a faculty member of the Department of Spanish and Portuguese at Stanford University. Born in Texas, he taught at the University of Washington, where he initiated courses on Chicano literature and culture and founded a Chicano theater group, "El Teatro del Piojo". He is co-editor of *Chicano Literature: Text and Context* (1972), and has published articles on Chicano literature in *Latin American Theatre Review* and the *New Scholar*. His research interests include Chicano art, theater and popular culture.

JUAN BRUCE-NOVOA is Assistant Professor of Spanish at Yale University, where he introduced the teaching of Chicano literature. He has published a collection of poetry, *Perverse Innocence* (1974), and numerous articles of literary criticism in *De Colores, Revista de la Universidad de México, Latin American Literary Review, Tejidos*, and *Revista Chicano-Riqueña*. His present research interests include structuralism and Chicano literature, and modern Mexican narrative.

CARLOTA CÁRDENAS DE DWYER, born in Illinois, completed her Ph.D. at State University of New York, Stony Brook. She is Assistant Professor of English at the University of Texas, Austin. She has edited an anthology, *Chicano Voices* (1975), and has had articles in *English Journal, La Luz, The American Pen, Review*, and *The Literary Criterion*. She is presently preparing a study on modern Chicano literary expression.

C. BARCLAY GOLDSMITH, a theater person, completed the M.F.A. at Carnegie-Mellon University. Currently a drama teacher at Pima Community College in Tucson, Arizona, he is member and stage director of Teatro Libertad, in Tucson.

JUAN GÓMEZ-QUIÑONES is Associate Professor of History at the University of California in Los Angeles. His literary interest is evident in a published volume of poetry, *5th and Grande Vista* (1974), and in his Preface to Alurista's *Floricanto* (1971). Among his historical writings are *Flores Magón: Eulogy and Critique* (1975), and articles in *Western Historical Quarterly, Aztlán, Historia y Sociedad, Revista Chicano-Riqueña*, and *Controversia*. In addition to his activity as editor of *Aztlán*, he has held numerous positions of leadership in community movements in East Los Angeles.

RALPH GRAJEDA, born in Colorado, completed his Ph.D at the University of Nebraska, where he is now Associate Professor in the Department of English. His dissertation treated the figure of the *pocho* in selected Chicano narratives.

Luis Leal, born in northern Mexico, received his Ph.D. at the University of Chicago, and went on to achieve a record of distinction as Professor of Latin American literature at the University of Illinois. Since official retirement, he has continued to teach at several University of California campuses. Among his long list of books, the most notable are *Mariano Azuela, vida y obra* (1961), *Historia del cuento hispanoamericano* (2nd. ed., 1971), and *Cuentos de la Revolución* (1976). His articles have appeared in virtually every journal of excellence in Latin America. All research on the short story in Mexico and Latin America must use Luis Leal's work as a point of departure. He himself continues to be active in research projects in Mexican and Chicano literature.

Felipe de Ortego y Gasca, born in Chicago, completed his Ph.D. at the University of New Mexico, with one of the first dissertations on Chicano literature. At present he is Professor of English at Angelo State University, and senior vice-president of La Luz Publications, Denver. A broadly gauged scholar, he has published articles on American and Old English literatures, as well as on Chicano themes. He edited an anthology, *We Are Chicanos*, in 1973.

Américo Paredes is Professor of English and Anthropology at the University of Texas. Currently he is acting director of the Center for Intercultural Studies in Folklore and director of the Center for Mexican American Studies at that university. He is past editor of the *Journal of American Folklore*. Born and raised on the Texas-Mexican border, he has been a collector and scholar of folklore and the *corrido* for decades. Among his most noted publications are *With a Pistol in His Hand: A Border Ballad and Its Hero* (1958); *Folktales of Mexico* (1970); *A Texas Mexican Cancionero* (1976); and (coedited with Raymund Paredes) *Mexican American Authors* (1972).

Juan Rodríguez, born in Texas, is presently a faculty member at the University of Washington, having earlier taught at the universities of Arizona; California, San Diego; and California, Berkeley. His articles have appeared in *Mester, New Scholar*, and *Bilingual Review*. He edits *Carta abierta*, an informal news and bibliographical letter.

Marta Sánchez, born in Los Angeles, is presently Assistant Professor of Spanish at the University of California, San Diego, where she completed her Ph.D. in 1976. She has published on Chicano and Latin American themes in *Diacritics* and *Latin American Literary Review*. Her present research centers on Chicana poets and on the modern Latin American narrative.

Rosaura Sánchez is Assistant Professor of Spanish at the University of California, San Diego. Born in Texas, she received the Ph.D. in Romance Linguistics from the University of Texas in 1974. She has published articles on Chicano bilingualism in *New Scholar, El Grito*, and the *Journal of the National Association of Bilingual Educators*. Her own short stories have appeared in *Bilingual Review, Maize, Caracol*, and *Revista Chicano-Riqueña*.

Daniel Testa is chairman of the Department of Spanish and Portuguese at Syracuse University. He has coedited *Spanish Writers of 1936* (1973) and a translation of Luigi Pirandello's *On Humor* (1974). His articles have appeared in *Modern Language Notes, Studies in Philology, Romance Notes, Revista de Estudios Hispánicos*, and *Revista Chicano-Riqueña*.

Ignacio Orlando Trujillo, born in New Mexico, is completing his Ph.D. at Stanford University with a dissertation on Chicano poetry. He is the only contributor to this volume with an extensive background in amateur prizefighting.

Yvonne Yarbro-Bejarano, born in Oklahoma, is Assistant Professor of Spanish at the University of Washington. She completed her Ph.D. at Harvard University in 1976 with a dissertation on Golden Age drama of Spain. An article on sixteenth century theater has appeared in a volume of essays honoring Jorge Guillén (1977). She has founded a Chicano writing workshop in Seattle and is editor of a journal of Chicano literature, *Metamórfosis.*

Selected Bibliography

Bibliographies

Heisley, Michael. *An Annotated Bibliography of Chicano Folklore from the Southwestern United States.* Los Angeles: Center for the Study of Comparative Folklore and Mythology, U.C.L.A., 1977.

Lomelí, Francisco A., and Donaldo W. Urioste. *Chicano Perspectives in Literature.* Albuquerque: Pajarito Publications, 1976.

Pino, Frank. *Mexican Americans: A Research Bibliography.* 2 vols. East Lansing: Latin American Studies Center, Michigan State Univ., 1974.

Tatum, Charles. *A Selected and Annotated Bibliography of Chicano Studies.* Manhattan, Kansas: Society of Spanish and Spanish American Studies, Kansas State Univ., 1976.

Trejo, Arnulfo D. *Bibliografía Chicana: A Guide to Information Sources,* Detroit: Gale Research Co., 1975.

Anthologies of Literature

Cárdenas de Dwyer, Carlota. *Chicano Voices.* Boston: Houghton Mifflin, 1975.

Castañeda, Antonia, Tomás Ybarra-Frausto, and Joseph Sommers. *Chicano Literature: Text and Context.* Englewood Cliffs, N.J.: Prentice-Hall, 1972.

Harth, Dorothy E., and Lewis Baldwin. *Voices of Aztlán.* New York: New American Library, 1974.

Ortego, Philip D. *We Are Chicanos.* New York: Washington Square Press, 1973.

Valdez, Luis, and Stan Steiner. *Aztlán: An Anthology of Mexican-American Literature.* New York: Vintage, 1972.

Literary Journals

Aztlán. Chicano Studies Center, U.C.L.A. Los Angeles, Calif. 90024.

Caracol. P. O. Box 7577, San Antonio, Texas 78207.

De Colores. Pajarito Publications, 2633 Granite NW, Albuquerque, N.M. 87104.

Grito del Sol. Tonatiuh International, 2150 Shattuck, Berkeley, Calif. 94704.

Revista Bilingüe/Bilingual Review. York College, CUNY, Jamaica, N.Y. 11451.
Revista Chicano-Riqueña. Indiana University Northwest, Gary, Ind. 46408.

Special Journal Issues on Chicano Literature

Latin American Literary Review, 5 (Spring-Summer 1977).
The New Scholar, 5, no. 2 (1977).